1

Sensitivity to People

Sensitivity to People

HENRY CLAY SMITH / *Michigan State University*

McGRAW-HILL BOOK COMPANY / *New York* / *St. Louis*
San Francisco / *Toronto* / *London* / *Sydney*

To my daughter Barbara,
who has tried hard
to improve my sensitivity

PREFACE

ONE QUESTION dominates the book: How can the ability to understand people be improved? Present training methods, as we see in Chapter 1, give us a far from satisfactory answer. In pursuit of a better one, the book examines what sensitivity is, its components, ways of measuring these components, the personality traits of sensitive people, the processes we go through in judging others and the errors we make in the process, and old and new ways of reducing the errors. The examination is based upon a wide range of theories, methods, laboratory and field findings, and experiences in clinical training, sensitivity training, and the teaching of psychology.

The question seriously concerns many people in many fields. Consequently, I have tried to make my ideas clear to those who are not psychologists. The question particularly concerns those whose daily work involves training clinicians and counselors, executives and labor leaders, or college students to understand people better than they do. However, the reader I have had most clearly in mind is one who wants to *do* something about sensitivity training: to expand our knowledge about sensitivity through research, to try new ways of improving the ability through training, or to evaluate the success of existing programs.

With this reader in mind, I have tried to present the facts that are most relevant to the question but have tried to avoid drowning him in empirical data. I have presented a theoretical framework for placing these facts in meaningful relationship to each other. And I have pushed the facts and the framework to the limit in the search for concrete suggestions for the improvement of training.

I have made heavy use of the work of graduate students and colleagues who have been involved with me in the study of various aspects of the question for more than a decade: Ernest Bruni, Donald Dunbar, Burton Grossman, Ward Harris, Gerald Hershey, Donald Johnson, Ronald Johnson, Sherwin Kepes, James Linden, Donald Livensparger, David Silkiner, Don Trumbo, John Wakeley, and Albert Zavala. I thank them for their help and tolerance. I want, in particular, to thank Prof. Victor Cline of the University of Utah for the generous use of his films and for his help in providing bibliographical materials. I wish also to express my appreciation to the Ford Foundation, which, through a grant to International Programs at Michigan State University, provided financial assistance in various phases of the project, and the School of Labor and Industrial Relations for providing assistance and encouragement.

HENRY CLAY SMITH

CONTENTS

PREFACE   vii

PART ONE   EDUCATION FOR SENSITIVITY

1 *The Problem*   3
What we mean by sensitivity   Education and sensitivity   The
generality of sensitivity   A component approach   Perspective.

2 *Goals of Training*   17
A theory of sensitivity   Objectives of sensitivity training   The
measurement of sensitivity.

3 *Methods of Training*   35
How we form impressions of a person   Training principles   Guides
to better training.

PART TWO   THE PERCEIVER

4 *Level*   59
The measurement of level   The generality of level   The personality of the high leveler   Level accuracy   Elimination of the
level component   The improvement of level accuracy.

5 *Spread*   77
The measurement of spread   The personality of the wide spreader
Spread accuracy   The general problem of spread accuracy in train-
ing   The improvement of spread accuracy.

PART THREE   THE INTERACTION BETWEEN
PERCEIVER AND PERSON

6 *Empathy*   93
The measurement of empathy   The people with whom we em-
pathize   The personality of the empathizer   Empathic accuracy
The improvement of empathic accuracy.

7 *Observation*   113
The nature of observation   The measurement of observational

accuracy   Sex and accuracy   The ways we look at people   The improvement of observational accuracy.

PART FOUR   THE PERSON

8 *Stereotypes*   133
The nature of stereotypes   The measurement of stereotype accuracy   Stereotype accuracy and leadership   The social sciences as a source of accurate stereotypes   The improvement of stereotype accuracy.

9 *The Individual*   153
The battle for uniqueness   The measurement of individual accuracy   Social roles versus psychological traits   The improvement of individual accuracy   A training proposal.

PART FIVE   IMPLICATIONS AND APPLICATIONS

10 *Questions and Answers*   175
What is sensitivity? Who is sensitive? What are the causes of insensitivity? How can selection be improved? How can training improve sensitivity?

11 *Sensitivity for Education*   193
The value of sensitivity   Clinical training   Sensitivity training   The teaching of psychology   Sensitivity as an educational goal.

BIBLIOGRAPHY   205
NAME INDEX   215
SUBJECT INDEX   221

Part One

EDUCATION FOR SENSITIVITY

Chapter One

THE PROBLEM

EVERYONE IS concerned with understanding others: the parent wants to understand his child; the teacher, his students; the doctor, his patients; the therapist, his clients; the executive, his employees; the politician, his constituents; and the novelist, his characters. Our cave-dwelling and club-wielding ancestors saw few people and had simple human relations problems. We, on the other hand, are becoming part of a complex world society of billions. More and more, we spend our days with others and with the problems created by being with others. As a consequence, the development of mutual understanding has steadily grown in importance as a goal of education. Our problem is that these educational efforts are less effective than we would like them to be and less effective than we think they could be. In exploring the problem in this chapter we first define "sensitivity," then consider the value of some of the major educational programs designed to improve it, and finally outline the major elements in a new approach to sensitivity training.

What We Mean by Sensitivity

Definitions are more like wet clay than rock, for they can be molded to serve the purpose at hand. Sensitivity and its brother terms, social perceptiveness and empathy, have been used to serve many purposes. While the varying definitions are natural they are also confusing. We need immediately, therefore, to give our definition: *Sensitivity is the ability to predict what an individual will feel, say, and do about you, himself, and others.* Our basic purpose is to examine present sensitivity training programs to develop better ones. This purpose is not exactly the same as that of psychotherapists concerned with helping disturbed people, nor the same as that of training directors concerned with developing executives to be more effective in their human relations, nor the same as that of teachers in the social sciences concerned with imparting our increasing knowledge of human behavior and experience.

Psychotherapists are more concerned with sensitivity as a process than as an outcome. They are primarily interested in understanding the immediate experiences of their clients during the therapeutic hour and in using their understanding to help their clients. They are *not* primarily concerned with predicting how their clients behaved before the hour or how they will behave afterward. They are interested in the process by which we become sensitive. They are therefore likely to prefer definitions of sensitivity like the following (Blackman, Smith, Brokman, & Stern, 1958):

> . . . the ability to step into another person's shoes and to step back just as easily into one's own shoes again. It is not projection, which implies that the wearer's shoes pinch him and that he wishes someone else in them; it is not identification, which involves stepping into another person's shoes and then being unable or unwilling to get out of them; and it is not sympathy, in which a person stands in his own shoes while observing another person's behavior, and while reacting to him in terms of what he tells you about shoes—if they pinch, one commiserates with him, if they are comfortable, one enjoys his comfort with him.

It is often more enlightening to work with terms that designate the process which creates the various forms of the outcome rather than with the outcome itself. The trouble with such definitions for our purpose is that the evaluation of training requires measures of what the training is supposed to do. How can we measure sensitivity as defined above and how can it be measured in a way that distinguishes it from projection, identification, and sympathy? The only present answer seems to be to measure outcomes: predictive accuracy. Thus, Fox and Goldin (1964), after pointing out the limitations of predictive accuracy as a measure of processes going on during psychotherapy, reluctantly conclude that more direct measures of these processes "have yet to be developed." Our strategy, therefore, is not to stress the process and then to look for the outcomes; it is to stress the outcomes and then to look for the processes that cause them.

Instructors of psychology, human relations, and social science courses have as one of their aims the development of their students' ability to understand people. However, they stress more remote processes than do psychotherapists. They assume, sometimes only implicitly, that a mastery of the vocabulary, the facts, the principles, and the theories of the behavioral sciences will lead to the outcome of increased sensitivity. They often have excellent measures of these assumed antecedents of sensitivity; they almost never measure sensitivity itself.

Sensitivity Training has grown from the work of applied group dynamicists, members of the National Training Laboratory in Group Development, and group psychotherapists and nondirective counselors. The program stresses sensitivity: "The ability accurately to sense what others think and feel." It is relatively unconcerned with the formal knowledge that the social sciences assume to be a necessary antecedent to the development of sensitivity. In fact, it stresses that sensitivity itself is an antecedent to the more important trait of behavioral flexibility: the ability to behave appropriately in interpersonal relationships. We stress sensitivity so that the validity of these assumed *consequences* can be explored. We shall, incidentally, have many occasions to refer to this program which stresses intense interaction between members of a small unstructured *T group* (i.e., training group). We shall also be referring to many other kinds of training designed to improve predictive accuracy. We shall refer to the former as Sensitivity Training; to the latter, as sensitivity training.

Our definition of sensitivity and its difference from those stressing assumed antecedents or consequences of it may be clarified by an illustration (Cobb, 1944):

> I remember well, when acting as a clinical clerk at Queen Square for Kinnier Wilson, I saw him present a new case to a group of students in the out-patient clinic. I was seated at the table taking notes, Wilson was standing, having just dismissed a patient, and there was an empty chair beside my table. Wilson rang for the next patient, the door opened and a man entered, followed by his wife. He walked across the fifteen feet of classroom, smiled at the students and at me, and sat down. Wilson turned to me instantly and said, "Write G. P. (paresis) as the diagnosis." Probably my jaw dropped, for he went on, "Well, Cobb, what else could it be? Here is a middle-aged man coming to a nerve clinic. He enters the room smiling, pushes ahead of his wife, does not take off his hat, takes the only chair without asking and likes an audience!" Subsequent neurological and serological studies proved the correctness of the diagnosis.

In this situation, the psychotherapist might be most interested in the immediate processes which led Wilson to his accurate prediction; the college instructor, in the educational background which led to his accuracy; and the sensitivity trainer, in the effective behavior of the doctor in treating the patient as a consequence of his accuracy. Like the therapist, the instructor, and the trainer, we are interested in the antecedents and consequences of sensitivity. Unlike them, we place sensitivity in the bright foreground, antecedents and consequences in the background.

Education and Sensitivity

A wave of educational effort with mounting enrollments has as one of its aims the development of sensitivity. The number of college students being graduated annually with a major in psychology is now approaching 10,000 and the total far exceeds 100,000. In 1949, 4 per cent of those who were granted a Ph.D. received it in psychology; by 1959, the percentage had doubled, largely because of the increasing demand for clinical psychologists. Human relations programs in business and government have been accelerating, probably at an even more rapid rate. Sensitivity Training, a dot on the waves a decade ago, is now high in the skies. Its use is expanding in colleges, in business, in military establishments, and in medical schools.

The tide has not advanced without its critics and pessimists. It has been called a "fad" and a "cult" which encourages people to "pick at the scabs of their psychic wounds" and to become "little tin Freuds." Fromm (1957) has raised larger issues:

> Beyond "market psychology" another new field of psychology has arisen, based on the wish to understand and manipulate the employee. This is called "human relations". . . . what Taylor did for the rationalization of physical work the psychologists do for the mental and emotional aspect of the worker. He is made into a *thing*, treated and manipulated like a thing, and so-called "human relations" are the most inhuman ones, because they are reified and alienated relations.

While the professionals have not viewed the trend with such dismay, they have sometimes been pessimistic about its effectiveness. A psychoanalyst, for example, has said (Watson, 1938):

> I am betraying no secret when I say that the degree of man's unstudied insight into his fellows has no relation to his "scientific" training or achievement. Nothing is clearer to the outsider than that a great deal of "scientific" psychology is the work of men singularly lacking in the capacity to enter into another foreign way of life. . . . The first principle of psychology and sociology must then be "live it" if you want to understand. . . . In this respect, the innkeeper, the oldfashioned medical clinician, or the literary worker, unencumbered by the shackles of a counterfeit "rigor," are in a better position to "get around" and to keep eyes and ears open to the flux of a turbulent world.

What *is* the relationship between "studying" and man's "insight into his fellows?" Exhibit 1-1 summarizes evidence dealing with aspects of the question. The answers are clear-cut. Are undergraduates who have had psychology courses more sensitive than those who have not? No. Are professional psychologists more sensitive than graduate students in psychology? No. Are clinical psychologists more sensitive than experimental psychologists? No. Are professional psychologists more sensitive

EXHIBIT 1-1   *The Influence of Training on Sensitivity*

EXPERIMENTER	METHOD	DID TRAINING INCREASE SENSITIVITY?
1. Estes (1938)	Two-minute silent movies of each of six subjects were shown to 56 judges (including 9 psychologists) who were then asked to match a subject to one of six personality sketches.	No. Psychologists did worse than musicians, painters, actors, and personnel managers.
2. Luft (1950)	After reading the verbatim record of an hour's interview with a subject, 28 psychologists and 28 physical scientists predicted the answers that the subject had made to a variety of personality tests.	No. In some comparisons, physical scientists were superior.
3. Wedell and Smith (1951)	Two hundred employees were each interviewed by three psychologists with advanced degrees and three without advanced degrees. The interviewers then tried to answer 55 questions on a job satisfaction questionnaire as the employees themselves had answered them.	No. Those with advanced degrees showed more frequent and serious discrepancies than those without.
4. Kelly and Fiske (1951)	Experienced psychologists and trainees predicted the eventual professional success of graduate students by means of a wide variety of materials in various combinations.	No. Trainees "utilized the materials as effectively as the more mature."
5. Soskin (1954)	Graduate students and experienced clinical psychologists answered a personality inventory as they thought a twenty-six-year-old mother had answered it. They were given her responses to projective tests.	No. The graduate students were as accurate in their predictions as the clinicians.

EXHIBIT 1-1 *(Continued)*

EXPERIMENTER	METHOD	DID TRAINING INCREASE SENSITIVITY?
6. Trumbo (1955)	The sensitivity scores of 44 students who had just completed the introductory course were compared with the scores of 44 students of the same intelligence who had completed five courses in psychology.	No. The advanced students did no better than the beginning students.
7. Taft (1955)	Psychologists and graduate students in and out of psychology made trait ratings and predicted inventory responses of subjects in a large assessment program.	No. The small differences found were largely due to the superiority of experimental over clinical psychologists.
8. Crow (1957)	Medical students in Colorado hospitals first saw sound motion pictures of physicians interviewing patients and made predictions about the patients, then took a training course designed to sensitize them to individual differences, and finally took the film test again.	No. "Contrary to expectations, a training program in interpersonal relations for medical students decreased the trainees' accuracy in judging others."
9. Grossman (1963)	The scores of 130 undergraduates on a variety of written and film tests of sensitivity were correlated with the number of credits they had had in psychology.	No. There were no significant correlations between credits and the median correlation was approximately zero.
10. Weiss (1963)	Sixty clinical psychologists and 60 physical scientists predicted the behavior of three undergraduates, sometimes with only identifying information and sometimes with the typescript of a half-hour taped interview.	No. "Physical scientists perform more accurately than psychologists when a greater amount of information is available."

than physical scientists, actors, personnel managers, and members of other professional groups? No. Does intensive training designed to increase sensitivity actually do so? No. Indeed, more than one of these studies shows that the less well-trained groups do significantly *better*.

To demonstrate the care with which many of these studies have been carried out, let us consider the last in more detail (Weiss, 1963). The author first gained the cooperation of three undergraduates: Ray, Ron, and Ruth. Each of them recorded a half-hour structured self-interview which covered the major areas of his life: family background, educational and occupational experience, etc. These interviews were then typed from the recording tapes. Each subject next participated in a lengthy interview with a psychologist to gather information about his actual behavior in a variety of life situations. The behavior reported by each of the volunteers was verified by interviews with two of his friends. From the accumulated information a series of questions was constructed like the following:

> There was a lot of talk at the restaurant where Ruth works about something she had done. The incident involved:
>
> 1. Ruth's necking with a Negro employee at a party
> 2. Ruth's organizing a strike for higher wages
> 3. Ruth's reporting to work one night drunk
> 4. Ruth's keeping tips left for other waitresses

The items thus constructed were administered to a pilot group and the results analyzed to eliminate poor items, correct for response bias, etc. Finally, 28 test questions like the one above were constructed for each of the volunteers. Letters were then sent to 120 professional clinical psychologists listed in the directory of the American Psychological Association and to 120 physical scientists listed in *American Men of Science*. Sixty from each group agreed to cooperate. Half of each group received a test with only minimal information about the person they were judging: age, sex, education, and occupation. The other half received this information plus the typescript of the self-interview. The completed tests were returned, scored, and subjected to thorough statistical analysis. Results: The psychologists *were* superior to the physical scientists under the conditions of minimal information. The physical scientists, however, made better predictions than the psychologists from the complete typescripts of the interviews—just the situation in which one might expect the psychologists to do better.

Kahn and Santostefano (1962) have wryly described the reaction of clinical psychology to facts of this kind:

> Clinical psychology presents itself in a state of chronic anxiety, great ambivalence, insecurity, and self-doubt. Clinical psychology states that it is a science, and then says that it is an art. It asserts that it is an independent and self-contained field, but then confesses that it is ancillary and in need of close relationships with other sciences and professions. It shows wide mood swings from expansive, grandiose plans, on the one hand, to agitated depression and low self-esteem on the other. A variety of defenses have been mobilized in the struggle to maintain ego integration.

Name-calling is one of these defenses. Clinicians describe their method as "dynamic," "global," "sympathetic," "genuine," "live," and "true-to-life." They describe experiments like those in Exhibit 1-1 as "cut-and-dried," "dead," "rigid," "oversimplified," and "pseudoscientific." They express confidence that the "right kind of study" will exhibit their prowess. The answer to this expression is obvious: *Do* the right kind of study and back up the claim with evidence. The defense of some teachers who are not clinicians is that they are not trying to increase the sensitivity of their students. To most students, this defense would be like saying that they were kids playing cowboys who were not expected to understand cows.

The Generality of Sensitivity

Is sensitivity a specific or a general ability? If it were specific, then the studies reported in Exhibit 1-1 would be meaningless, for one could draw no confident conclusions about a person's general sensitivity from his performance in one situation on a particular test of sensitivity. Thus, in most of the studies, the perceivers were asked to predict the responses of very few people. If sensitivity is specific, then one can tell nothing about a perceiver's general sensitivity from his accuracy in judging one student, one patient, or one 26-year-old mother. In most of the studies, the perceiver has contact with the people he is judging in only one situation—in social interaction, in a movie, in a case report, or over a tape recorder. If sensitivity is entirely specific, then accuracy in one situation would have no relationship to accuracy in others. In most of the studies, the perceiver is asked to predict only one kind of behavior about the person he is asked to judge—how he filled out an inventory, what his friends said about him, or how he behaved in a series of social situations. Again, if sensitivity is specific, then one cannot generalize from one kind of prediction to others.

The criticism is plausible. Few would wish to bet much that the perceiver who is accurate in predicting the questionnaire responses of a few women he sees briefly in a movie while he sits in a darkened classroom with several hundred others would also be accurate in making predictions about the behavior of people in everyday social situations. Even if the criticism were true, it would not appeal to the trained, for they are not interested in defending the position that they are as good as the untrained; they are interested in asserting that they are better. It is vital, however, in clarifying the nature of sensitivity to answer the question: Is sensitivity a general trait?

The answer of Crow and Hammond (1957) was "no." They had 65 medical students make 15 different kinds of predictions about student attitudes toward each other and about patients they saw on sound films: their reticence, their vocabulary level, their scores on personality inventories, etc. The authors intercorrelated these 15 measures of sensitivity. Of the more than one hundred correlations only a handful were large enough to be significant and some of these were negative. Conclusion:

> Failure to find support for the hypothesis of a general ability of interpersonal perceptiveness in this study makes the *assumption* of generality untenable. Consequently, comparison of the results of interpersonal studies based on different measuring techniques can be justified only when the comparability of such results has been empirically demonstrated.

Applied to the studies of Exhibit 1-1, this conclusion means that there is no reason for assuming that sensitivity as measured in one study would have any relationship to sensitivity as measured in another.

A more recent study of Cline and Richards (1960) is more hopeful:

> The results of this study, in other words, indicate that there is a general ability to perceive others accurately. This general ability, however, consists of two (at least) independent parts: Sensitivity to the Generalized Other and Interpersonal Sensitivity. . . . It may appear paradoxical (or inappropriate) to conclude that at the same time the ability to perceive others accurately is general and that it consists of two independent components. The authors are of the opinion, however, that these seemingly conflicting conclusions mean that the ability to perceive others accurately is factorially complex and that the independent components reflect this complexity.

The critical difference between this study and the earlier one is that Cline and Richards exercised great care in the development and pretesting of their measures of sensitivity: They eventually selected only 10 from 25 available film interviews; they had each interviewee complete a dozen different inventories and scales, some as many as three times to ensure the stability of their responses; and they pretested all aspects of their measures for internal consistency. As a consequence, the final measure of sensitivity had considerable generality: Perceivers who were good in judging one person were good in judging others, and perceivers who were accurate in making one kind of prediction were accurate in making other kinds.

The results of the two studies are supplemental. The latter says that sensitivity measures of high generality can be developed; the former says that unless care is taken to ensure that measures have generality, they will not have it. Most important of all, they both suggest the need for a component approach to sensitivity.

A Component Approach

The ability to make accurate predictions about people is not a single, global, and unified trait. Rather, a number of relatively independent components determine accuracy. In this respect, sensitivity is comparable to intelligence. Until 1938 it was assumed that intelligence was a general trait and that a single IQ score was adequate for measuring it. In this year, Thurstone published his analysis of the components of intelligence. The analysis revealed that general intelligence scores were widely varying mixtures of such primary mental abilities as verbal comprehension, word fluency, number ability, space ability, memory ability, perceptual ability, and reasoning ability. These abilities are so loosely related that it is quite possible to be very high on one and very low on others. Thus, a person may have high verbal comprehension and low rote memory, high space ability and low word fluency, etc.

The independent measurement of primary mental abilities permits us to view an individual's intellectual abilities more analytically and more realistically. Potentially even more important, it permits a new and more hopeful approach to an unanswered question about intelligence: How much can it be modified by training? Now the same question may be asked in a simpler and more concrete way for each separate component. For example: How and how much can rote memory be improved by training?

Cronbach (1955) did for sensitivity what Thurstone has done for intelligence: He isolated, defined, and measured components of sensitivity. Five of the components he isolated were accuracy of elevation (the habitual tendency of a perceiver to rate at low or high level), accuracy of differential elevation (the habitual tendency of a perceiver to spread or not spread his ratings), accuracy of assumed similarity (whether a perceiver assumes or does not assume that the person he is judging is like him), accuracy of stereotypes (understanding of group behavior), and differential accuracy (the perceiver's accuracy in differentiating between individuals). He concluded:

> Social perception research has been dominated by simple, operationally defined measures. Our analysis has shown that any such measure may combine and thereby conceal important variables, or may depend heavily on unwanted components. Only by careful subdivision of global measures can an investigator hope to know what he is dealing with.

Cronbach's method was mathematically sophisticated and involved in its details. His general approach, however, is suggested by the following simple example. Eight men are candidates for the job of employment interviewers. As part of the selection process, each man interviews the other seven men. After each interview, he answers questions for himself like the following:

To what extent did you feel at ease during the interview?

1. Very much
2. A good bit
3. Only slightly
4. Not at all

In addition, each interviewer also answers the questions as he thinks each of the *other* seven men had answered them. The correct answer for a man was assumed to be the average answer for his seven interviews. After all the ratings had been made, Cronbach calculated for each man his overall accuracy in predicting the answers of the other men as well as his accuracy in predicting their elevation, differential elevation, stereotype accuracy, and differential accuracy.

Each man's rank (1 is most accurate) in overall sensitivity and on each of the components is shown in Exhibit 1-2. Note that the interviewer with the best overall sensitivity had the best elevation accuracy. That is, the average elevation of his ratings was exactly the same as the average elevation that the people he interviewed used in describing themselves. Note also, however, that the elevation component is not perfectly related to overall accuracy: The worst overall rater was fifth in elevation accuracy, the rater ranking sixth in overall accuracy was third in elevation, etc. In general, the components of sensitivity are only loosely related to each other and to overall sensitivity.

EXHIBIT 1-2   *General Sensitivity Scores and Scores on Sensitivity Components for Eight Interviewers*
(Adapted from Cronbach, 1955)

	RANK ON COMPONENTS OF SENSITIVITY			
RANK IN GENERAL SENSITIVITY	ELEVATION ACCURACY	DIFFERENTIAL ELEVATION ACCURACY	STEREOTYPE ACCURACY	DIFFERENTIAL ACCURACY
Albert 1	1	5	1	1
Bert 2	4	6	3	6
Charles 3	2	4	4	7
Don 4	7	7	2	4
Elinor 5	6	8	6	2
Frank 6	3	1	8	3
George 7	8	2	5	8
Harry 8	5	3	7	5

The component approach of Cronbach so dominates the general framework of the present book that it will be helpful to indicate at the beginning the ways in which they differ. In the first place, while the same components are used, terminology and definitions are somewhat different. In the second place, Cronbach measured all the components simultaneously by the elaborate statistical analysis of ratings which are influenced by all the components; we have tried to measure each component separately and as independently of the other components as possible. This method has meant the rigid avoidance of ratings. Finally, Cronbach's primary purpose was to isolate the components; our purpose has been to criticize, reinterpret, and integrate by means of these components a wide range of studies dealing with sensitivity training.

This book deals in detail with the applications of the component approach to sensitivity and sensitivity training. The general nature of the approach may be suggested by returning to Wilson, who accurately predicted that his patient was paretic. What accounted for his accuracy? The component approach suggests questions like the following: How often did he diagnose patients as paretics and how frequently were they actually so? What was his typical diagnosis of a patient and how often and how widely did he vary from it? How well did he observe and what did he observe about this particular patient? Did he see any kind of similarities or dissimilarities between his own behavior and that of the patient? What does he believe to be the critical differences between a paretic and a nonparetic patient, and how accurate are his beliefs? Does he make any differentiations between different kinds of paretic patients, and how accurate are these differentiations? Complete answers to these questions would help us to tell whether Wilson was an excellent diagnostician or just a lucky guesser; they might enable us to understand better the requirements of a good diagnostician; and they might provide clues to better training methods for interns. The best guess in this case is that Wilson had an accurate knowledge of the critical differences between paretic and nonparetic patients. That is, he had high "stereotype accuracy."

We turn to a less speculative question: Why did the psychologists in Weiss's study make more accurate predictions about the three college students than the physical scientists when both had little information but make less accurate predictions when both had more information? The superiority of the psychologists under the first condition seems most likely to be due to their more accurate stereotypes of college students. That is, they had a more accurate and detailed picture of how typical college students behave. This fact is not surprising when we consider that most of the psychologists were college teachers but that few of the physical scientists were. But why should the psychologists have been less accurate with *more* information? It seems most likely that the psycholo-

gists made more serious errors than the physical scientists in their elevation ("level" in our terms). Assume, for example, that the incidents of
behavior used for the college students could be placed on a scale from
extremely abnormal to extremely normal and that the typical behavior
of the students was closer to normal than abnormal. The psychologists'
predictions were more often below the actual level than those of the
physical scientists. That is, psychologists, sensitive to abnormalities in behavior, saw more abnormality in the students than was there. If this finding is generally true, then it has important implications for the training
of psychologists.

Perspective

Our general purpose is to examine the applications of the component
approach to sensitivity training. In examining the goals of training in
the next chapter, we consider in more detail each of the components
and the devices available for measuring them. In the following chapter,
we consider the general training principles whose application seems most
critical for the improvement of training. In the remaining chapters, the
six components are considered separately: their general nature and significance, ways of measuring them, the origins of individual differences
in them, the consequences of these differences, and the most likely ways
of improving an individual's ability in them. In the end, we draw these
separate threads together in an effort to evaluate their overall significance
for the improvement of the ability to understand people.

Chapter Two

GOALS OF TRAINING

Only with a knowledge of goals can the instructor know what he is to teach, the student what he is to learn, and the evaluator what he is to use as a criterion of training success. The more realistic and measurable these goals become, the better the training becomes. In this chapter, we consider what determines the predictions we make about people, the training goals that such determinants imply, and ways of measuring sensitivity.

A Theory of Sensitivity

Assume that a perceiver is rating the intelligence of a person on a scale from 1 (very low) to 7 (very high). What determines the rating he makes? Figure 1 pictures the six determinants that provide the framework of the present book. Two of them concern the perceiver; two, the interaction between the perceiver and the person; and two, the perceiver's knowledge of the person he is judging. The perceiver determinants have little to do with the person being perceived, much to do with the perceiver. They involve the perceiver's general ideas about people and his general habits in judging them. The interaction determinants grow out of the relationship between the particular perceiver and the particular situation in which he is perceiving a particular person. The last two determinants focus upon the person being judged and concern the facts that the perceiver has about the person and his ability to use these facts to differentiate between people. The accuracy of a perceiver's judgments is the product of *all* these relatively independent causes. We turn first, therefore, to a brief consideration of each.

A perceiver's *level* is his general tendency to rate others as low, average, or high; as poor, fair, or superior; as possessing few, some, or many desirable traits; or as deserving an F, C, or A grade. The leveling habits

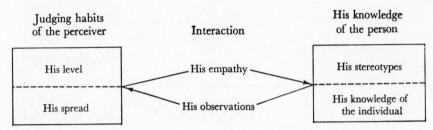

Judging habits of the perceiver	Interaction	His knowledge of the person

Figure 1   What determines the perceiver's predictions about a person

of instructors, for example, are so different, so well known, and so stoutly defended that Goldberg (1965) tried to determine their academic consequences. Cooperating instructors used the varying levels shown in Exhibit 2-1 in assigning midterm grades to more than six hundred students in an introductory psychology course. He used subsequent achievement test scores to determine the motivational influence of these different leveling tendencies on later learning in the course. There was none: "The findings . . . should force proponents of a particular grading policy to make a thorough reappraisal of their beliefs." The study is mentioned here, not to support such an unlikely reappraisal, but to illustrate the level determinant and to suggest the pervasive influence it may have in judging people.

A perceiver's *spread* is his general tendency to rate himself and others over a narrow or a wide range. The narrow spreader sticks close to his level, tending to give all people on all traits about the same rating. The wide spreader tends to rate at the extremes, rating people as very high *or* very low, very good *or* very bad, F *or* A, etc. Variations in spread from perceiver to perceiver are large and important. Zax, Lowen, Budin, and Biggs (1962), for example, gave college students, schizophrenics, hospital patients, and alcoholics more than a hundred desirable and undesirable adjectives. They asked each subject to fit each adjective in turn into the blank in the sentence, "I am a _____ person,"

EXHIBIT 2-1   *Percentage of Students Assigned Each Letter Grade by Low, Average, and High Levelers*
(Adapted from Goldberg, 1965)

	PERCENTAGE OF STUDENTS WHO RECEIVED				
TYPE OF INSTRUCTOR	A	B	C	D	F
Low leveler	00	05	25	40	30
Average leveler	10	20	40	20	10
High leveler	30	40	25	05	00

after which they rated each adjective on a scale from 1 (very undesirable) to 7 (very desirable). The alcoholics had a narrower spread than any of the other groups: "A generalized and relatively homogeneous response set by members of this group to avoid the use of extreme scores." The narrow spread of the alcoholic was interpreted as his way of dealing with his anxieties: "Although . . . this has the effect of making his pleasures less enjoyable, it has the highly desirable effect of making his anxiety less intense."

The core idea of *empathy* is the ability to transpose oneself imaginatively into the feeling, thinking, and acting of another. It is the best-known, but most elusive idea in the field of sensitivity. It is used to refer to specific components of sensitivity but also to sensitivity in general; to predictive outcomes but also to the determinants that lead to these outcomes; to differences between individuals but also to a phenomenon referring to all people. Empathy is often talked about but rarely measured. We shall consistently use the term to mean *the tendency of a perceiver to assume that another person's feelings, thoughts, and behavior are similar to his own.* It will be used to refer to a specific determinant of predictions made, to an outcome rather than a process, to individual differences in this outcome, and to measurable aspects of these differences. Empathy thus defined varies with the particular perceiver, with the particular person he is perceiving, and with the particular interaction between them. Above all, empathy thus defined is a determinant of predictions, not a synonym for predictive accuracy. That is, the similarities we assume between ourselves and others may be wrong as well as right—and often are.

Observation is obviously an important determinant of sensitivity, for what we hear a person say and see him do has much to do with the inferences we make about him. However, psychologists have shown a curious lack of interest in this determinant. For example, Bruni (1963) in his investigation of observation in relation to sensitivity found only a few studies that had any relevance and none concerned with the effectiveness of training in the observation of people. Scott (1955), a biologist, has noted a more general and striking neglect of observation by psychologists. He suggests that the explanation may lie in the development of psychology from philosophy. The younger discipline, he feels, has been excessively dominated by the a priori reasoning methods characteristic of philosophy. Whatever the reason, our observations about people play too central a part in determining our judgments of them to be neglected here.

Our present judgments of an individual are influenced by our past judgments of the groups to which the individual belongs. Thus, the business executive who thinks that the typical union leader is egotistical and emotional is likely to have similar thoughts about each individual union leader he meets. In a similar way, our judgments of a particular woman are influenced by our impressions of women in general; our judgments of a particular man, by our impressions of men in general; etc. We shall refer to this influence on our judgments as *stereotyping*.

Our level, spread, empathy, observations, and the differentiations we make between groups exert an independent influence on the predictions we make about a person. What remains as a determinant of our judgments is the influence of our *differentiations between individuals*. Many important judging situations show this determinant in a nearly pure form: The admissions officer must select freshmen from a group that all have equally good grades and references, a clinician must select individual patients for therapy from a group of patients that all have equally good prognoses, and a man picks a wife from a group of girls that are of the same age, looks, and background.

Objectives of Sensitivity Training

We have defined the determinants of the predictions we make about people. Predictions, however, may be right or wrong. The basic goal of sensitivity training is to *increase the accuracy* of the trainee's predictions. We turn, therefore, to the task of translating each of these determinants into a training objective.

THE IMPROVEMENT OF LEVEL ACCURACY

In any given rating situation, some raters have a characteristically low, some a moderate, and some a high level. However, there is only *one* accurate level. To take a simple and extreme example, assume that a group of raters is asked to judge how fast each of 100 men will run 100 yards. Assume, further, that the average man actually runs the distance in fifteen seconds. Fifteen seconds, then, is the accurate level. The rater whose average estimate for the 100 men is closest to fifteen seconds has the most accurate level. The rater whose average prediction is ten seconds will be making a constant error of underestimation that will invade all his individual judgments. The rater whose average prediction is twenty seconds will be making a constant error of overestimation that will invade all *his* judgments. One important goal of sensitivity training, therefore, is to increase the level accuracy of the trainee.

The above illustration is simple. The ramifications of level accuracy as a goal, however, are complex. In the first place, an individual's level pervades his way of thinking about people, has a profound but largely unconscious influence, and may be highly resistant to change. In the second place, the influence of level errors may be invisible to even the trained eye, as, for example, in the apparent case of the clinician's tendency to overestimate the abnormalities in the behavior of others. In the third place, there is no level that is regularly more accurate than other levels. In some situations, the low level is the accurate one, whereas in other situations it is the average or high that is accurate.

The improvement of level accuracy is not only one way of increasing sensitivity, it may well be the best way—at least to start. Cronbach (1955) is of this opinion:

> An argument can be presented for concentrating attention on constant processes, taking up interactions between J and O only after the constant processes characteristic of J are dependably measured. Constant processes in the perceiver have potentially great importance because they affect all his acts of perception. Individual differences in constant processes need to be measured dependably so that their influence can be discounted in studies of variable processes. Moreover, *identifying constant errors should permit training to eliminate such biases;* this may be the most effective way to improve the social perception of leaders, teachers, and diagnosticians.

In Chapter 4, we return to a detailed consideration of this goal.

THE IMPROVEMENT OF SPREAD ACCURACY

While raters may vary in the spread of their ratings, there is only one accurate spread for a given situation. Returning to our male runners whose average speed for 100 yards is fifteen seconds, assume that the standard deviation of their speed is two seconds. From this statistic, we can infer that the fastest man did the 100 in less than ten seconds and the slowest man took more than twenty seconds while two-thirds of the men ran the distance in some time between thirteen and seventeen seconds. The closer a rater's spread approaches 2, the closer it comes to the actual spread.

The spread of a rater that minimizes his predictive errors is *not* identical with the actual spread. The optimum spread is almost always *less* than the actual spread and is generally considerably less. Suppose, for example, that the rater of runners has no information about individual runners that would help him to predict their speed. What spread in this situation would minimize errors? The answer: *No* spread. He would make fewer and less serious errors by assuming that *all* runners would run the distance in fifteen seconds.

The goal of spread training is to teach trainees to adjust their spread to the knowledge they have of the person they are judging: no knowledge, no spread; a little knowledge, very little spread; and much knowledge, a moderate amount of spread. This principle is generally violated.

The most experienced violate it the most seriously. Psychologists seem to have excessive confidence in their ability to make accurate predictions about individuals on the basis of little knowledge about them. Chapter 5 returns to this goal.

THE IMPROVEMENT OF EMPATHIC ACCURACY

Empathy is the similarity we *assume* between ourselves and others. It provides the foundation of understanding. Without any special reflection, we assume that others have sensations, feelings, and thoughts similar to our own. We see red and assume that others see the same; we love and hate and assume that others do too; and we think and assume that others also think. All of us assume some similarity, but some of us consistently assume much more than others. An important goal of sensitivity training is the improvement of *empathic accuracy,* the ability to judge in what ways we are similar and in what ways we are dissimilar to other people.

A basic source of empathic error lies in the *level of empathy.* That is, some of us consistently assume too much and others too little similarity between ourselves and others. Another common source of error is to assume too much similarity to those who are like us in obvious and superficial ways and too little similarity to those who are not. Again, we too readily assume similarity between ourselves and those we like and dissimilarity between ourselves and those we dislike. Possible ways of correcting errors such as these are explored in Chapter 6.

THE IMPROVEMENT OF OBSERVATIONAL ACCURACY

While no one questions the importance of better observation for better understanding, it is the exceptional program that has improving observation as a central aim. One such exception is a course developed over six years for the teaching of observational skills in child psychiatry to fourth-year medical students (Shapiro, 1964). It consists of 6 two-hour sessions. The first three are based on twenty-minute edited tapes of family interactions, the fourth consists of observing a child in play therapy through a one-way screen, and the last two consist of observing the instructor interviewing members of a family. In commenting on the aims of the course, the instructor says:

> The students tend to interpret the observed facts in terms of such theoretical concepts as Oedipus complex, penis envy, or castration anxiety. It is the instructor's task to hold them to an accurate description of behavior first, before they try to account for it. They soon discover that sharp

disagreements often develop over simple behavioral items. It is not so easy to notice that a father uses words his son does not understand.

The improvement of observation requires a fuller appreciation of its critical importance, a better understanding of common types of observational errors, and clearer ideas of what to observe and how to observe it. These are the problems discussed in Chapter 7.

THE IMPROVEMENT OF STEREOTYPE ACCURACY

Everyone makes, and uses, generalizations about groups. An incident in the life of a personnel worker suggests how we do it (Tannenbaum, Weschler, and Massarik, 1961, pp. 52–53):

> This was Jean Krugmeier's first day on her job. She liked being an employment interviewer. People were interesting, and it would be a novel experience to sit behind a desk all day. The initial two interviews proceeded uneventfully. The third applicant wanted to be a foremen of the shipping gang. He was a young, burly 250-pounder who said that he used to work in the steel mills near Gary. He spoke loudly, with much self-assurance. "Some sort of a bully—a leering Casanova of the hot-rod set," Jean thought. Jean always did dislike guys like this, especially this sort of massive redhead. Just like her kid brother used to be—"a real pest!" The more he bragged about his qualifications, the more Jean became annoyed. It wouldn't do to let her feelings show; interviewers are supposed to be friendly and objective. She smiled sweetly, even if she did have a mild suspicion that her antagonism might be coming through. "I am sorry, we cannot use you just now," she said. "You don't seem to have the kind of experience we are looking for. But we'll be sure to keep your application in the active file and call you as soon as something comes up. Thank you for thinking of applying with us."

Social scientists have defined, and generally condemned, group generalizations as "stereotypes": ". . . a false classificatory concept to which, as a rule, some strong emotional-feeling tone of like or dislike, approval or disapproval is attached" (Young, 1944). The question, however, is not whether we should or should not use group generalizations. We do. The question is whether they are valid or invalid. Much social science research aims to discover valid generalizations about groups: men, women, Jews, Negroes, college students, psychologists, executives, workers, neurotics, alcoholics, etc.

Courses in the social sciences aim to increase the ability to differentiate between groups. Anthropology aims to increase understanding of the differences between cultural groups; sociology, differences between members of various social classes; political science, between political groups within the society; economics, between economic groups; and psychology, between personality groups. The more comprehensive theories and principles of these sciences aim to increase understanding of men in general. Is the aim achieved? We have few facts that bear upon the question, but the few we have are not very encouraging. The purpose of Chapter 8 is to consider how the growing store of information about group differences can be used more effectively to develop the student's ability to understand people.

THE IMPROVEMENT OF INDIVIDUAL ACCURACY

The training of the historian, the biographer, and the novelist stresses the importance of understanding the unique individual in the unique situation. The training of counseling psychologists, psychiatrists, and social workers also stresses the importance of understanding the unique individual. As far as predicting the responses of people are concerned, however, it is easy to overstate the case. To begin with, some of the predictions we make about an individual we would make for practically all persons and some we would make for all individuals in the group to which he belongs.

Even more critical: Considering a person as a unique individual may lead to *less* accurate predictions about him than if he is considered as a member of a group. We shall be reviewing a nearly overwhelming body of evidence that leads to this conclusion. Soskin (1959), as one example, had psychologists make predictions about the behavior of David in a wide variety of situations. They were first given only his age, race, religion, marital status, education, and occupation and asked to make the predictions. One subgroup then observed him in an extensive series of especially designed role-playing sessions. On the basis of the individual information thus obtained, they were asked to make the predictions for David again. Result: No increase in predictive accuracy. Another subgroup was given an interpretation of David's Rorschach test and asked to make predictions again. Result: They were *less* accurate after seeing the Rorschach interpretation.

The first training objective is to learn when to and when not to try to judge a person as a "unique individual." Once this goal is achieved, training may then focus on finding and correcting errors in the differentiating process.

A COMPOSITE VIEW

Figure 2 summarizes the training goals we have outlined. It also applies them to the fictional scores of a psychologist and a physical

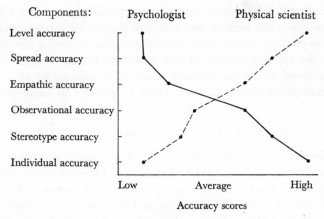

Figure 2 Accuracy scores of psychologist and a physical scientist on the sensitivity components (hypothetical)

scientist in predicting the behavior of a person like David. The profile of the psychologist indicates he has perceived very clearly the differences between David and other men like him (very high accuracy in individual differentiation) and quite clearly the differences between the group of men to which David belongs and other groups (high accuracy in group differentiation). His scores also suggest that he is observant but that he underestimates the similarity between himself and David. The low level and spread accuracies mean that he is far from the norm in judgments of David's typical behavior and inclined to spread his predictions over too wide a range.

The physical scientist, while relatively poor in differentiating between individuals and groups, is shown as observant, inclined to assume sufficient similarity between himself and David, sensibly cautious in his spread, and very accurate in estimating the norms of David's behavior. In sum, while the overall predictive accuracy of these two men is about the same, the sources of their errors are very different. The ultimate aim of training is to increase the trainee's accuracy on all of these components.

The Measurement of Sensitivity

Goals without measures of goal achievement are of dubious worth. Without measures we cannot select those who need training most, design programs to enhance goal achievement, give trainees knowledge of the progress they are making, or evaluate the effectiveness of the training. It is, therefore, to the questions involved in the measurement of sensitivity that we now turn: How can the persons to be judged be presented to the perceivers? What kinds of predictions should the perceivers be asked to make about the persons and how can their accuracy be determined? How should they record their predictions? The following sections summarize the varying answers in 100 studies involving measures of sensitivity analyzed by the author. Each summary is followed by an evaluation that attempts to define the best kinds of answers to each question.

METHODS OF PRESENTING THE PERSON TO BE JUDGED

The first step in the development of a measure of sensitivity is to present a person to be judged to a perceiver. Figure 3 shows the various ways in which experimenters have presented the person to be judged: live interaction between the person and the perceiver, written records, silent and sound films, photographs, and taped interviews. These are discussed in the order of the frequency with which they have been used.

Interaction

The majority of the studies (56 per cent) asked the judge to make predictions about people he had seen and talked to. In a few, as in the case of married couples asked to make predictions about each other, the period of interaction was quite long. In most, however, the period was short; in about half of the interaction studies, the period was less than one hour. The interaction period in the study by Bronfenbrenner, Harding, and Gallwey (1958) is representative. Since we will have other occasions to refer to the study, we describe the method of presentation in some detail.

The experimenters invited 72 Cornell students to dinner at the Statler Inn on the Cornell campus. Upon arrival at the Inn, the students were divided into 12 discussion groups. Each group consisted of three

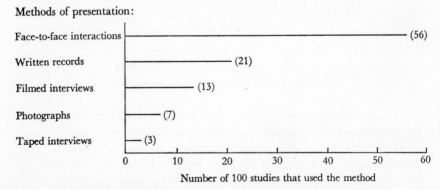

Methods of presentation:

Face-to-face interactions	(56)
Written records	(21)
Filmed interviews	(13)
Photographs	(7)
Taped interviews	(3)

Number of 100 studies that used the method

Figure 3 Methods of presenting the person to the perceiver

men and three women who were strangers to each other. Each group participated in one discussion before dinner and in another after dinner. In one period, the groups discussed the question: What three courses should be required of every Cornell student? In the other period, they discussed the question: What three things would you wish to have along if you were marooned on a desert island? Each group ate together with no talking between groups, and each group met in a separate room for the discussion period. Each group member was thus exposed to the other five members during two discussion periods and a dinner, a total of about four hours. At the end of this time, the individuals were asked to make predictions about the other members of the group.

Written Records

Next to direct observation, the most frequent method (21 per cent) of presenting the person was in a written record: the judge was given some information in writing about the subject and then made predictions about him. The amount of information given ranged from a few hundred to thousands of words. The method employed by Trumbo (1955) illustrates the shortest type of presentation. He developed a test based on eight cases like that shown in Exhibit 2-2. After reading the thumbnail sketch, the judge was asked whether he thought each of the 15 statements about the individual was true or false.

Filmed Interviews

Thirteen per cent of the studies used either silent or sound films, some in color. The films developed by Cline and Richards (1960) are among the best. Their original films were in black and white but their more recent ones have been in color. From 25 interviews actually filmed they selected 6 on the basis of technical excellence of the film, significance of the content of the interview, and extent to which the interview discriminated in pilot studies between sensitive and insensitive judges.

The 25 interviews represented a cross section of the adult population in Salt Lake City. The camera was in full view of the interviewee during the filming of the interview. A member of the University of Utah theater staff conducted all the interviews. The interviewer asked each interviewee similar questions concerning his religious beliefs, his ideas about his strengths and weaknesses, his reactions to the interview, and his interests and hobbies. All the filmed interviews have a running time of less than five minutes. After seeing a film, the judges predicted how they thought the person had filled out numerous questionnaires and how they thought his friends had rated him.

Exhibit 2-2   *The Case of Karl Schultz*
(Adapted from Trumbo, 1955)

Karl was twenty-four at the time he entered a private New England college. He was of average height and weight, but had a powerful physique. He was energetic, competitive, physically courageous, and loved to be with people. His grades on the College Entrance Examination Board tests were highest in social studies and science, lowest in languages. His overall score was about the average of other freshmen.

He was raised in a small country town by parents of German and Swiss origins. He has two brothers—one 3 years older and one 2 years younger. His father, a skilled mechanic, is conscientious, but somewhat suspicious and anxious. Karl said his mother is "an industrious but worrisome woman." He also said that he "would like to see the world remodeled on the Christian ethical standard with the law of love pervading the hearts of men."

Which of the following statements about Karl is true, which false? (The correct answers are in italics)

T F   1. He thinks that his father was strict but friendly and helpful.
T   *F*   2. Karl graduated near the middle of his high school class. At the age of seventeen, he completed the Strong Vocational Interest Blank. He said he liked the following occupations:
T F   3. Hotel manager
T   *F*   4. Artist
T   *F*   5. Printer
T F   6. Chemist

He made the following statements about himself:

T F   7. I usually start activities in my group.
T F   8. I win friends easily.
T   *F*   9. I have more than my share of new ideas.
T   *F*   10. I am always on time with my work.

During his college career:

T F   11. He did a good deal of drinking.
T   *F*   12. He reported that his philosophy of life was primarily concerned with religion.
T   *F*   13. He felt that the Bible could be accepted as literal truth.
T   *F*   14. In his senior year he was interviewed by a psychiatrist who reported that Karl has good insight into his problems.
T   *F*   15. Karl married two years after he was graduated.

Photographs

Seven of the one hundred studies used pictures of people. Most of these were concerned with the judgment of emotional expression, but the study of Wedeck (1947) was an exception. He showed several hundred paintings and photographs to English secondary school children. After seeing a picture, the children were asked to select from four alternatives the one they thought best suited the picture. For example, a child is shown crying and the subject had to choose the one of the following alternatives that he felt was the most appropriate: (1) slightly uncomfortable; (2) very unhappy; (3) gloomy; (4) sulky. In another picture a young woman is shown in the act of using her powder puff and the perceivers again were asked to pick the most descriptive statement from four alternatives. The correct answers for each picture were the ones agreed upon by three psychologists who also took the test.

Taped Interviews

Three of the studies used recorded interviews that were later played to the judges. Chance and Meaders (1960), for example, tape-recorded forty-five-minute interviews with men who had previously completed the Edwards Personal Preference Schedule. The instructions to the judges were as follows:

> You will hear two short interviews. The two students interviewed were seen by the same interviewer and were asked to talk about five minutes on each of the following topics: If you had a vacation with plenty of time and money, how would you spend it? If you were working for someone, what kind of boss would you like to have? If you were hiring people to work for you, what kind of people would you look for? What kind of girl do you hope to marry? What qualities do you like in close personal friends? In general, what kind of people do you like less than others? What qualities in people do you dislike? In general, what qualities in people do you admire and value very highly?
>
> After the interview outlined above, each person interviewed took the test you have just taken. Each was told to answer the way he felt at the time. The interviewer stayed in the room with him, but did not look at his answers. Now I am going to play the first person's interview for you. I want you to listen carefully and to see how he describes his likes and dislikes. See what sort of person he seems to be. After the interview has been played, you will be asked to take the test as you think he took it—to try to predict what *he* said on the test, *not* what he is really like or what he really would *do*. There *may* be differences. Try to get a general impression of what the person is like. You probably will not get information about specific items on the test.

Evaluation

Of all the ways of presenting persons to judges, the interaction method has been most frequently employed and seems closest to everyday reality. From a measurement point of view, however, the method presents almost insurmountable obstacles: The same person is not presented to different judges in the same way; the method is time-consuming; and experiments using the method cannot be duplicated because a person appears in a face-to-face study and then disappears, seldom being available again. For the selection of trainees or for the evaluation of training programs, the method is very time-consuming. Photographs, while quite practical, are so limited in the amount of information they give judges that they are useful for only limited purposes. Written records, taped interviews, and sound films have different weaknesses and strengths. Tests based on written records can be made quite reliable, are easy to develop, and are flexible in use. They have less face validity than the taped interview and much less than the film interview. The development of film tests, on the other hand, is expensive; once developed, however, they are simple and convenient to use.

The measure of sensitivity with the greatest generality would expose judges to a large and heterogeneous sample of people by different methods: personal interaction, written records, taped interview, sound film, etc. Making such measurements, however, is severely restricted by the small number of suitable tests available as well by the limited time that a group of perceivers has available to complete them. For this reason, no experimenter has used more than one method of presentation. Some have used only one person to be judged, most have used a few, and practically none have used more than ten.

KINDS OF PREDICTIONS MADE

What kinds of predictions are the perceivers to make about a person? Predictions can be conveniently divided into four types (Bronfenbrenner et al., 1958): (1) *first person,* in which the perceiver predicts what the person thinks of him; (2) *second person,* in which the perceiver predicts what the person thinks of himself; (3) *third person,* in which the perceiver predicts what other people think of the person being perceived; and (4) *nonpersonal,* in which the perceiver predicts how the person actually behaved. Estimates of the weight of John by a perceiver give a simple example: What will John think my weight is (first person)? What will John think *his* own weight is (second person)? What will other people think John's weight is (third person)? What will the scales say his weight is (nonpersonal)? In the 100 studies, first-person predictions were rarely used; second-person, third-person, and nonpersonal predictions were used with about equal frequency. About one in ten studies employed some combination of these types.

In one well-known study using first-person predictions, Dymond (1949) first had each of her perceivers rate himself on six traits:

1. Superior-inferior
2. Friendly-unfriendly
3. Leader-follower

4. Shy–self-assured
5. Sympathetic-unsympathetic
6. Secure-insecure

The traits were rated on a five-point scale, from 1 (very friendly) to 5 (very unfriendly). Then each perceiver interacted with nine other persons during the course of an evening by rotating from one group of four to another group of four. At the end of each group meeting, each perceiver rated the other three members of the group on the six traits. He also rated himself *as he thought each of the other members of the group had rated him.* That is, he originally rated himself as he thought he was and then he rated himself nine times as he thought the others would rate him—once for each of the nine people with whom he interacted. The first-person accuracy score was the number of times that a person's rating of how he thought another had rated him on a trait corresponded with the actual rating. Since there were six traits and nine persons, the highest possible score would have been 54. The highest score actually obtained among a group of eighty students was 28; the lowest, 11.

Cline and Richards (1960), who presented persons to be perceived through the use of sound-color film, required their perceivers to make second-person, third-person, and nonpersonal predictions. Consequently, we can illustrate these kinds of predictions within the framework of a single study. The persons filmed checked on a five-point scale their degree of agreement or disagreement with religious statements such as the following:

1. No one who has experienced God like I have could doubt his existence.
2. God does marvelous things which are called miracles by some.
3. I have sometimes been very conscious of the presence of God.

A perceiver, after seeing a filmed interview, filled out the religious questionnaire as he thought the person in the film had completed it. The accuracy of a perceiver's second-person predictions was measured by counting the differences between how he thought the person had filled out the questionnaire and how the person actually had.

Friends of Mrs. P., a typical interviewee, were asked to rate her on such traits as cooperative and stubborn. After seeing Mrs. P. in the film, a perceiver rated the person on the traits as he thought Mrs. P. had been rated by her friends. The accuracy of the judge's third-person predictions was measured by counting the differences between how the judge thought her friends had rated Mrs. P. and how they actually had rated her.

In nonpersonal predictions, the judge is required to make predictions about a person that are *not* concerned with the person's opinions of himself or the opinions of other people about him. Clear cases of nonpersonal prediction would involve answers to such questions as: Is she married? Does she have children? Did she graduate from high school? Data for nonpersonal prediction questions were gathered by visiting the interviewee at home, discussing aspects of her behavior with acquaintances, and observing the person. From these data, predictive items like the following were constructed.

In paying bills and debts, Mrs. P. is:

1. Usually late or delinquent
2. Only average in this regard
3. Quite punctual and conscientious

A perceiver's accuracy in predicting such items was measured by comparing his predictions about the behavior of the interviewee with what was found out from her friends about her actual behavior.

Evaluation

First-person prediction studies are limited to personal interactions, for we cannot sensibly ask a perceiver to predict what he thinks a person in a written case, a film, a photograph, or a tape-recorded interview thinks of him. The studies are also awkward to plan and time-consuming to conduct. Yet self-insight, a highly prized human trait, is measured through determining the accuracy of first-person predictions. Furthermore, what we think a person thinks of us has a decisive influence on what we think of him. A convincing case can also be made for the importance of second- and third-person sensitivity, at least in certain situations. It is, for example, vital for the psychotherapist to understand what the client thinks of himself (second person). In most human relations situations it is equally vital to know what others think—rightly or wrongly—of a person. Scientists seek, however, to know what kind of an individual a person *really* is—regardless of what he thinks he is or what other people think he is. The most convincing test of the reality of a person is what he actually *does*. It is difficult to construct a good measure based on actual behavior, although, with increasing frequency, investigators are developing such measures (Cline and Richards, 1960; Soskin, 1959; Weiss, 1963). The ideal measure would include subscores for each type of prediction.

METHODS OF RECORDING PREDICTIONS

Experimenters have asked perceivers to record their predictions of persons by ratings, by choosing from multiple-choice alternatives, by matching, and by ranking. The apparently minor matter of the method of recording has a major influence on judgments.

In almost half of the studies (45 per cent), predictions were recorded solely by ratings. The method Cline (1955) used in his trait ratings is typical. Friends of each of his interviewees were given 12 traits: cooperative, stubborn, careful, impractical, ambitious, etc. They were then asked to rate the interviewee on the following six-point scale:

1. Very unlike him
2. Rather unlike him
3. A little unlike him
4. A little like him
5. Rather like him
6. Very like him

The average of the ratings given an interviewee by friends was used as the criterion of the "correct" rating. Perceivers who saw the interviewee in the film rated him on the same traits in the way they thought his friends had rated him. The perceiver's accuracy was measured by subtracting the differences between his ratings and the actual ratings given the interviewee by his friends.

Objective questions, either the multiple-choice or the true-false–yes-no type, were the second most widely used method of recording predictions (28 per cent). One reason for their popularity lies in the relative ease with which an interviewee can be given a standard personality test and the perceiver can be asked to predict how he filled it out. Cline used many judging instruments of this type: the Strong Vocational Interest Blank, the Minnesota Multiphasic Personality Inventory, the California Psychological Inventory, the Gough Adjective Check List, and a multiple-choice sentence-completion test.

Seven of the one-hundred studies used the matching method of recording judgments. The method requires the judge to match some data about a person with some other data about the same person. In contrast to the rating and objective questionnaire methods which require many concrete, detailed, and often quantified judgments about a person, the matching method may require only a single global judgment. Estes (1938), for example, presented to his perceivers two-minute silent films showing two college students in a variety of expressive movements: playing slapjack, building a house of cards, trying to push each other off balance, etc. Then the perceivers were given three thumbnail sketches to read: two of these were based on long study of the students in the film; the third was a "joker." The task of the perceivers was to match a sketch to the student in the film that it fitted. The experiment as a whole required the judges to repeat the process for seven different pairs of persons. A perceiver's score was the percentage of correct matches made. It was in this experiment, incidentally, that judges interested in painting, dramatics, and personnel were significantly superior to psychologists: the former averaged over 60 per cent correct judgments; the latter only 42 per cent.

The matching method has substantial merits: The criterion of accuracy is objective; the method is flexible; and it is easy to use. It is also likely to seem more realistic to the respondent for it requires him to make a single judgment rather than many detailed judgments. The method also seems closer to the global ways in which we normally make judgments of people (Asch, 1946). The ranking method is similar to the rating method, but it has been used much less frequently (5 per cent). Instead of having a perceiver rate each person in a group separately, the ranking method requires him to rank the members of the group from the highest to the lowest.

The ranking method is simple and practical. Its general merit, however, lies in the fact that it *eliminates* the influence of level and spread habits on predictions. By contrast, rating stresses their influence. Consequently, the use of rating makes it almost impossible to assess the relative influence of habit, interaction, and differentiation determinants on the predictions. If rankings had been used in all the studies where ratings were used, we would now know more about sensitivity than we do. The moral: Use ratings where the primary concern is with level and spread habits; never use ratings where this is *not* the primary concern.

Chapter Three

METHODS OF TRAINING

OUR LIVES FORCE us to spend much of our time from the cradle to the grave learning about people and trying to predict their behavior. Formal training is a little and a late addition to our understanding. In fact, such training seems as likely to result in a subtraction as in an addition. In the search for better methods, therefore, we first look for the elements that are involved in forming *all* of our impressions about people—both correct and incorrect. With this as a basis, we then try to formulate guides for making them more correct through training.

How We Form Impressions of a Person

Lawson (1966) suggests that the function of learning is to enable the human being to predict the outcome of behavior relative to other objects in the world and on the basis of that prediction to guide or direct behavior so that behavior of the person fits the environment. The basic form in which *all* learning takes place consists of "(1) the perception of some whole or unity that holds the attention of the perceiver and toward which the perceiver behaves, (2) behavior relative to the unity guided by some known behavior pattern, (3) differentiation of new elements of the unity as a result of the behavior, and (4) the relating of these elements within the context of the initial whole, and with the guidance of the known behavior pattern." Whether the pattern is adequately fitted to all learning may be doubted. However, it certainly seems to fit the facts about how we form our impressions of people.

WE REACT TO A PERSON AS A UNITY

We first perceive a person as a unit, as a whole. We do not see his specific traits and then fit them together to form a general impression; we get an almost instantaneous general impression. Allport (1937, p. 500) has suggested how one might convince himself of this:

> While riding in a public conveyance close your eyes and turn your head toward some fellow passenger not previously observed, perhaps someone sitting obliquely opposite. Open your eyes for a brief glimpse lasting two or three seconds, and then with the eyes closed introspect upon the impressions as they arise. Here is a person, never before seen and completely unknown. With but the briefest visual perception, a complex mental process is aroused, resulting within a very short time, thirty seconds perhaps, in judgments of the sex, age, size, nationality, profession, and social caste of the stranger, together with some estimate of his temperament, his past suffering, his "hardness," his ascendance, friendliness, neatness, and even his trustworthiness and integrity. With further acquaintance many of the impressions would no doubt prove to be erroneous, but the exercise serves to call attention to the swift "totalizing" nature of our judgements.

Asch (1946) provided extensive experimental support for the idea that we see people as a unity. In a varied series of studies, he gave his subjects instructions similar to these:

> I shall read to you a number of characteristics that belong to a particular person. Please listen to them carefully and try to form an impression of the kind of person described. You will later be asked to give a brief characterization of the person in just a few sentences. I will read the list slowly and will repeat it once.

The following is one such list: energetic, assured, talkative, cold, ironical, inquisitive, persuasive. Here are two typical characterizations:

> He is the type of person you meet all too often; sure of himself, talks too much, always trying to bring you around to his way of thinking and with not much feeling for the other fellow.

> He seems to be the kind of person who would make a great impression upon others at first meeting. However, as time went by, his acquaintances would easily come to see through the mask. Underneath would be revealed his arrogance and selfishness.

None of the hundreds of subjects in the different experiments ever merely repeated the list of traits as a description of the person or replied merely with synonyms of the words in the list. Although their impressions varied, they got a unified picture of the man behind the traits: They could not form an impression of a quarter or half a person; they could not experience an anonymous trait—a trait apart from a person; and they could not determine the quality or value of a trait apart from the person. Thus, the entire person always spoke through his individual qualities: "One strives to form an impression of the entire person. The impression tends to become complete even when the evidence is meager. It is hard not to see the person as a unit."

So powerful is the impulse toward unity that it can blind us to obvious facts. Gollin (1954), for example, showed 79 college students a film in five scenes of a young woman. Two scenes suggested that she was promiscuous and immoral: (1) being picked up in front of a run-down hotel and (2) entering a glass-fronted store that might have been a bar and coming out with a man who was not the same man who had picked her up in front of the hotel. The middle scene was neutral: (3) walking along and talking to a female companion. The other two scenes suggested that she was kind and considerate: (4) giving money to a beggar and (5) helping a woman who had fallen on a public stairway.

After they had seen the film the students were asked to "write down on the paper given to you the impression you have formed of the person who appears in all the scenes. Please be as detailed as you can, that is, write your impression as if you were telling someone about this individual's personality." Some gave *simplified* impressions by describing the girl as immoral *or* kind, but not both; some gave *aggregated* impressions by describing the girl as immoral *and* kind, but not trying to show how the two qualities were related; and some gave *related* impressions by both describing the two qualities and accounting for their presence in the same girl. Of the descriptions, 49 per cent were classed as simplified; 30 per cent, aggregated; and 21 per cent, related.

OUR IMPLICIT THEORIES GUIDE OUR IMPRESSIONS

People are so complex that we are easily dazzled by the vast array of things to describe, explain, and predict. Scientists, faced with the same problem, have developed a variety of ways of dealing with it. Mechanical devices provide one solution: The telescope limits the astronomer's attention to one part of the heavens; the microscope fastens the attention of the biologist upon one part of his environment. Theories provide an even more powerful way of preventing the scientist from being paralyzed and confused by complexities, for a theory tells him not only what to look for but also what *not* to look for or worry about.

A scientific theory defines a set of terms and assumes relationships between the terms. Freudian theory, for example, defines the id, ego, and superego and assumes relationships between them. A theory unifies the facts we have and suggests new facts to look for. It is, therefore, not so much true or false as it is useful or not useful. The utility of a theory is determined by the ease with which predictions can be made from it and by the ease with which it is possible to determine whether they are false. Its strength is determined by its resistance to efforts to falsify it.

We all use theories in dealing with people: We invent concepts, assume relationships between them, and make predictions from our assumptions. Our theories are not, however, useful in the scientific sense, for they are implicit rather than explicit. That is, we are only dimly aware of our theories. As a result, we rarely make any real effort to test them. Yet they rule our impressions and our judgments.

We have implicit theories about the relationship between appearance and psychological traits. McKeachie (1952) had six men rate six women on 22 different personality traits. They were told that the purpose of the study was to determine the reliability of personality ratings made on the basis of a ten-minute interview. Actually, the purpose was to determine the influence of lipstick on personal impressions. Each man interviewed three girls with and three without lipstick; each girl appeared in three interviews with and three without lipstick. Result: Without lipstick, a girl was more often judged as being conscientious, serious, talkative, and not interested in men. After the interviews the men were asked what things they thought had influenced their ratings. None mentioned lipstick.

The reverse is also true: We have implicit theories about the relationship between psychological traits and physical appearance. Students were given these two descriptions (Secord, 1958):

A. This man is warmhearted and honest. He has a good sense of humor and is intelligent and unbiased in his opinion. He is responsible and self-confident with an air of refinement.

B. This man is a ruthless and brutal person. He is extremely hostile, quick-tempered, and overbearing. He is well known for his boorish and vulgar manner and is a very domineering and unsympathetic person.

The students were then asked to rate 32 facial *features* of the two fictitious men on a seven-point scale. The students not only did this quickly and without difficulty but also generally agreed on the differences between them. The warmhearted man had a more direct gaze, a smoother brow, more relaxed nostrils, and hair more neatly groomed. The ruthless man had a darker complexion, more tense face, a squarer jaw, and a rougher texture to his skin.

Our theories are structured: a few central traits organize the peripheral ones within a unified framework. The warmth of a person is one of these central traits. Asch (1946) read list *A* to one group and list *B* to another:

List *A*: Intelligent, skillful, industrious, *cold,* determined, practical, cautious

List *B*: Intelligent, skillful, industrious, *warm*, determined, practical, cautious

The two groups were asked to write an imaginative sketch of the kind of person who would have such a combination of traits. The substitution of warm for cold made a big difference in how the other traits were viewed. The following sketches are typical:

> COLD GROUP: A very ambitious and talented person who would not let anyone or anything stand in the way of achieving his goal. Wants his own way, he is determined not to give in, no matter what happens.
> WARM GROUP: A person who believes certain things to be right, wants others to see his point, would be sincere in an argument, and would like to see his point won.

The groups were also given a list of additional traits and asked to check those which fitted their impression of the person. The warm person was more often checked as generous, wise, happy, sociable, popular, and humorous. The cold person was more often checked as shrewd, irritable, ruthless, and self-centered. Asch concludes:

> The moment we see that two or more characteristics belong to the same person they enter into dynamic interaction. We cannot see one quality and another in the same person without their affecting each other. . . . From its inception the impression has structure, even if rudimentary. The various characteristics do not possess the same weight. Some become central, providing the main direction; others become peripheral and dependent. Until we have found the center—that part of the person which wants to live and act in a certain way, which wants not to break or disappear—we feel we have not succeeded in reaching an understanding.

OUR THEORIES DETERMINE OUR PREDICTIONS

We strive to complete the incomplete, to unify, to achieve *closure*. When we are shown a circle with a tiny gap, we see a complete circle; when we are shown a face in profile without a nose, we perceive a complete face; and when we hear an unfinished story, we finish it ourselves. Our implicit theories help us to close the gaps in our knowledge about a person, to finish his story. They not only help us to complete our present picture of him; we predict his past and his future by means of them.

At least some of the means we use for prediction are remarkably stable. Secord and Berscheid (1963) presented 79 students with traits sometimes assumed to be characteristics of the typical Negro (lazy, dishonest, happy-go-lucky, superstitious, and deeply religious) and also with traits not commonly associated with the Negro (sportsmanlike, sincere, generous, conceited, moody, and quarrelsome). The assumed relationships between each pair of traits was measured by having the students fill out ratings like the following:

A person is *lazy*. How likely is it that he is *also*:
Sportsmanlike

0   1   2   3   4   5   6   7   8   9   10
Impossible   Certain

Each trait was rotated into the "lazy" and "sportsmanlike" slots. The mean ratings for a pair were used as a measure of the assumed relationship between the two traits. The higher the rating, the greater the relationship. The ratings were repeated, but this time the students were asked to assume that the person was a Negro. That is: "A Negro is *lazy*. How likely is it that he is . . ." It was the assumption that a comparison of the relationships between the traits under the two situations would provide an acid test for the stability of implicit theories. If the assumed relationships between traits were changeable, they would change when the students shifted from whites to Negros. Result: No change. Conclusion: "If implicit personality theory biases remain unaffected in the type of quantitative judgment employed here, as they seem to, they will be even more likely to operate in the everyday situation where there is usually little pressure for precision in judgment and more freedom for biases to operate."

Implicit theories, like scientific theories, vary in acceptance. Some relationships, such as those between the traits considered above, are widely accepted. Some are accepted by one group but not by another. Teachers, for example, assume that quietness is related to good adjustment and loudness to poor adjustment. Psychologists assume the reverse, i.e., that quietness is related to poor adjustment. And some individuals have their own unique theories.

Exhibit 3-1 illustrates these variations in the implicit acceptance of relationships as well as the variations in strength of the relationships. Chelsea (1965) had five sorority sisters rank ten other members on five traits: boldness, calmness, extroversion, control, and empiricism. The five traits and their definitions were derived from a factor analysis of 22 personality inventory measures.

The bold cluster included measures of dominance, energy, self-confidence, and optimism; the calm cluster—calmness, amiability, emotional control, and warmth; the extroverted cluster—low artistic and high economic values as well as a measure of outward-oriented thinking; the controlled cluster—ambition, organization, and emotional control; and the empirical cluster—readiness for change, religious skepticism, nonconformity, and scientific values.

The correlations in the table show the relationships assumed varied with the traits and with the girls. Boldness and extroversion were assumed by all of the girls to be closely and positively related (median *r* of .88), whereas calmness and empiricism were somewhat negatively related (median *r* of —.30). The median correlations at the bottom

EXHIBIT 3-1   *Individual Differences in the Acceptance of
Implicit Personality Theories*
(Chelsea, 1965)

	CORRELATIONS BETWEEN RANKINGS FOR TRAITS					
TRAITS ASSUMED TO BE RELATED	ANNE	BABS	CLARE	DONNA	EVELYN	MEDIAN CORRE- LATION
Bold and extroverted	.86	.88	.89	.88	.79	.88
Controlled and empirical	.78	.78	.79	.49	.65	.78
Bold and empirical	.23	.27	.50	.55	.68	.50
Bold and controlled	.07	− .21	.43	.36	.45	.36
Extroverted and empirical	.14	.39	.18	.35	.71	.35
Controlled and extroverted	.03	− .12	.23	.37	.57	.23
Bold and calm	− .30	.30	− .10	− .09	.59	− .09
Extroverted and calm	− .05	− .15	.21	− .20	.79	− .05
Calm and controlled	− .20	− .01	− .43	.13	.60	− .01
Calm and empirical	− .47	− .01	− .30	− .30	.60	− .30
Median correlation	.05	.13	.22	.35	.62	

of the exhibit indicate that the general level of relationships between the traits varied a great deal from girl to girl. Overall, for example, Anne assumed the least positive relationship between the traits (.05),
whereas Evelyn saw the traits as closely related (.62). That is, Evelyn
saw the boldest girl as also the most extroverted, empirical, controlled,
and calm. As a consequence, each girl had a somewhat different implicit theory from every other girl, and some of the girls had conflicting theories. Anne, for example, saw calmness and empiricism as
being negatively related, whereas Evelyn saw them as being quite positively related (.60). From such implicit theories about the relationships
between physical and psychological traits and between one trait and other
traits we quickly fill out our picture of a person and make predictions
about him. Our focus is upon the *discrepancy* between assumed and actual relationships. All the girls, for example, assumed some relationship
between some of the traits. Yet correlations between measures of the
five traits among 100 students showed no significant relationship between
any of the traits (Linden, 1965). The implicit theories of the girls were
wrong.

OUR PREDICTIONS FIT THE INITIAL UNITY

At the beginning, we see a person as a whole. By means of our
theories, we differentiate elements from the whole and make predictions

from these elements. The predictions, however, are cut to fit the whole we originally perceived—we move from a homogeneous whole to a differentiated whole.

We *perceive* a person. Our observations, our theories, and our predictions from the theories are interwoven to give us our conviction of what a person *is*. We perceive people, in other words, in the same general way that we perceive everything else.

In our perceptions we are so used to predicting the substance from its sensory shadow that we normally feel that the shadow is the substance: We do not see green, but a pea; we do not smell smoke, but a cigar; and we do not hear a high-pitched voice, but a child. So it is with our perceptions of people. We do not see lipstick, but a girl interested in men; we do not hear a loud voice, but a dominating man; and we do not see a dark complexion and a tense face, but a ruthless person. We do not normally separate the facts we have observed about a person from the inferences we make from the facts. They are interwoven and the result of the interweaving is, for us, what the person *is*. The novelist Proust (1922) has tried to describe the process:

> Even the simple act which we describe as "seeing someone we know" is, to some extent, an intellectual process. We pack the physical outline of the creature we see with all the ideas we have already formed about him, and in the complete picture of him which we compose in our minds those ideas have certainly the principal place. In the end they come to fill out so completely the curve of his cheeks, to follow so exactly the line of his nose, they blend so harmoniously in the sound of his voice that these seem to be no more than a transparent envelope, so that each time we see the face or hear the voice it is our own ideas of him which we recognize and to which we listen.

Training Principles

What we have said about people can be said again about the way we solve a puzzle. Consider the following crypt-arithmetic puzzle:

$$\begin{array}{r} \text{S E N D} \\ + \text{M O R E} \\ \hline \text{M O N E Y} \end{array}$$

Each letter stands for a particular number from 0 to 9. The problem is to infer the correct numbers. The theoretical system used in solving the problem concerns the arithmetic operations involved in addition. The solution is achieved when each letter has been replaced by a number and where collectively they satisfy the rules of addition. The puzzle solver begins by inspecting the pattern of letters, looking for some clue that will suggest a number for a letter. For example, in this puzzle M can only be 1. The letters are gradually replaced by numbers until we finish with:

$$9,567$$
$$+1,085$$
$$\overline{10,652}$$

As in our reactions to a person, the letters represent the initial unity that attracts and holds attention. As in our implicit theories, arithmetic allows us to find unity and meaning in the puzzle. As in our predictions about people, arithmetic allows us to make predictions concerning the numbers represented by the letters. Also, as in our predictions about people, each possible number is tested for its fit and accepted or rejected on this basis. As in our efforts to understand people, the initial unity persists throughout the solving process. Each part of the puzzle is differentiated as one discovers the correct number for each letter until finally all the letters are replaced by numbers and the puzzle is solved. Perhaps the most critical difference lies in the fact that we have one common theory of arithmetic but innumerable theories about people.

The basic implication for sensitivity training is this: If learning about a person necessarily involves the initial perception of him as a unity that gradually becomes differentiated, then the most effective training would also involve organizing the training so that the student is first presented with a person as a unity and then required to differentiate within the unity in a manner that leads the student to make more correct predictions than he made before. But how does one do this?

THE UNIFIED PERSON

The more the training requires students to attend to people as unified wholes, the more effective it will be. If the principle is correct, one would expect that those individuals who are motivated to see people as wholes and trained to do so would be more accurate in their judgments. Allport (1937) has suggested that people in the arts are most likely to be of this type:

> The esthetic attitude seeks always to comprehend the intrinsic harmony of an object that is the center of attention. The object may be as trivial as an ornament or as substantial as a human being; in any case the singleness and the symmetry of the structure are what interest the esthetic person. . . . As a qualification, it seems to stand above all others, especially in the case of the most gifted judges.

Some empirical evidence provides significant support for the view. Estes (1938), for example, concluded: "Judges who have strong interests in either the graphic arts or dramatics are more successful than those whose dominant interests are in the sciences and philosophy." Cline (1955) also discovered that those whose tastes in pictures coincide most closely with those of painters were most accurate in their predictions.

Sensitivity training should focus on people as unified wholes. Failure to apply this principle offers a ready explanation for the repeated failures of reading, lectures, and discussions of psychology to have any appreciable impact on predictive accuracy. It may also account for the repeated failures of such approaches to have any influence on the development of interpersonal competence. For example, an extensive evaluation of a human relations program for foremen at the International Harvester Company arrived at this conclusion (Fleishman et al., 1955, p. 101):

> With reference to training in human relations, our study yields one clear implication. . . . Our foremen developed a point of view in school but lost it on their return to the plant if their superior had a different point of view. . . . this suggests that to improve social relations almost anywhere, it is important to work on the *whole social setting*. It is not possible to pull people out of this setting, tell or teach them some ideas, and then return them to the setting and consider everything fixed.

A similar evaluation of a similar lecture program at the Detroit-Edison Company reached a similar conclusion (Hariton, 1951).

Human relations programs over the past decades have focused ever more sharply upon the consideration of actual persons as unified wholes. They have moved from lectures to conferences, from conferences to case studies, from case studies to role playing, and from role playing to Sensitivity Training. This particular trend is related to the general trend toward stressing unified wholes in *all* kinds of instruction. Instruction in arithmetic has moved from a stress upon the multiplication tables to a stress upon solving problems; instruction in reading, from a stress upon the alphabet to a stress upon sentences; and instruction in foreign language, from a stress upon grammar to a stress, from the beginning, upon speaking and reading.

THE FACILITATION OF CHANGE

We fill out our picture of a person and make predictions about him on the basis of our theories. Some theories lead to correct predictions, some to erroneous ones. *The easier the training program makes it for a student to shift to a better theory, the more effective it will be.* We stick much too tenaciously to even our poor theories about people. We view people as wholes and differentiate the parts within a whole that rapidly becomes immune to change, for we select facts that fit the whole and ignore facts that do not. Furthermore, our impressions of a person are not so much a tentative hypothesis as a firm conviction about reality, and we tend to fight for our convictions. Most important of all, we generally have little or no idea about the theories that we use in judging people.

The importance for training in the ease-of-change principle is indirectly but strongly supported by comparisons of sensitive and insensitive perceivers. The largest and most consistent difference is between those perceivers who are ready for change and those who are not; Grossman (1963), for example, obtained the scores of 130 students on a sound-film test of the ability to differentiate between individuals and a written test of the ability to differentiate between groups. These scores were correlated with several dozen inventory measures of personality. Scores on a readiness-for-change scale were more highly correlated with all the measures of sensitivity than any other trait. That is, those most ready for changes in meals, measurement systems, the calendar, methods of burial, women's clothing, etc., were most accurate in their differentiations between both individuals and groups.

The major finding of Cline (1955) stresses the importance of resistance to changes. The *least* sensitive were the most fascistic ($r = -.46$), the most ethnocentric, and the most conservative. Furthermore, the longer both an authoritarian and a nonauthoritarian have known a person, the greater the differences in their sensitivity (Newcomb, 1963). Freshmen living in the same cooperative house were give the F scale when they first arrived. During the first week, they attempted to predict each other's responses to various scales and inventories. Those with high F scores were somewhat less accurate. They made the same predictions after they had known each other for a month. This time, the high F scores were strikingly less accurate ($r = -.56$).

Authoritarians are less accurate than nonauthoritarians even in judging traits that are more important to the authoritarian. Navy recruits took the F scale. They then heard recordings of an authoritarian recruit and a nonauthoritarian one. After hearing the recordings, the recruits judged each of the two on 30 personality traits. Conclusion: "In the perception and judgment of others, authoritarians seem to be more insensitive than nonauthoritarians to the psychological and personality characteristics of others. It is true even with the attributes of personal power or forcefulness, to which authoritarians are allegedly sensitive" (Jones, 1954). Why should authoritarians be more insensitive? The most likely explanation is that they are more defensive and therefore more resistant to changing their theories about a person. Two groups of subjects, one defensive and one nondefensive, were selected by measuring the time it took them to "recognize" threatening and unthreatening words that were flashed on a screen: the longer the time, the greater the perceptual defensiveness. A study of the defensive and undefensive groups led to the following conclusion (Chodorkoff, 1954):

> The better adjusted individual attempts to obtain mastery over threatening situations by getting to know, as quickly as possible, what it is that is threatening . . . for the well-adjusted person threat is a relatively momentary phenomenon. He is only threatened initially; then he extends himself in order to handle the threat. As a result, the threat is minimized. For the maladjusted person, threat persists because he cannot deal with it directly. Instead he tries to remove himself from it by denial or misperception.

The authoritarian does not "see" qualities in other people that are a threat to him.

KNOWLEDGE OF RESULTS

Suppose we genuinely and deeply wanted to know whether our theories and predictions about a person are true or false. How could we find out? Our informal interactions with people rarely give us a check. The greatest potential advantage of formal training is that it *can* provide us with systematic tests of our theories about people. *The more frequently and the more precisely training provides the student with tests of his theories, the more effective the training will be.*

Of 20 studies found by the author where a measure of general intelligence was related to a measure of sensitivity, *all* were positive. The median correlation was .30. More specifically, verbal comprehension and reasoning ability appear to be primarily responsible for the relationship. Rote memory ability is not even related to the ability to remember names and facts (Witroyl and Kaess, 1957) and differences in the speed and flexibility of perception are unrelated (Grossman, 1963; Newbigging, 1953). All the results are consistent with the commonsense conclusion that we find out about a person and check what we think about him by listening to what he says about himself or to what others say about him. The more intelligent we are, the better we can do these things.

Knowledge of results (reinforcement, feedback, reward, etc.) is universally accepted as essential for learning about anything. However, there is doubt about why it is effective, when it is effective, and what kind is most effective. It has, for example, been assumed in programmed instruction that a program facilitated learning by requiring a response that was immediately reinforced. Facts do not fit the assumption. Tobias and

Weiner (1963), for example, tested subjects with a program in which one group wrote all the responses and checked each response immediately after it was made. A second group responded by "thinking" the response and checking their thoughts against the correct answer. A third group read the items on a ditto manuscript where all the blanks requiring a response were filled in and did not check their responses. A posttest was given to subjects immediately after they completed the program and again after six weeks. Result: No differences between the various methods of reinforcing.

Interpretation: Knowledge of results in sensitivity training provides the essential service of focusing the perceiver's much needed *attention* on the person he is trying to understand. It also encourages the development of *self-competition* and *game-playing attitudes,* which are of great help in encouraging the student to overcome his strong resistance to change.

Guides to Better Training

Sensitivity training should focus upon the unified person, make it easy for trainees to shift their theories, and provide feedback. The effective application of these general principles in actual programs is a difficult and still largely unsolved problem. None of the following suggestions are either novel or controversial. They are, however, critical; no program has applied them all with even minimal success.

FORMULATE MORE REALISTIC GOALS

The goals of the typical college course are content-centered: "The aim of this course is to cover the theories, methods, facts, and principles of (for example) abnormal psychology." The question of whether changes in the sensitivity of students occur as a result of mastering the content is ignored. In human relations programs and Sensitivity Training, the goals are more trainee-centered but also more vague. As a consequence, the trainer does not know exactly what he is supposed to be teaching or the trainee what he is supposed to be learning.

As goals become more specific, the failures of training to reach them become clearer. The goal of one program, for example, was to improve the trainee's skill as a good listener and his ability to get people to "open up" (Maier, Hoffman, and Lansky, 1960). To achieve these aims students participated in weekly role-playing sessions and had practice in reflecting feeling. The criterion of success was the quality of performance in a role-playing scene at the end of training. Results: A modest improvement in listening; no improvement in the ability to get people to talk. Conclusion:

The implication of these results for the amount and type of training received by supervisors and executives in the typical industrial course in human relations is obvious. Training is a slow process of reorientation and of the accumulation of new concepts, attitudes, and skills . . . we can conclude that where management is seriously interested in training supervisory personnel in effective human relations, they might expect to invest considerably more time then is presently customary.

The component approach indicates the specific goals which training may try to develop: level and spread accuracy, empathic and observational accuracy, or accuracy in differentiating between individuals and groups. By considering specific traits and specific kinds of people these may be even more concrete: accuracy in observing the social traits of disturbed children, accuracy in differentiating the interpersonal competence of neurotic adults, etc. It is part of the task of the following six chapters to explore these possibilities in relation to each of the components.

DEVELOP BETTER MEASURES OF GOAL ACHIEVEMENT

Measurement is the *sine qua non* of effective training. The effort to develop measures before training clarifies the goals; the use of measures during training gives trainees the knowledge of results that is essential for learning; and the use of measures after training shows how successful the training has been and indicates how it might be made more effective.

Accuracy in predicting how a person will think and behave is not just a good measure of sensitivity; it is *the* measure. However, efforts to measure predictive accuracy have generally assumed that sensitivity was a single dimension. The results have been confusing. The relatively independent influences of level and spread, of empathy and observation, and of differentiation between groups and individuals have been intermixed in unknown and varying ways. Consequently, what is thought to be a measure of accuracy in differentiating between individuals turns out to be a measure of the ability to differentiate between groups; what is thought to be a measure of accuracy in differentiating between groups turns out to be a measure of level accuracy. Although a single index of sensitivity may eventually be possible, the greatest present need is for the improvement of pure measures of the components.

Measures must fit the specific goals of the actual training situation. There are, however, general criteria for determining the goodness of any measure: reliability, validity, generality, and practicality. The criteria are so widely ignored in the measurement of sensitivity that a brief review of them is in order. The more reliable a measure, other things being equal, the better the measure. The reliability of a test is the self-consistency of its scores. Self-consistency may exist between the parts of the test (internal consistency) or between the same test from one time to another (stability). If people who get high scores on one part of the test also get high scores on another part of the test, then the test is internally consistent. If people who get high scores the first time they take the test also get high scores when they take the test at the later time, the test is stable. The reasonableness of this criterion is apparent: if scores on the same measure of sensitivity are not related to each other, it is very unlikely that they will be related to anything else. The more valid a measure, the better. A measure of low reliability cannot be valid; a test of high reliability may or may not be. The validity of a test is the degree to which it measures what it is supposed to measure. A test of sensitivity is supposed to measure predictive accuracy. But how is accuracy to be determined? In everyday life, we rarely have any good way of telling whether our predictions are correct or not.

One way of getting correct answers is through using expert opinion. Mahoney (1960), for example, developed a sensitivity test that consisted of four selections from fiction portraying markedly different personalities. Those taking the test are instructed to read the selection, to get "feel" for the individual portrayed, and then to complete 20 multiple-choice incomplete statements as they think the individual in the selection would have completed them. Mahoney had 23 psychologists take the test who had been picked as being particularly sensitive people. The answer most often given by them was taken as the correct answer. The internal consistencies and stabilities of scores on the test were quite high: a respondent who agreed with the experts on one question at one time agreed with the experts on other questions at other times. So the test was reliable, but was it valid, i.e., did the answers of the experts agree with the answers that the fictional personalities would have given? There is no way of knowing in this case. There is, however, a way of measuring sensitivity so that the answers can be known. The method consists of having respondents judge actual people who have already answered the questions or whose behavior is known from observation. Then the accuracy of a respondent's predictions can be checked against the actual responses. Because of its greater validity, the method is being used with increasing frequency in the development of sensitivity measures. The more generality a measure has, the better. Even though a test is reliable and valid, it may have little generality. Thus, scores on a test may be a reliable and valid measure of sensitivity to men but may not have any relationship to sensitivity to women. Again, scores on a test measuring sensitivty to what a person thinks of another may not be related to scores on a test measuring sensitivity to what the person thinks of himself.

The less time it takes to develop and take a test, the better. In theory, practicality is the last and least important criterion to be considered, for there is no point in giving a test that can be easily constructed and taken in a brief time if it is not reliable and valid. In general practice, practicality is the first and most important criterion; if a test cannot be developed in the time available or if it takes too much time to finish, it will not be used.

SEQUENCE THE GOALS

In the process of achieving the general purpose of training, the trainee must inevitably learn many different things. Which of these things is it most efficient to learn first? second? third? Finding the best order of learning the various things he must know is the problem of *sequencing*.

The relationship between didactic and practicum training is a central and unsolved sequencing problem in the education of clinical psychologists. Should didactic training precede, follow, or be intermingled with the practicum work? Some experts are quite sure that a mastery of general psychology, personality theory, and experimental methods must precede actual clinical experience. They hold that such knowledge is essential if the trainee is to be ready to observe adequately what goes on in the clinical situation, to interpret properly what he sees and hears, and to understand fully the professional setting and its requirements. Other experts are just as sure that some clinical experience should precede most, if not all, of the academic training. They believe that students should first encounter clinical phenomena, should be puzzled by them, and should then raise questions which give his academic study more meaning and direction. Still other experts feel that the two types of training should run along together: As the classroom training proceeds from general to specific, practicum experience proceeds from the simple to the complex. As there are no decisive facts that bear on this question, the controversy continues. As far as the development of sensitivity is concerned, the component view suggests that all the experts are right: Attempts to improve sensitivity without an adequate theory are ineffective; the mastery of abstract theory apart from concrete people is ineffective; and, therefore, the simultaneous exposure to both theory and people is the most effective way of increasing sensitivity. The unanswered question is: How can this be done?

Part of the answer is to concentrate on the components one at a time. Within the framework of a particular component, the training can then focus on unified wholes, facilitate the shift from less to more adequate theories, and provide the trainee with knowledge of his progress in mastering the component. Within such a framework, the student can be exposed to a wide variety of persons, traits, and situations.

How should the components themselves be sequenced? An argument can be advanced for various sequences. Improvements in level and spread may be produced more quickly; improvements in empathic and observational accuracy may have the most pervasive and enduring influence; and improvements in the ability to differentiate between groups and individuals may be of greatest clinical importance. It is our guess that the sequence as given in the following chapters will be most efficient: level, spread, empathy, etc. It seems even more certain that any sequence is preferable to an attempt to deal with all of the components simultaneously.

REDUCE DEFENSIVENESS

For his sensitivity to increase, the trainee must change some of his beliefs about people. As the evidence of both psychology and Sensitivity Training amply testifies, the process of changing one's beliefs can be very stressful. In fact, it is widely assumed that such stress is both inevitable and necessary if changes in our perceptions of ourselves are to occur. It seems to be a dubious assumption, for as stress increases, resistance to change increases. At any rate, the component approach provides several ways of reducing stress and the consequent rigidity.

Sequencing goals reduces stress. The more important a goal is to a trainee and the more uncertain he is about his achievement of it, the more stressful the situation is likely to be. Since general sensitivity is both more important and more uncertain than any of its components, stress can be reduced by considering the components one at a time rather than all at once. The components also vary in the importance that trainees attach to them. People are likely to be less concerned about the accuracy of their level than about their sensitivity to the differences between people. In general, then, stress can be reduced by taking up the goals one at a time, beginning with the one least likely to generate stress. Stress can also be controlled by varying the training methods. Who is judged? What kind of predictions are to be made? And how are the predictions to be recorded? As Exhibit 3-2 suggests, stress varies with the answers to these questions. A person is unlikely to be disturbed when

EXHIBIT 3-2 *Variations in Stress with the Methods of Training*

	LOW STRESS	AVERAGE STRESS	HIGH STRESS
Presentation of the person	Written case	Tape recording Filmed interview	Social interaction
Type of prediction	Nonpersonal	Third person Second person	First person
Recording of predictions	Rating	Matching	Ranking

he finds out about his errors in rating a person he has read about. He is more likely to be disturbed when he finds out that others do not think he had as much sense of humor as he thinks he has. Generally, the closer we feel to the person we are judging, the more stressful the situation; the more relevant the predictions are to our opinions of ourselves, the more stressful; and the more we are compelled to discriminate the good people from the not-so-good, the more stress. Ranking forces people to discriminate; rating does not, since all people can be given the same rating. The popularity of rating over ranking is due in part to the distaste for making the discriminations required by ranking.

Stress also varies with the social desirability of the quality being considered: less stress is generated by judgments about the neatness of our handwriting than about our self-insight and sense of humor. We assume that the trainee is more likely to develop skill in dealing constructively with stress if the level of stress is raised gradually. We also assume that a person is more likely to deal effectively with the fact that his acquaintances think he is too talkative and humorless if he has already dealt with similar but less powerful facts about himself.

FIT THE METHOD TO THE GOAL

Many methods are used in sensitivity training: lectures, group discussions, case studies, role playing, T groups, etc. Training methods are ways of reaching training goals, and the method used should be one adapted to achieving a particular goal. In practically all training, however, it is the method that dominates. For example, Sensitivity Training as evolved by the National Training Laboratory stresses a method, not a goal. The method demands the use of small unstructured groups, focuses upon the trainee rather than upon the trainer, and stresses emotional rather than conceptual learning.

Stress upon a method leads to fuzziness about aims. Thus, the goals of different NTL-type programs vary a great deal depending upon who sets them up, who pays for them, who conducts them, and where they are held. Tannenbaum et al. (1961, p. 232) complain:

> The trainers may value greater insights into defenses, more realistic perception of others, understanding of communication processes, or newly found awareness of the forces operating in a group. Fellow participants may stress willingness to understand and listen to others, effectiveness in role playing, recognition of the trainee's impact on a discussion, or his efforts to help the group achieve its goals. The trainee himself may most wish to develop feelings of confidence and security, to improve his ability to handle tough situations, to gain skills in interviewing and listen-

ing, and to experience relief from some of the tensions and anxieties with which he feels himself saddled.

It may be that some training methods are good for nothing and others are good for everything. However, the value of even a good method varies with the training goal: a method that is good for developing level accuracy may be valueless for developing empathic accuracy. Those who develop training programs and those who take them have limited time. When in doubt, therefore, the simplest, quickest, and most flexible method should be preferred. Some form of the written case seems to best meet these criteria. Cases are easier to develop than tape recordings or sound films and much more flexible to use. Unlike social interaction methods that are limited to the immediate situation, written cases can be used indefinitely. The critical question is not what is *the* best method but what is the best use for any particular method. Such time-consuming methods as role playing and T-group sessions are often used when forms of the written case study would be both quicker and more effective. Combinations of methods would probably be still more effective. Thus, learning programs utilizing written case study material might eventually prove to be the best way of teaching the elements of sensitivity; the more time-consuming methods could then be limited to advanced training. In general, the question of what we are trying to do comes before the question of how we are going to do it.

EVALUATE THE SUCCESS OF TRAINING

We have outlined how we form impressions of people, listed three general principles whose application in training should lead to the formation of more accurate impressions, and translated these principles into a set of guides for the development of sensitivity training programs. Whether the translation works in any given program can only be confidently determined by evaluating it. A good evaluation must meet two difficult requirements: (1) it must use valid criteria for measuring success in achieving the goals of training, and (2) it must use an experimental design which ensures that any apparent improvement is due to the training and not to something else. Our concern here is with the problem of experimental design, for the problem of developing adequate criteria pervades the entire book. Before proceeding, however, it is well to stress a point that the reader may find hard to believe. In the typical program in our educational system, there is no evaluation that can, by the most generous scientific standards, be called adequate. What is true of training in general is even more true of sensitivity training.

Four general types of designs have been used to evaluate training:

1. Measures after training without a control group
2. Measures before and after training without a control group
3. Measures after training with a control group
4. Measures before and after training with a control group

The first of these designs is the most often used but the poorest; the last is the least often used but the best.

Measurements are widely used after training without a control group. For example, students attend a course in human relations. At the end, they take a test covering their knowledge of the facts and principles of human relations. From their test scores, what can be confidently concluded about the effectiveness of the training? While the test scores report how much different students know about the course content, they tell nothing for certain about when, where, and how they learned it. It is quite possible that the students learned all they know *before* they took the course. Even if they did learn the facts and principles in the course, this increased knowledge may have no relation to sensitivity. It is, however, not the inadequacy of the criterion but the inadequacy of the design that we are now stressing. Measures taken after training without a control group are better than nothing—but not much better.

The use of before-and-after measures does not show clearly whether changes did take place during the training period. To this extent, it represents an improvement. Thus, if the same test that was given at the end of a human relations course had also been given at the beginning, the *difference* in knowledge would measure the changes that had taken place. Its weakness is that it does not establish with certainty that the change was due to the training. Thus, it is generally true that just taking the same test a *second* time results in improvement. It may be that the students learned what they learned outside of the training situation. Designs using measures before and after training without a control group are better than those using just measures after training without a control group. Such designs, however, are not as adequate as those that use measures only after training but do use a control group. In fact, after-training measures with a control group can give quite trustworthy evidence about both the impact of training and the reasons for the results. Its remedial weakness is that it is hard to make sure that the experimental and control groups were the same at the beginning of training. This difficulty can be overcome by matching the experimental and control groups before training begins. Even when careful matches are made, however, some critical initial difference in experience or intelligence may be overlooked and bias the results. The assignment of trainees on a strictly random basis is another way of eliminating the weakness. The remedy, however, requires relatively large numbers of trainees in order to reduce the influence of chance.

The design that uses measures before and after training with a control group avoids these common pitfalls in training evaluation:

1. Matching the experimental and control groups on the before-training measures avoids the danger that the groups may not be comparable at the beginning.
2. Taking the difference between before-and-after measures in the trained group indicates what changes took place during the training period.
3. Comparing these changes with the changes that took place in the untrained control group during the training period isolates the changes caused by the training itself.

The exactness of the design has the advantage, among others, that confident conclusions can be drawn from a study based on a small number of trainees. The following study, for example, while not concerned with the development of sensitivity, does illustrate the economy of the before-and-after measures with a control-group design. In 1953, the Bell Telephone Company of Pennsylvania sent 17 of its executives to the University of Pennsylvania for a special ten-month program. The following year it sent 19, and a year after that, 21. The executives took courses in history, science, philosophy, and the arts that required an unusual amount of reading. The aim of the program was to meet the need of business for managers "with breadth and depth, with a broad knowledge of the world in which business exists and operates, with a sensitivity to the forces that affect our business system, and with an understanding of people and their motivations." The measures used to evaluate the effectiveness of the training included two standard achievement tests (the Graduate Record Examination Profile Test and the Cooperative General Culture Test) and measures of artistic, economic, and liberal values (Viteles, 1959). The tests were given at the start and at the end of the ten-month training. They were also given to 16 carefully matched excecutives of the company who did not participate in the training program.

In spite of the small number of trainees involved, the results were decisive. All the trained groups made much higher scores on the achievement tests at the end of the training than they had at the beginning. They also made much higher scores in artistic and liberal values and much lower scores in economic values at the end of the training than at the beginning. For example, 53 per cent of the control group disagreed with the statement "Individual liberty and justice . . . are not possible in socialistic countries." At the end of the program, 95 per cent of the trained executives disagreed. Another example: 67 per cent of the trained group agreed with the statement, "Democracy depends fundamentally upon the existence of free business enterprise." Among the control group, 94 per cent agreed with the statement.

The use of different designs permits us to answer with varying confidence the question: How effective has the training been? The answer determines whether the training program is worth repeating. Even more important, it helps answer the question: How can the training be improved?

Part Two

THE PERCEIVER

Chapter Four

LEVEL

WE PERCEIVE a person as a unified whole. The wholes we perceive, however, are heavily influenced by differences in our levels. One instructor sees a student as mediocre while another sees him as outstanding. Furthermore, the first instructor may find few students that are commendable while the second finds many. In the same manner, one clinician finds few signs of abnormality in people while another finds many; one sales manager searches intensely for qualified salesmen but finds few while another manager finds many; and one conscientious professor sees few instructors that are qualified for promotion while another, equally conscientious, finds many. The nature of level and ways of improving level accuracy are the concerns of the present chapter.

The Measurement of Level

A perceiver's level is his general tendency to make favorable or unfavorable ratings. Assume that a perceiver has rated a series of people on a series of desirable traits from low to high. Then his level is his average rating of all the people on all the traits.

Exhibit 4-1 shows the first of three cases used by Grossman (1963) in the development of a measure of level. The information given about Jim Nelson and the other two men was made ambiguous so that the ratings would more fully reflect the influence of level differences. In addition, the 30 ratings were selected from an original group of 90 on the basis of their ability to discriminate between low and high levelers. Each rating was on a five-point scale. The average rating of each of 100 students on the 30 traits for the three men was computed by adding all of his ratings and dividing by 30. While the average for all students was high (4.0), the variations around the average were still wide. The students were extremely consistent in their leveling habits—the correla-

Exhibit 4-1 *A Test Measuring Differences in Level*

Directions: This is a study of how people rate other people. You are given a brief sketch of three employees: George Drake, Harry Maynard, and Jim Nelson. On the basis of the sketch rate each on the personality traits, give your evaluation of their worth as employees, and answer the inventory statements as you think they did.

JIM NELSON—FOREMAN

For the last ten years Jim Nelson has been the foreman in the shipping department of an automobile parts manufacturing company. When Jim was appointed foreman, several others with more seniority were also considered for the job. Jim got the job because he had had more education than the others. Some of the men resented this and made Jim's task as supervisor a pretty tough one at first. However, this has been forgotten now and Jim gets along with the men very well. Jim's greatest handicap as a supervisor is the fact that he is somewhat shy. Also, he occasionally has difficulty expressing himself. His strongest quality is his sincere interest in his job.

Personality Ratings

On the basis of the information given, do you think Jim has the following qualities? Mark each one as follows: (1) Quite unlike him; (2) A little unlike him; (3) A little like him; (4) Rather like him; (5) Quite like him.
1. Realistic
2. Ambitious
3. Flexible
4. Practical

Evaluation

Assume that you are Jim's supervisor and must give him a merit rating on the following qualities. Mark each quality as follows: (1) Poor; (2) Fair; (3) Average; (4) Good; (5) Superior.
5. Initiative
6. Potentiality
7. Industriousness

Inventory

Jim filled out an anonymous personality inventory when he was hired. He responded to each of the statements below by marking them: (1) Strongly disagree; (2) Disagree; (3) Neither agree nor diagree; (4) Agree, (5) Strongly agree. Answer the following three statements as you think Jim answered them.
8. I like reading about business trends.
9. I am systematic in caring for my personal property.
10. I never neglect serious things in order to have a good time.

tion between the averages of the 15 odd-numbered ratings and the 15 even-numbered ratings was .90.

The scale in Exhibit 4-1 used only desirable traits. Therefore, the higher the ratings, the higher the level. If undesirable traits were included in the measure, then the weights of these traits would be reversed. Suppose, for example, that perceivers are asked to rate a person on the traits of friendliness (a desirable trait) and egotism (an undesirable trait). The high levelers would give the person a high rating on friendliness and a low rating on egotism; the low levelers, a low rating on friendliness and a high rating on egotism. Assume that a five-point scale is used: very low, low, average, high, and very high. If "very low" is counted as 1 for the desirable traits, then it would be counted as 5 for the undesirable traits. If "very high" is counted as 5 for the desirable traits, it would be counted as 1 for the undesirable traits, etc.

The more desirable a trait, the more it is influenced by level. Consequently, the most efficient measure of level is one which uses very desirable or very undesirable qualities and avoids relatively neutral ones. However, no matter how neutral one may think a quality is, some will see it as favorable and others as unfavorable. Further, some qualities viewed as generally favorable, such as ambition or affection, will be viewed by others in an unfavorable light. The ideal in the selection of items for the measurement of level, therefore, is to obtain a set that is most widely viewed as favorable or unfavorable.

The Generality of Level

The influence of level is dependent upon its generality. If a perceiver's level on one trait is unrelated to his level on another, its overall influence on his own predictions is small; if closely related, its influence is great. The same trait may be rated from quite different orientations:

SELF-ORIENTATION:	How do I rate myself?
FIRST-PERSON ORIENTATION:	How do I think he rates me?
SECOND-PERSON ORIENTATION:	How do I think he rates himself?
THIRD-PERSON ORIENTATION:	How do I think others rate him?
PERSONAL ORIENTATON:	How do I think he rates?

Evidence regarding level generality within some of these orientations is presented below.

SELF-ORIENTATION

How general are the self-oriented ratings? How likely is a person who rates himself high on one desirable trait to rate himself high on other desirable traits? Here is the answer for one person (Maslow and Mittelman, 1951, p. 143) :

> I usually feel self-confident and am sure of myself and am practically never bashful or shy, and I can remember only once ever being really self-conscious and that was in my one try at amateur acting when I had to say some awful things. . . . You could call me a strong person. . . . As I look over the qualities you asked me to rate myself in, it looks as if I were pretty well satisfied with myself (intelligence, attractiveness to the opposite sex, appearance, etc.). People do sometimes call me conceited, but I think it is only because they envy me. After all, I am successful in most things I want to do, and can usually do my job better than the other people around me.

Differences in the level of self-evaluations appear to be one of the most central and stable aspects of personality. Widely varying efforts to outline the basic dimensions of personality regularly reveal a self-evaluation factor: self-confidence, self-acceptance, social presence, boldness, dominance, etc. The level factor also has a remarkable stability. Kelly (1955), for example, found that scores in self-confidence after a twenty-year period had a correlation of .61, higher than for any other trait.

SECOND-PERSON ORIENTATION

In a test of the generality of second-person levels, Gross (1961) showed half-minute films of 30 men and women aged twenty to forty to 60 perceivers. After seeing the film, each perceiver rated each person on seven traits. Each perceiver's average level was determined for each trait. Result: A high rating of any person on any one of the traits was related to a high rating of any other person on any of the other traits. The reliabilities for individual scales ranged from .24 to .75 (masculinity-femininity). Further, the median correlation between level on one scale and level on another was .57. That is, the tendency of a perceiver to be a low or higher leveler was remarkably general from person to person and from trait to trait.

Unexpected but strong support for the generality of second-person ratings comes from the findings of Gage, Leavitt, and Stone (1956). They were primarily interested in the relationship between the sensitivity of teachers and their teaching effectiveness. In measuring sensitivity, they showed teachers filmed interviews with 8 fifth graders. After seeing an interview, the teacher predicted the child's response to a long personality inventory that the child had previously filled out. The results were, at first, puzzling: the accuracy of a teacher in predicting the responses of one child had no relationship to his accuracy in predicting the responses of another. The teacher who was very accurate in predicting one child might be very inaccurate with another. Why? The accuracy of a teacher was largely the result of the chance meshing of his rating level with the rating level of a particular child. Thus, a high-leveling teacher gave all the children a high rating on all the inventory traits. His predictions for a high-leveling child suggested great understanding of that child; his predictions for a low-leveling child, little understanding. This kind of accuracy is like the accuracy of a stopped clock that gives the correct time—twice each day.

Crow and Hammond (1957) found more direct support for the high generality of second-person levels. Medical students were shown films of 10 patients being interviewed by their doctors. They saw the films three times: at the beginning of the academic year, six months later, and twelve months later. Altogether, 30 films were used. That is, the students saw *different* doctors and different patients on each occasion. Each time the students completed a series of rating scales for each patient as they thought the patient himself had completed them. In one scale, for example, the patient was asked to complete a rating of how concerned he thought the doctor was about him as a person. The seven-point scale ranged from "extremely concerned" to "doesn't care at all." One major finding of the study: little generality of *accuracy* scores. The correlation between accuracy in predicting the responses of the first 10 patients and the second 10 patients was .21; between the first 10 and the last 10, .19; and between the second 10 and the last 10, .31. The fact that a student did well in judging the first 10 patients was only slightly related to his accuracy in judging six or twelve months later.

The generality of second-person level scores, in spite of the low generality of accuracy scores, was very high. Measures of level for each student were computed in a manner similar to that used by Grossman—a student's average rating for 10 patients on a scale was used as a measure of level. Level scores were calculated for 16 different scales. Correlations of level scores from 10 patients at one time to 10 *different* patients six months later ranged from .39 to .67 with a median of .53; to different patients twelve months later, from .36 to .66 with a median of .47. Considering the facts that the patients were entirely different groups, that the lapsed time was from six to twelve months, that the highest generality among the accuracy scores was less than the lowest generality among the level scores, and that the scales themselves were somewhat unreliable, the authors conservatively concluded that the generality was "very high."

PERSONAL ORIENTATION

The generality of personal levels accounts for the confusing findings in some employee attitude studies. Workers at the Buchsbaum company, for example, rated the favorableness of their attitude toward both the company and the union (Gottlieb and Kerr 1950). Result: The significant and vitally important finding of this research comes in an unexpected but entirely plausible quarter. Apparently, mutual emotional acceptance and cooperation between management and union tend to structure employees' satisfaction attitudes along integrated rather than divisive lines. Evidence for this is a positive Pearsonian coefficient of correlation between the total scores on management ballot and union ballot of .74.

The worker, it seemed, has a dual allegiance—the stronger his loyalty to the company, the *stronger* his loyalty to the union. Was this, however, just an example of the generality of level: the more favorable a worker is to his company, the more favorable his attitude toward everthing else is likely to be—union, wife, children, church, car, etc.? To answer the question, the influence of level differences had to be controlled. Stagner (1954) did so. He correlated union and management attitudes, not between individuals but between companies. In each of eight companies in Illinois, he measured the *average* satisfaction with the management and the *average* satisfaction with the union, thus eliminating the influence of individual differences in level. Result: Only a slight relationship between satisfaction with the management and satisfaction with the union. The high correlation at Buchsbaum seems largely due to the high generality of personal levels.

GENERALITY ACROSS ORIENTATIONS

There are 10 possible combinations of level generality across orientations: self-orientation with first-person orientation, with second-person orientation, with third-person orientation, and with personal orientation; first-person with second-person, etc. Of these logical possibilities, the relation between self-orientation (self-acceptance) and personal orientation (other-acceptance) has been most fully studied. Fey (1955) measured the level of self-ratings among college women with their ratings of other women. Result: $r = .50$. The degree of self-acceptance, incidentally, had no relationship to *actual* acceptance by others. While self-levels were related to levels in rating others, they were not identical. Some had high levels for themselves and low levels for others; they saw themselves as poised and socially effective but others saw themselves as egotistical and smug. Some had low self-levels and high levels for others; they lacked self-confidence but were very popular with other people.

Comprehensive studies have not yet been made of all areas within and between which levels might generalize, nor have we presented all that have been done. It seems already clear, however, that a perceiver's level is a central and stable quality of his personality and has a pervasive influence upon his judgments of others. In other words, each individual tends to have a strongly developed implicit theory about level which he uses in making most of his judgments about himself and others.

The Personality of the High Leveler

The personality differences between low and high levelers still seem best pictured by the results of Dymond (1949). Her original aim was to study personality differences between the generally sensitive and the insensitive. Results of later investigations, however, clearly suggest that the personality differences she found were largely due to differences, not in general sensitivity, but in level. After considering the interpretation suggested by these later investigations, we shall return to her study.

Investigators who tried to measure sensitivity, like Dymond, found that they were primarily measuring level. Gage (1958), for example, used as a measure of sensitivity the accuracy with which elementary school teachers predicted the attitudes of their students toward the curriculum, school plant, classroom activities, etc. The competence of the teacher as measured by the favorableness of student ratings was closely related to the sensitivity measure ($r = .60$). In spite of the high correlation, the sensitivity scores were completely unreliable, i.e., a teacher's accuracy in one area had no relationship to her accuracy in another. Why? The best interpretation appears to be as follows: (1) the generality of student ratings was high, so that if they rated school life low or high, they consistently rated the curriculum, the school building, as well as the teacher, low or high; (2) the generality of teacher ratings was also high, so that if they predicted that the students would have favorable attitudes toward school life they also predicted that the students would like the curriculum, the school building, etc.; (3) some teachers had classes whose average level was higher than that of others; and, thus, (4) the teacher who happened to have a high level and a class of high levelers turned up simultaneously with high "sensitivity" and high "competence" as a teacher. That is, the apparent measures of both sensitivity and competence were the result of the chance meshing of the general level of the teacher with the general level of her students.

Level has been confused with sensitivity and leadership competence in the same way. Many studies report findings that seem to show that good leaders have high sensitivity. They may, but the results of these studies do not prove it. Campbell (1955) has explained the source of error:

> In these studies, the measure of social perception has been based upon the very measure of leadership or group adjustment with which it has been correlated. Let us use I to represent Insight (social perceptiveness,

interpersonal knowledge); L to represent leadership status, sociometrically derived in these studies; and G to represent the person's guess as to the leadership status ascribed him by others. Then $I = L - G$. In a study of individual differences, I will be found to correlate with both L and G just because it has been made up from them.

In her study, Dymond (1949) first divided 80 people into 20 groups of 4 members each. Each group met separately for a brief period of acquaintanceship. They then rated each other on a five-point scale on each of six traits: self-assurance, leadership, friendliness, sympathy, superiority, and security. Each member rated himself and the other members on the six traits in four different ways:

1. A rating of himself
2. A rating of each of the other three
3. A rating of how he thought the other three would rate him
4. A rating of how he thought each of the other three would rate themselves

A measure of first-person accuracy was obtained by totalling the differences between how he thought the others would rate him (rating 3) and how they actually did rate him. A measure of second-person accuracy was obtained by totalling the differences between how he thought the others would rate themselves (rating 4) and how they actually did rate themselves.

Lindgren and Robinson (1953) shattered Dymond's belief that she was measuring general sensitivity. These authors simplified her procedure in order to use students in a large lecture class. Like her, they found the test as a whole reliable, the scores on first-person and second-person accuracy related.

Unlike her, however, they tested the hypothesis that a student's accuracy was not a product of his sensitivity, but a product of his level. First, they found the average rating 100 students had given themselves on each of the six traits (they were high). They then found how much each student differed in his average rating on that trait from the actual average rating. In getting the student's level discrepancy score by this method, the authors *completely disregarded how he had rated himself or how he had rated the other individuals in his group*. Finally, these level accuracy scores were correlated with accuracy scores computed by Dymond's method. Result: The correlation was about as high as it could possibly be. It seems almost certain, therefore, that Dymond's measure of sensitivity was a measure of level accuracy. Furthermore, the average student gave himself a high rating on these desirable traits. Consequently, the measure of level accuracy was primarily a measure of the tendency of a student to make high ratings of himself and others on desirable traits.

Finally, after these complexities, we return to Dymond's findings on personality. She contrasted the Rorschach test and Thematic Appercption Test scores of low and high scorers. The low levelers were "rather rigid, introverted people . . . who prefer to get along without strong ties to other people. Their own early emotional relationships within the family seem to have been so disturbed and unsatisfying that they feel they cannot afford to invest their love in others as they need it all for themselves. They seem to mistrust others. . . ." The higher levelers, on the other hand, were "outgoing, optimistic, warm, emotional people whose emotional relations have been sufficiently satisfying so that they find investing emotionally in others rewarding." Her findings are consistent with those of Grossman (1963). He correlated a measure of level (Exhibit 4–1) with a long battery of sensitivity, ability, and personality inventory measures. Two traits were related to level: the high leveler was both more considerate and more observant of others.

Level Accuracy

We have, thus far, been preoccupied with level. In training, however, our concern is with level *accuracy,* with the agreement of a perceiver's level with some good external criterion. Such criteria are rare in everyday life. As a result, the teacher does not know whether his grade for his average student is objectively correct; the supervisor, whether his merit rating for his average subordinate is correct; or the clinical psychologist, whether his estimate of the maladjustment of his typical client is correct.

Exhibit 4-2 illustrates the steps in the measurement of level accuracy. The hypothetical perceiver (H) has rated Mrs. Palmer on five desirable traits on a scale from 1 to 5. Note that the average level of the judge is 4, i.e., he thought that Mrs. Palmer's friends would say that "cooperative," "confident," "friendly," "affectionate," and "careful" were "rather like her." Note that the actual level of the ratings of her friends was consistently higher, i.e., they thought that all of these traits provided a *very* accurate description of her. The judge's level accuracy score is the difference between the average level of his ratings and the average level of the ratings of Mrs. Palmer's friends (5 minus 4). An adequate measure of level accuracy, of course, would be based on a perceiver's ratings on more traits and on more people. The necessary ingredients, however, are exemplified: (1) an independent criterion for determining accuracy level (in this case the judgments of friends) and (2) the com-

EXHIBIT 4-2   *An example of a Measure of Third-person Level Accuracy*

Directions: You are about to see a brief filmed interview with Mrs. Palmer, a middle-aged and soft-spoken woman. She was rated on each of the traits below by people who knew her well. Rate Mrs. Palmer as you think she was rated by her friends.

TRAITS ON WHICH MRS. PALMER WAS RATED	1 VERY UNLIKE HER	2 A LITTLE UNLIKE HER	3 A LITTLE LIKE HER	4 RATHER LIKE HER	5 VERY LIKE HER
1. Cooperative				H*	Fs†
2. Confident				H	Fs
3. Friendly				H	Fs
4. Affectionate				H	Fs
5. Careful				H	Fs

* H, rating given by a hypothetical perceiver who saw the film.
† Fs, average rating by friends of Mrs. Palmer.

parison of the level of the perceiver with actual level over a series of traits.

Measures of third-person level accuracy are readily obtained and can be a stimulating aspect of group conferences and discussions. For example, at the beginning of a series of meetings for the directors of a large New Jersey corporation, the directors completed a scale indicating the favorableness of their attitudes toward the demands of their employees (Bingham, 1953). The directors differed a great deal in their average level, some indicating very favorable and others very unfavorable attitudes. A measure of the actual level of the group could have been obtained by averaging the ratings of the individuals in it. Individual measures of level accuracy could then have been obtained by comparing each director's estimate of what he *thought* the average attitude of the group was with the actual attitude. Second-person level accuracy can be determined by comparing what a perceiver thinks a person will say about himself with what he actually says.

A perceiver's level is relatively constant; the relationship between his level and level accuracy is very inconstant. A low leveler, for example, will be more accurate in predicting what other people think of him (first-person level) but less accurate in predicting what other people think of themselves (second-person level). The high leveler, on the other hand, will be less accurate in predicting what other people think of him but more accurate in predicting what they think of themselves. The realistic goal of training, therefore, is *not* to establish the trainee at a particular level; it is to develop a *flexible* level. The aim is to train the individual to adapt his level to the orientation, to the person, to the behavior, and to the situation in which he is making his predictions.

Elimination of the Level Component

A perceiver's level, while central to him, is generally peripheral to his purpose. As a director of admissions, for example, his purpose is to pick those students most likely to succeed at his college, not to determine how well they will succeed. As a clinical diagnostician, his purpose may be to pick those clients most likely to improve under therapy, not to determine how much they will improve. And as a man looking for a wife, his purpose is to pick the woman most likely to be a good one, not to determine how good she will be. In general, level judgments are not necessary for most purposes, and they introduce large errors in judgments. They can be easily eliminated by the use of ranking instead of rating. In most cases, they should be.

In rating, a judge rates a *man* from low to high on a trait; in ranking, he ranks *men* from low to high on the trait: Tom Jones, first; Dick Thomas, second; Harry Smith, third, etc. While the ranking is commonly done on a single overall quality, it is just as adaptable to a series of qualities. Sometimes, the rankings on separate qualities are then converted into an overall ranking by adding the rankings on separate traits and then ranking the composite scores. Since every ranker must use every rank, it is impossible to have low or high rankers as we inevitably have low or high raters.

The larger the group being ranked, the more difficult become the problems of ranking: it is easy to rank five men, hard to rank twenty-five. The *paired-comparisons* method is one way out of this difficulty. The perceiver is given a series of pairs and, for each, predicts which one of the two is more likely to think, feel, or behave in a given way. Each man to be judged is thus paired with every other man, the total number of times each man is picked is determined, and these are then converted into a ranking. This method also becomes impractical as the size of the group increases: in comparing 20 men, the perceiver must make almost two thousand comparisons; in comparing 100 men, almost five thousand comparisons.

The *forced-distribution* method modifies the ranking principle so that it can be conveniently used with large groups. The key is that the judge using the forced-distribution method must assign a definite percentage of the people he is judging to each category. Assume, for example, that a judge using an ordinary scale is asked to rate 100 people on a five-point scale: (1) poor, (2) below average, (3) average, (4) above average, and (5) excellent. He can, and generally does, rate few men below average and many men above average. Using a forced-distribution system, he would also have five categories. He is now, however, required to put an assigned per cent into each category, for example: (1) 10 per cent, (2) 20 per cent, (3) 40 per cent, (4) 20 per cent, and (5) 10 per cent. That is, instead of ranking men individually, he classifies them into ranked categories.

An evaluation of procedures for selecting managerial personnel revealed the superiority of ranking over rating (Albrecht, Glasser, and Marks, 1964). Two staff members of a firm of consultants used an intensive interview, personal history data, and scores on a variety of ability and personality tests to predict the success of 31 recently promoted managers. On the basis of this information, each consultant rated the probable success of each manager. He also *ranked* the managers from the one most likely to be most successful to the one least likely. The ratings and the rankings of the two consultants were combined and correlated with a composite criterion of actual success on the job. The ratings were not related to success ($r = .09$); the rankings were ($r = .46$). The authors concluded: "The rating-form procedure, in contrast to ranking, adds the uncertainty of interpretation of a scale with possibility for central tendency or leniency biases to enter the picture."

The advantages of ranking over rating have been well understood for decades. Still, ratings are used in the majority of studies of sensitivity. It is hard to understand why. Perhaps too few studies have pitted the methods against each other. Perhaps researchers have been misled by the very high correlations between a *particular* perceiver's ratings and rankings (sometimes over .90). Most likely, the excessive use of ratings is another evidence of the pervasive importance and naturalness of leveling tendencies in people. In any case, judgments are improved by substituting rankings for ratings wherever possible.

The Improvement of Level Accuracy

Where differences between *persons* are the issue, level differences are an irrelevant source of error. Where differences between *perceivers* of the same person are the issue, then differences in level are of central importance and cannot be avoided by ranking procedures. Such differences are frequent and vital. Thus, parents are more generous in their ratings of their child than are his teachers (Levinger, 1961). Graduate students in psychology are consistently more generous in their ratings of another student than are professional psychologists (Soskin, 1954).

And employees are more generous in their ratings of themselves than are their supervisors (Parker et al., 1959). The following training experience indicates the practical difficulties created by differences in the level of perceivers.

General Electric managers attending a series of small conferences were divided into a John group and a Manager group (Kellogg, 1962). Both groups were given the following information:

JOHN:

John Jones is a young man in his thirties, with a liberal arts degree, and a law degree. He was in the top fifth of his class in arts, but only in the top half in law. He was originally hired on a relations rotating program and was placed in union relations for his first job. After about a year there, he went into salary and wage administration and has been in this field for about three years. He is bright, quick, outgoing; he is quite a leader; he is persuasive both orally and in writing. He is not very detail-minded, dislikes routine and records very much. He wants to be eventually at least a relations manager and possibly a general manager. He had had some assignments in manufacturing and he liked them very much, so that he is torn between relations and manufacturing and really would welcome advice on this point.

MANAGER:

John's manager is about fifty years old. He has been in the salary and wage field all his life. He would like to be promoted but has been passed over twice, so that he feels it is not very likely. He is personally very methodical, detail-minded, and a little withdrawn and reserved. He feels that John's records are not as accurate as they could be and that John does not spend enough time at his desk doing his paper work. He does recognize some excellent results—John has won the confidence of managers, his advice on pay levels and rates is frequently asked, and better understanding about pay administration has been achieved.

The Manager group was asked to pretend that it was the evening before a discussion with John to help him make a plan for his development. In addition to the above descriptions, the group was given details about his education, work history, past performance appraisals (average or better), and a few test results. The members of the John group were asked to pretend that they were John, faced the next day with a discussion of his development needs and plans. After the two groups had discussed the situation and made their plans, a chairman of each group presented them to the class.

In 11 different conferences, the Manager and John groups invariably saw the situation in quite different ways. The managers saw John as a below-average employee even though they knew he had received above-average ratings from his former supervisors. The Johns saw the manager as a person impossible to work for who blocked his advancement and failed to give rewards for good work. The managers and Johns set widely different aims for their discussion. The managers planned to get John to be more exact, keep his records better, and develop more self-discipline. The Johns planned to get out from under the manager without making him an enemy.

The conflicts grew out of differences in level: the Johns judged the managers at a generally lower level than the managers judged themselves; the managers judged the Johns at a generally lower level than the Johns judged themselves. Similar kinds of problems grow out of the level differences of parent and teacher, student and professor, employee and supervisor, client and therapist, husband and wife, etc. The question is: What principles embedded in a level-training program and learned by trainees will improve their level accuracy? The following suggestions are derived from the principles discussed in the last chapter and have at least some factual support.

DELAY THE FORMATION OF IMPRESSIONS

We naturally form a unified impression of a person with great speed. Once formed, the impression firmly molds our judgments. Still, some people form impressions more slowly than others, all people form impressions more slowly under some circumstances than under others, and all can learn to slow down the process. Snap judgments tend to be poor judgments, particularly when they are based on impressions formed from unimportant data. One goal of level training, therefore, is to teach trainees to *slow down the process of impression formation.*

Dailey (1952) documented the errors resulting from the formation of premature judgments. He gave two groups of perceivers a little information about a person. The first group was asked to make predictions on the basis of trivial information and the second group was not asked to make such predictions. Both groups were then given more complete information and again asked to make predictions. The second group, which had *not* made initial predictions, made more accurate final predictions. The result was not due to the first group's sticking rigidly to its earlier specific predictions for the perceivers made more serious errors in new predictions about the person: "The effect appears to be on the observer's understanding of the *person* rather than of the person's traits or behavior." In fact, the result seemed to be due primarily to being given time to form an impression. In one part of the study, perceivers who were given some information about a person and a waiting period before they received the rest made less accurate predictions than perceivers who did not have the waiting period. In general, perceivers who were given time and encouraged to form quick impressions formed wrong impressions. The results of Hyink (1955) support the same conclusion.

Premature judgments fix the perceiver's opinions. They also give him an unfounded confidence that he can use additional information effectively. In one study (Oskamp, 1965), psychologists first read a few general facts about a man and then predicted how he would behave in 25 different situations. They were asked: How many of your predictions do you think were correct? The average psychologist expected 33 per cent to be correct and actually 26 per cent were correct. The same psychologists were then given more than a thousand words of additional information, asked to make their predictions again, and asked how many of their predictions they thought were correct. Result: Expectation, 53 per cent; actual, 28 per cent. Conclusion: "The judges' confidence ratings show that they became convinced of their own increasing understanding of the case. . . . Their certainty about their own decisions became entirely out of proportion to the actual correctness of those decisions."

What techniques might aid in delaying the formation of impressions? As we have seen, a core aspect of impression formation is the level at which we put the person on the bad to good dimension. One way of avoiding this powerful tendency is to train perceivers to avoid leveling by *ranking within the individual.* Suppose, for example, that the manager of John was asked to evaluate him on the following traits:

1. Effectiveness in promoting high worker morale
2. Effectiveness in instructing, training, and developing subordinates
3. Effectiveness in directing, reviewing, and checking the work of subordinates
4. Effectiveness in setting and obtaining adherence to time limits and deadlines

If he recorded his impressions by rating, he would rate John on a scale from poor to excellent. If he recorded them by normal ranking methods, he would rank John on each of the traits in relation to other subordinates. In ranking *within* the individual, however, he would rank as 1 that quality in which he felt John was highest and as 5 that quality in which he felt John was lowest. The approach would both disrupt the manager's natural leveling tendency and encourage him to seek more information before crystallizing his impression. In the above case, incidentally, the procedure would provide a more constructive basis for discussions between the manager and John.

MOVE FROM NONPERSONAL TO PERSONAL LEVELS

Once formed, our impressions are resistant to change. Some impressions, however, are more resistant than others. We have less resistance to changing our attitudes about ourselves in unimportant than in important areas; we are less resistant to changing our opinions about strangers than about ourselves; and we are less resistant to changing our opinions about someone we read about than about someone with whom we live.

Level training should proceed by gradual steps *from less stressful to more stressful situations.* Training can begin with quite neutral situations. For example, trainees could be given a written thumbnail sketch of a man and asked to predict from a series of interests those for which he had expressed a liking. They could then be given information about their level accuracy, i.e., whether they were indicating too few or too many interests for the man. Additional series of interests and additional feedback could be given until the trainees had reached an acceptable level of accuracy for the man. Thumbnail sketches of other men could be presented, predictions made, and knowledge of results fed back until the trainees had developed adequate internal norms for judging the interests of men.

The training could then proceed to more stressful situations. The training may be made more stressful by moving the perceivers closer to the person being judged—from a man in a written sketch to the voice of a man on a tape recording, to a man introduced by sound film, to a man viewed by a group, to a man met in an interview. Stress may also be increased by moving from the prediction of neutral to the prediction of highly desirable qualities—from height to sense of humor—and by varying the orientation—from what do other people think of him to what does he think of me. The most stressful kind of situation would be one in which the perceiver was expected to predict the level at which his superiors would rate his intelligence, warmth, humor, etc.

MOVE FROM GENERAL TO SPECIFIC LEVELS

We perceive people as unified wholes and make ratings on specific traits that are consistent with that whole. The basic sources of leveling errors are general rather than specific. For example, the problem with John and his manager lies not in their disagreements over specific points but rather in their disagreements about the general level at which they rate each other. Effective training, therefore, should start with the correction of general leveling errors. The following studies indicate the importance of the principle for developing level acuracy.

Psychologists and psychiatrists predicted the behavior of David in 37 different situations (Soskin, 1959). They read what the situations were that David had been in and then predicted in which one of four ways he behaved. The situations and the correct answers were determined from interviews with David, his wife, and his friends. The first time predictions were made, the group was told only David's age, race, religion, and marital, educational, and occupational status. On the basis of this limited information, the average number of accurate predictions was 14.8. Then some of the perceivers were given an interpretation of David's Rorschach test to read, and others saw him perform in a role-playing situation. Both the Rorschach and the role-playing groups again predicted David's behavior in the same 37 situations. Result: "None improved accuracy beyond the level achieved by the study of the biographical facts alone." In fact, the Rorschach group was *less* accurate than they had been the first time. Why?

The answer: Both the Rorschach and the role-playing information caused the judges to shift their level in erroneous but opposite directions. The answer was obtained in the following way. First, independent judges rated the abnormality of behavior that would be indicated by each of the four behavioral alternatives in each of the 37 situations. The 12 alternatives that were judged to be most indicative of serious maladjustment were isolated. Then the frequency with which the judges chose these alternatives before and after seeing the Rorschach interpretation or role-playing session was determined. Result: The Rorschach group chose almost 50 per cent *more* of these alternatives after seeing the interpretation; the role-playing group chose almost 50 per cent *fewer* of these alternatives after seeing the role playing. The Rorschach group erred "quite consistently in overestimating the degree of maladjustment"; the role-playing group "developed a positive effective response toward the subject which caused them to evaluate his behavior with a selective bias." Errors of the psychologists and psychiatrists lay not so much in their specific predictions as in the general *level* of their predictions. In turn, the way of correcting these errors lies in correcting the general level of prediction.

It may be that clinicians develop a deep and general "maladjustment" bias. Policemen, at least, seem to develop their own occupational bias. Toch and Schulte (1961) exposed for a half second a violent picture to one eye of policemen and nonpolicemen and a nonviolent picture to the other eye. Under such circumstances, all people perceive only one of the two pictures. The 16 policemen saw twice as many violent pictures as the 43 nonpolicemen.

> Unusual experiences, after all, become 'familiar' in the course of *any* specialization. The funeral director or the medical intern, for instance, may learn to accept corpses as part and parcel of everyday experience. The dedicated nudist may acquire a special conception of familiar attire. The air pilot may come to find nothing unusual about glancing down out of a window at a bank of clouds. In the same fashion . . . the law enforcer may come to accept crime *as a familiar personal experience*, one which he himself is not surprised to encounter. The acceptance of crime as a familiar experience in turn increases the *ability or readiness to perceive violence where clues to it are potentially available*.

While such biases may help the specialist act more appropriately in his special world, it may also lead to increased errors in the world outside his specialty.

Nothing is clearer in the area of level training than the fact that specific level errors can be easily corrected. With a few hours of training, students improved their accuracy in rating emotional states from photographs by 50 per cent (Guilford, 1929). In a similarly brief time, students improved their accuracy in rating height, weight, age, introversion-extroversion, and intelligence: "Typical trial-and-error learning curves are found for each of the traits tried" (Martin, 1938). Two graduate students in clinical psychology rated a series of three-year-olds after an hour's observation on cooperation, sociability, hostility, etc. Initially, they agreed on only 25 per cent of their ratings. After examining and discussing each other's ratings on four different children, their level of agreement climbed to 88 per cent (King, Ehrmann, and Johnson, 1952).

In many practical situations, improvement on specific traits may be highly desirable. However, the rapid improvement on specific traits may also rapidly disappear. For example, after reaching an 88 per cent agreement level, the two clinical students were asked to read the case folders of a series of 15 children before observing and rating them. Result: The level of agreement *dropped* from 88 to 68 per cent and the mean difference in their ratings tripled. Conclusion: "The information may be organized as a background or frame of reference against which the observed behavior is interpreted . . . . If the mother indicates that her boy is aggressive, the observer may interpret the child's social contact as a sign of aggression." That is, the record of the child may have created a unified but different impression in the observers and they interpreted what they saw in the light of their overall impression.

The training method implied by the principle of starting with general levels is: Ignore the specific levels and stress the average level. Thus, if the manager is rating John on 10 desirable traits, start with the average level of rating and its accuracy. If the clinician is rating the adjustment of David in a variety of specific situations, start with the average rating and its accuracy. And if the observer is rating the social behavior of a child on a series of traits, start with the average rating and its accuracy.

Chapter Five

SPREAD

WE DIFFER in the generosity of our estimates of others; we also differ in the variability of our estimates. Some stick close to their level from trait to trait and from person to person while others vary widely around their level. Thus, the narrow spreader rates the intelligence of Tom, Dick, and Harry about the same while the wide spreader may rate Tom as very intelligent, Dick as very unintelligent, and Harry about average. The nature of the spread component, the reasons for the differences between narrow and wide spreaders, the impact of spread differences upon predictive accuracy, and ways of improving spread accuracy are the major themes of the present chapter.

The Measurement of Spread

Although the arithmetic is somewhat more involved, the same ratings that are used for calculating level can be used for calculating spread. Grossman (1963), for example, using the ratings from his scale (Exhibit 4-1), first found the average level for the 30 five-point ratings made by each person. He then found the deviation of each of the 30 ratings from this average, squared each of them, and found the sum of the squares. The sum was his measure of spread. Suppose, for example, the average rating of a respondent on all 30 traits was 3 but that his rating of Jim Nelson on initiative was 2 (fair) and on industriousness, 5 (superior). The deviation of 2 from 3 is 1 which, when squared, is still 1. The deviation of 5 from 3 is 2 which, when squared, is 4. The spread score for the respondent would then be 1 plus 4 plus the squares of the deviations for the other 28 ratings. Crow and Hammond (1957) used essentially the same method in measuring the spread of ratings by medical students of patients shown in films:

. . . the inverse of the average variance of an *S*'s estimations for the scales. An *S* may perceive wide differences among people in the characteristic under consideration, or, he may perceive people as being very much alike. He may, in other words, cluster his estimations closely around his stereo-type (mean estimation) or he may vary them widely. The variance of the estimations for each scale was computed and averaged for the seven scales as a measure of perceived individual differences.

Gross (1961), who had perceivers rate 30 persons shown in films on 10 personality traits, used a more complex statistical method for calculating differences in spread.

Like level, the differences in the spread of perceivers are very reliable and stable. It is, in fact, uncertain which is *more* reliable and stable. The reliability of Grossman's measure of spread was somewhat less than the reliability of his measure of level ($r = .57$). Gross, on the other hand, found greater consistency in his measure of spread (.91 versus .57). Crow and Hammond also found their measures of spread more stable than their measures of level. The correlation between spread scores of medical students six months apart was .60, twelve months apart .53. With remarkable consistency, considering the conditions of the study, the low spreaders at the beginning were low spreaders at the end; high spreaders at the beginning were high spreaders at the end.

The Personality of the Wider Spreader

We first see a person as a unified and simple homogeneous whole. It is only slowly and gradually that we learn to differentiate the parts within the complex whole that is the complex person. The narrowing of spread parallels the movements from simple to complex perceptions, the widest spreaders having the simplest perceptions and the narrow spreaders having the most complex.

Adults saw films of a woman engaged in both desirable and unde-sirable activities. They were then asked to write their impressions of the woman (Gollin, 1954). About half gave simplified impressions by ignor-ing either the desirable *or* the undesirable behavior. About a fourth gave aggregated impressions in which they mentioned both the good and bad activities but did not try to relate them. Another fourth did attempt to relate the good and bad activities. The result is by no means a surprise. For example, the novelist Somerset Maugham (1938) reached the same conclusion:

I suppose it a natural prepossession of mankind to take people as though they were homogeneous. . . . It is evidently less trouble to make up one's mind about a man one way or the other and dismiss suspense with the phrase, he's one of the best or he's a dirty dog. It is disconcerting to find that the savior of his country may be stingy or that the poet who has opened new horizons to our consciousness may be a snob. Our natural egoism leads us to judge people by their relations to ourselves. We want them to be certain things to us, and for us that is what they are; because the rest of them is no good to us, we ignore it.

Children before the age of ten appear to be incapable of complex relational thinking about people. Gollin (1958) tested more than seven hundred elementary and secondary school students in Minnesota. A five-scene silent motion picture was used to present the behavior of an eleven-year-old boy. The first scene was a close-up of the boy. Two of the following scenes showed the boy engaged in socially approved behavior. One of these showed two other small boys playing catch when a larger boy breaks up their game by shoving them aside and taking their ball. The eleven-year-old enters and recovers the ball, drives the larger boy off, and returns the ball to the smaller boys. In the other good scene a small boy riding a tricycle falls into a heap of dry leaves and appears to have hurt himself. The eleven-year-old comes along, helps him up, rights his tricycle, brushes him off, and gets him started again. Two of the scenes show the boy engaged in socially undesirable behavior. In one, two boys are engaged in building a "soap-box" car. The eleven-year-old pushes over the boy who is sawing, snatches the paint brush from the other boy, and smears the number and the side of the car with the paint. In the other, the eleven-year-old grabs comic books from younger boys, tears some of them up, and scatters the others by kicking. At the end of the film, the judges were asked "to write as much about the boy as you can, that is, pretend you are telling someone about him. Give your opinion of the boy, write what you think about him." The statements were then classified as trying or not trying to account for the good and bad behavior of the boy by using relational concepts. To be classified as relational it was only necessary that the student had tried; it was not necessary that the attempt had been either satisfactory or complete. Still, only 2 per cent of the ten-year-olds used relational concepts.

Relational thinking increased with age: 2 per cent at ten; 15 per cent at fourteen; 51 per cent at seventeen. At ages fourteen and seventeen, however, twice as many of the girls as boys used relational concepts. Low-IQ girls of seventeen made more relational responses than high-IQ boys of the same age. The absence of a female superiority at ten and its dominating presence at the later ages strongly suggests a maturational element involving the more rapid physical and social development of girls in early adolescence.

Simple thinkers about people are simple thinkers in other areas. Also, complex thinkers about people are complex thinkers in other areas as the following study shows.

Over a hundred evening college students saw the film of the girl in the good and bad scenes and wrote their impressions (Gollin and Rosenberg, 1956). In addition, they were presented with the terms: Buddhism, Capitalism, Christianity, Communism, Democracy, Fascism, Judaism, Protestantism, and Socialism. After defining each of these terms, the students were given the following instructions: "Now that you have defined the terms, here is what we would like you to do next. In the blank space provided below we would like you to write a paragraph stating whether or not you feel that all of these terms are interrelated. If you feel that all of these are interrelated *describe the way in which you think they are interrelated.*"

The replies were then classified into those which did *relate* the terms under some concept like "social institutions," "beliefs," or "methods of group control" and those who did not. Of the total group, about a third used relational concepts and two-thirds did not. Of the one-third using the relational approach in describing the girl, more than two-thirds used the same approach in classifying terms. Of the two-thirds not using the relational approach in describing the girl, more than two-thirds did not use it in classifying the terms.

The evening college students who were simple thinkers were wide spreaders; those who were relational thinkers were narrow spreaders. All of the students who saw the film completed the following questions:

> Using the following scale (1. Yes; 2. Probably; 3. Don't know; 4. Probably not; 5. No) as far as the individual seen in all the sequences of the picture is concerned, do you feel that you:
>
> 1. Would admit her to close kinship by marriage?
> 2. Would admit her to your group as a personal chum?
> 3. Would admit her to your street as a neighbor?
> 4. Would admit her to your college as a fellow student?

The person who answered "Yes" to each question would have the minimum score of 4 and the minimum social distance; the person who answered "No" to each question, the maximum score of 20 and the maximum social distance from the subject.

The average scores of the simple and relational thinkers were nearly identical (20.4 and 20.3). The spread of the scores for the two groups was decidedly different (standard deviations of 8.2 and 5.6). That is, some simple thinkers saw the girl as good and some as bad. If they saw her as good they wanted to be close to her; if bad, they wanted to be distant. The average of these extreme scores gave a moderate score. On the other hand, the relational thinkers who saw both her good and bad qualities had generally moderate scores. Why do some adults not become relational thinkers and narrow spreaders? In addition to age factors Gollin (1958) found that men of low intelligence and poor social backgrounds were more often simple thinkers. One possible explanation of these facts is that wide spreaders have a high *speed of closure* (Thurstone, 1944). Shown a circle with a tiny gap, fast closers more quickly see a complete circle; shown a face in profile without a nose, they more quickly perceive a completed face; and told a few facts about a person, they more quickly complete their impressions of him. In part, fast closing is a function of personality. Pemberton (1952) found fast closers more often agreed with statements about themselves like the following:

> People regard me as self-confident.
> I seldom try to get the overall picture of a problem.
> I look for the "silver lining in every cloud."
> I admire and respect people in authority.

In general, fast closers are uninterested in getting the overall picture, impatient with abstract principles, and strongly inclined to accept authoritative judgments.

In part, fast closing is a function of parental thinking. Parents of social and economic marginality are prone to expect their children to learn rules which are rigid and often incomprehensible. The children learn that there is no time for fine discrimination or for attempts to obtain a full understanding; there is only time for speedy closure and quick action (Frenkel-Brunswik, 1949). The slow closers, on the other hand, learn in life that it is safe to say, "I don't know," and to wait for needed evidence. Germans who resisted Hitler appeared to come from homes which fostered slow closures. Their mothers were unusually demonstrative and affectionate, their fathers were generally well liked and were not harsh disciplinarians (Levy, 1948). The more confident a person is, the wider he is likely to spread his ratings (Grossman, 1963). Furthermore, the more experience a person has in a judging situation, the more confidence he is likely to have. Herein lies a real danger for the expert, for his confidence often is unjustified (Cronbach, 1955).

Spread Accuracy

How is spread related to predictive accuracy? The theoretical answer can be stated with precision. Assume that five judges are rating the intelligence of 10 people. Assume, further, that level accuracy is constant, that the average IQ of the 10 is 100, that all the judges know this, and that the actual ratings of each by the judges turn out to be 100. Assume, finally, that all the judges know the actual spread of IQs in the group to range from a low of 70 to a high of 130 and to have a standard deviation of 16. Will a judge's errors be smallest if he rates 10 people at an IQ of 100, spreads his ratings from 70 to 130, or compromises somewhere between the minimum and maximum spread?

The correct answer varies with how well the judge knows the 10 people. If he knows nothing about them, errors will be smallest if he rates them all at an IQ of 100. If he knows them perfectly, the errors will be smallest if he spreads the ratings over the entire range. While the answer is definite, it is neither complete nor very helpful, for we seldom rate people that we know nothing about and we never rate people that we know everything about. The critical question thus becomes: What is the relationship between amount of spread, degree of accuracy, and amount of knowledge about the people being rated?

Cronbach(1955) has given an exact and general answer to the last question. The spread accuracy is greatest when

$$\text{SD}j = \text{SD}a \times r_{ja}$$

Applied to the 10 people, j is the judge's estimates of their intelligence, a is their actual intelligence, SD is the standard deviation (the most widely used statistical measure of spread) and r is the correlation between the judge's estimate of intelligence for the 10 people and their actual intelligence. Thus, if a judge knows nothing about the intelligence of the 10 people, his ratings will be guesses, his guesses will have no relationship to the actual intelligence of the people, and r_{ja} will be zero. Zero times the SDa, which in this case is 16, will also be zero; consequently, SDj will also be zero. We reach the conclusion that we stated in the last paragraph: If a judge knows nothing about the people he is rating, he will make the fewest and smallest errors by assuming that *everybody* is average. The formula also applies to the opposite extreme, i.e., if the correlation between the judge's estimate of intelligence and actual intelligence is perfect (r_{ja} is 1.00), then he will make the fewest errors by having his spread (SDj) equal the actual spread (SDa, which is 16).

The formula fits our commonsense conclusions about the extreme cases. Much more important, it leads to some unexpected conclusions about the in-between cases that make up practically all life situations. As an example, let us continue our assumptions about the case of the 10 people. Assume that our five judges have brief interviews with each of the 10 people and then rate their intelligence. Assume further that the correlation between the *best* judge's estimates of intelligence and actual intelligence is .50 (which is quite high under the circumstances) and the *worst* judge's estimates correlate .20 with actual intelligence. What does the formula indicate as the optimum spread for the two judges? For the best judge, the answer would be $16 \times .50$ or 8 (SD$a \times r_{ja}$). If he followed this recommendation, he would rate 7 of the 10 people between 92 and 108 and none of them as low as 76 or as high as 124. For the worst judge, the answer would be $16 \times .20$ or 3.2. If he followed this recommendation, he would rate 7 out of 10 of the people between 96 and 104 and none below 90 or above 110.

The General Problem of Spread Accuracy

Do we normally apply Cronbach's rule for achieving the most accurate spread? The evidence that we do not is truly overwhelming: Most people most of the time have too wide a spread and consequently make constant and serious errors in their judgments of people. The evidence has accumulated largely through an effort to settle the controversy over clinical versus actuarial prediction (Meehl, 1954).

The controversy has revolved about the best way to use information about a person in making a prediction about him. Is it better to combine the data mechanically, or is it better to combine the data individually? The general method used to answer the question and the nearly universal answer obtained is illustrated by the author's experiences in a small graduate course in interviewing. Over a period of years he has given his students an objective examination on the text.

Both the scores on the test and the general grade-point averages of the students are ranked from the lowest to the highest. The rankings on the test and on grade-point averages are then correlated, the correlations ranging over the years from .50 to .75. The students are next asked to try "to beat the formula." They are given the grade-point ranks of each student, the correlation with the test, and a lengthy interview with each of the other students. Finally, they rank themselves and the other students as they think they actually performed. Result: A student rarely ties the formula, and the typical student has a correlation considerably below that obtained by using the mechanical prediction. The procedure illustrates the basic steps in comparing no spread with some spread from a given level: (1) Raters are given a prediction for ratees on the basis of some information combined mechanically; (2) the raters are given both this information and additional information about the ratees; (3) the raters make their own subjective ratings on the basis of all the information; and (4) the validity of the subjective ratings are compared with the validity of the mechanically determined ratings.

Meehl found 20 studies that compared the accuracy of predictions based on mechanical combination of data with predictions based on the intuitive combinations of counselors, psychologists, psychiatrists, and social workers. In one study, for example, the problem was to predict the grades that more than five hundred freshmen would get in college. In prediction by the group method, rank in high school class and scores on a scholastic aptitude test were used. In predicting the grades for a particular student, it was assumed that his grades would be typical of those that every student with his high school record and aptitude would get. The accuracy of these predictions was compared with those made by trained counselors who had had an hour interview with a student, plus use of his high school rank, aptitude score, and other information in his record folder. Result: The predictions by the former method were more accurate than the counselor predictions. In summary, Meehl states: "We have here, depending upon one's standards for admission as relevant, from 16 to 20 studies involving a comparison of clinical and actuarial methods, *in all but one of which the predictions made actuarially were either approximately equal or superior to those made by a clinician.*"

When and how can a perceiver "beat the formula"? Meehl (1954) used only a global measure of predictive accuracy. Cline and Richards (1962) in a careful analytical experiment compared the accuracy of mechanical predictions with the clinical predictions of 56 judges. As they expected, the mechanical predictions were more accurate in differentiating between groups and were, overall, more accurate. The judges, however, were more accurate in differentiating between individuals. Conclusion:

> Contrary to common opinion among clinicians, the activity at which clinicians are most likely to exceed the actuary is *not* making predictions about an "unique individual." . . . appropriate activity for clinicians is predicting differences among persons who are grouped into the same class by statistical predictions, and it is easy to suggest many ordinary activities of clinicians that are of this type. An example of this might be a mental hospital in which ten patients had roughly the same statistically derived "predicted benefit from psychotherapy" score, but which had such a limited staff that only three of these patients could actually be given psychotherapy. The results of this study suggest that the clinician might be quite successful in picking the three "best bets" although all ten had been given an "equal" rating by the statistical prediction procedure.

How could the students in the interviewing class have used this conclusion to improve their predictions? Since the formula predicted the ranks of the students, no students would fall "into the same class by statistical predictions." Two students, however, might fall into very similar or very dissimilar classes, i.e., they might have adjacent ranks or one might be ranked 1 and the other 10 by the formula. The fullest possible application of the suggestion, then, would be for a student to consider changing only the position of adjacent ranks. A more flexible application would be: Freely interchange the ranks of adjacent students; cautiously, the ranks of students several ranks apart; and never, the ranks of students far apart. In general, a perceiver has the best chance of beating the formula by using *a narrow spread around the level predicted for a person by the formula*. The counselors who predicted the grades of the 500 college freshmen could also have done better by using the principle.

Suppose for example, that the formula predicted that 10 per cent would get A grades; 20 per cent, B; 40 per cent C; 20 per cent, D; and 10 per cent F. The counselors would then concentrate on those with a predicted A grade and indicate those that they thought would get A+, those that would get A, and those that would get A—. Students at each of the other levels would be handled in the same way. The method would use all that the formula had to offer and would also permit the subjective judgments of a counselor to play a helpful part.

The Problem of Spread Accuracy in Training

The spread of perceivers tends to be too wide. We would expect, therefore, that training which increased spread would decrease accuracy and training which decreased spread would increase accuracy. Training evaluations verify the expectation. Medical students, for example, saw films of physicians interviewing patients and made predictions about how the patients would rate themselves (Crow 1957). They then completed an intensive training course designed to increase their sensitivity to patients as individuals. They saw the films and made predictions about their ratings again. Result: "Contrary to expectations, a training program in interpersonal relations for medical students decreased the trainees' accuracy in judging others." Why? Most of the students increased their spread during training, and the increase seemed responsible for the decline in accuracy. A follow-up study established the relationship more precisely (Crow and Farson 1961). Air Force officers and civilian supervisors attended a week-long course designed to increase their sensitivity. The core of the program involved the use of the T-group method, interactions in small and unstructured groups. To evaluate the effectiveness of the program, the predictive accuracy of the members was measured before and after training.

Accuracy was measured in the following way. Prior to training, the trainees were assigned at random to eight testing groups of eight members each. The groups were composed so that only two members of the same training group were included in a testing group. At the end of the week the trainees were again assembled into entirely different eight-man testing groups. Trainees in each testing group became as well acquainted with each other as they could in thirty minutes. Each trainee then rated himself on a ten-point rating scale. Finally, each trainee rated the other

EXHIBIT 5-1   *The Relationship between Changes in Spread and*
Changes in Sensitivity
(Adapted from Crow and Farson, 1961)

	SMALLER SPREAD AFTER TRAINING, %	LARGER SPREAD AFTER TRAINING, %
More sensitive after training ($N = 38$)	73	54
Less sensitive after training ($N = 22$)	27	46
Total	100	100

seven members of the group as he throught they had rated themselves.
The agreement between a trainee's rating for the other members and
the ratings the other members gave themselves was the measure of sensitivity. More trainees increased than decreased their accuracy. This time,
however, as Exhibit 5-1 shows, more trainees decreased than increased
their spread. Among those who had a larger spread after training, as
many decreased as increased the accuracy of their rating. Among those
who had a smaller spread after training, almost three times as many
increased their accuracy. It seems clear that the unplanned decline in
spread among most of the trainees was primarily responsible for the
planned increase in accuracy.

Among the medical students, spread increased; among the Air Force
officers, it declined. Neither change was anticipated. It is clear, however,
that sensitivity training will become more effective as those involved become more aware of the potent influence of such changes. With only
minor reservations, the awareness should be guided by this principle:
The trainee who narrows his spread will increase his accuracy.

The Improvement of Spread Accuracy

The reasons for eliminating level, discussed in the last chapter, apply
with equal force to eliminating spread. In general, wherever the issue
is the differences between persons and not the differences between perceivers, spread as well as level are best eliminated. The ranking which
eliminates level at the same time eliminates spread; in addition, the training methods which help to improve level accuracy—delaying the formation of impressions, moving from nonpersonal to personal levels, and
moving from general to specific levels—also help to improve spread accuracy. To these methods may be added three that are particularly relevant
to spread: (1) practice in using the spread accuracy formula; (2) the

development of realistic internal norms; and (3) practice in the observation of discrepant facts.

THE SPREAD ACCURACY FORMULA

The principle derived from the formula is: *The spread of the perceiver's behavior predictions should never exceed the spread of the actual behavior and ordinarily should be much smaller.* How much smaller depends on the validity of his predictions: no validity, no spread; moderate validity, a little spread; and high validity, a moderate spread. There are both constant and variable errors of spread. A constant error: Most people have too wide a spread. A variable error: Most people maintain the same spread from situations in which their predictions are valid to situations in which they are not valid. Practice and feedback would seem to be the obvious essentials for the correction of constant errors. After understanding the formula and the principle behind it, trainees might be given a series of problems like the following: Predict the four-year grade average of the following beginning freshmen by reference to their standing in their high school graduating class and by their scholastic aptitude scores. The correlation between standing and college grades is .50; between aptitude test scores and grades, .40. The average grade obtained by the students you are rating was 2.5, the lowest student obtaining an average of 1.5; the highest 3.5.

After making the predictions, trainees could be given the actual grades of students and their errors calculated and related to their spread. The process could then be repeated until an acceptable level of accuracy had been reached.

THE DEVELOPMENT OF INTERNAL NORMS

To develop accurate spread, trainees must have accurate levels from which to spread. The results of Stelmachers and McHugh (1964) show the value of realistic norms. They had 42 psychologists, psychiatrists, and psychiatric social workers predict the responses two men and two women made to 171 items on the Minnesota Multiphasic Personality Inventory. One of the women was a normal college sophomore; the other was an elderly woman with a long medical and psychiatric history and the diagnosis of "conversion reaction." One of the men was a teen-age homosexual with a lengthy criminal record; the other, a psychiatric patient with a diagnosis of "depressive reaction." To aid them in making their predictions, the experts were given information from a biographical questionnaire, an interest and activities questionnaire, and a sentence completions test as well as hospital records and psychiatric interviews.

The accuracy of the predictions of the experts was compared with the accuracy of predictions based on the idea that each of the subjects would make the typical responses of the broad reference groups to which he belonged: college females, adult females, or adult males. The norms of the MMPI handbook give the percentage of each of these groups answering true and false to the 171 items in the prediction test. A special key was then made for each group where an item was called "true" if 50 per cent or more of the group answered it true and "false" if 49 per cent or less answered it true. The keys were applied to each of the four subjects. For example, if the college girl answered a statement "true" and the typical college girl had also answered it "true," the item was counted as correct, etc.

The accuracy of the predictions of the experts and the special keys are shown in Exhibit 5-2. In the words of the authors: "It is truly surprising how powerful these keys turn out to be!" For three out of four of the subjects, the special keys were more accurate than the predictions of the experts. The authors conclude:

> Psychologists would do well studying the base rates of various types of behavior in as many separate populations as is practicable. Apparently even a very approximate matching on a very few variables between subject and population can lead to a significant improvement in predictive accuracy if the population norms are known to the judge. For most pieces of behavior assumed to be relevant in personality assessment, such norms are not available. Therefore, it seems that the establishment of them for a select number of broadly defined populations could be beneficial to the clinicians' performance in the area of behavior prediction.

Oskamp (1962) verified the value of norms for training psychologists and undergraduates. He first classified 200 MMPI profiles—half of which were those of hospitalized psychiatric patients—as psychiatric or nonpsy-

EXHIBIT 5-2 *Comparison of the Predictive Accuracy of Experts and of Special MMPI Keys*
(Adapted from Stelmachers and McHugh, 1964)

SUBJECTS WHOSE MMPI RESPONSES WERE PREDICTED	ACCURACY OF EXPERTS	ACCURACY OF SPECIAL KEYS
1. Normal female sophomore (college female norms)	127	144
2. Elderly female patient (adult female norms)	106	129
3. Adult male depressive (adult male norms)	98	67
4. Criminal teen-age homosexual (adult male norms)	102	116

EXHIBIT 5-3 *A Measure of Norm Flexibility*

Directions: Each of several hundred Midwestern college men rated himself as he thought he compared with other college men on a series of traits. Rate the *average college man* on each of the traits below as you think he rated himself.

Mark "1" if you think he rated himself in the lowest 25%.
Mark "2" if you think he rated himself in the middle 50%.
Mark "3" if you think he rated himself in the highest 25%.

1. Rebellious	9. Stubborn	17. Cooperative
2. Impractical	10. Egotistical	18. Friendly
3. Unrealistic	11. Shy	19. Ambitious
4. Unpredictable	12. Affectionate	20. Adaptable
5. Socially poised	13. Serious	21. Wide range of interests
6. Easily upset	14. Talkative	22. Liberal
7. Timid	15. Imaginative	23. Adventurous
8. Irresponsible	16. Aggressive	24. Trustful

chiatric. The psychologists were much more accurate than the undergraduates. Undergraduates were given empirically determined rules for identifying profiles that were typically psychiatric as well as practice and feedback in applying these rules. Result: "This brief training raised accuracy to the level of the clinicians which suggests that techniques of specific training and immediate feedback may be profitably used in clinical training programs to speed the accumulation of internal norms."

The accuracy of a level varies with the situation; the levels of perceivers, however, tend to remain the same. The author, for example, administered an expanded form of the test shown in Exhibit 6-3. The correct answer for the traits in the left column is 1; in the middle column, 2; and in the right column, 3. The accuracy of students for each of the columns was measured separately and the scores intercorrelated. Result: The more accurate the student was in the left column predictions, the less accurate he was in the right column ($r = .49$). In general, people tend to stick to their levels. Consequently, they must learn norms that fit the situation in which they are judging. Such norms, however, may be useful in a wide range of situations. "Even a very approximate matching" of a norm to an individual may do much to improve the accuracy of the predictions made about him.

THE OBSERVATION OF INCONSISTENT FACTS

A core problem in spread accuracy lies in the drive that we have to see people as simple wholes. The drive leads us to ignore or distort facts that frustrate our desire for wholes: We see what we want to see, what we expect to see, and what we have learned to see. Once we have seen the person as a whole, we can, and often do, make extreme judgments about him. One discouraging consequence, as numerous studies indicate, is that we have a light appetite for facts and a tendency to get indigestion if we have too many. Stelmachers and McHugh (1964), for example, gave different judges widely different amounts of information upon which to base their predictions. Result: "The comparatively elaborate and individualized personality sketches failed to produce accurate predictions, were in fact no better than the knowledge of the subjects' age and sex."

One possible remedy for the situation is to train people to pay particular attention to facts that seem to conflict with each other or with their implicit theory about the person. Darwin once remarked that he never wrote down facts that fitted his theory and always wrote down facts that did not seem to fit, for he knew he would remember the former but tend to forget the latter. How people can be trained in Darwin's habit, or whether they can, is a matter for speculation. One suggestion arises from the findings of Gollin (1958). In writing their impressions of the kind *and* immoral girl, half of the students described her as kind *or* immoral. The relational thinkers, on the other hand, used both sets of facts in describing her. However, to relate facts we must both observe and remember the facts. The first step toward the development of relational thinking, therefore, would appear to be training in observing apparently inconsistent facts.

Training might begin with stress upon the importance of observing inconsistent facts. The actual practice could begin with films like that of the girl. After seeing the film, the trainees could be tested for their accuracy in observing the appearance, actions, and conversation of the individuals in *all* scenes of the film. As they became proficient in this type of observation, the stress could be increased. Trainees known to be anti-Negro, for example, might be shown a Negro in scenes where he was sometimes performing desirable and sometimes undesirable acts. Observational training of this sort has the merit of a perfectly valid criterion of accuracy: He did or did not have a blue sweater on, he did or did not open the car door, etc. There is little question that training of this sort would produce large improvements in the training situation. Whether the improvement would transfer to other situations is more doubtful.

Part Three

THE INTERACTION BETWEEN
PERCEIVER AND PERSON

Chapter Six

EMPATHY

WEBSTER'S THIRD New International Dictionary defines empathy as "The imaginative projection of a subjective state whether affective, conative, or cognitive into an object so that the object appears to be infused with it." Consistently, we have defined empathy for a person as *the tendency of a perceiver to assume that another person's feelings, thoughts, and behavior are similar to his own.* Freudians (Fenichel, 1945) and non-Freudians (Sullivan, 1956), sociologists (Mead, 1934) and psychologists (Rogers, 1961) stress that our similarity to others forms the foundation of our understanding of them. What they do not stress is that the similarities we assume can be wrong as well as right, can lead to mistaken as well as to correct judgments. Our focus is upon *empathic accuracy,* the ability to predict accurately in what ways we are like and in what ways we are unlike others. We first consider empathy and the processes that determine it and then consider empathic accuracy and ways of improving it.

The Measurement of Empathy

Everyone assumes some similarity between himself and others, but some assume more than others. The common way of measuring differences in assumed similarity is first to have people answer questions as they themselves would answer them and then to have them answer the same questions as they think someone else would answer them. The number of questions that a man answers for others in the same way he answers them for himself is his empathy score. Exhibit 6-1 illustrates this method of measuring empathy (Livensparger, 1965). Note that the respondent answers questions as he thinks other men and women would answer them. He then answers them (part 3) for himself. A perceiver's assumed similarity score is the number of items which he answers for

EXHIBIT 6-1 *Empathy Inventory*
(Livensparger, 1965)

This inventory measures three things: (1) your knowledge of the interests of the majority of men; (2) your knowledge of the interests of the majority of women; and (3) your own interests. Follow the separate directions for each part.

(1) KNOWLEDGE OF MEN

A large and representative group of educated men checked whether they liked or disliked the various occupations, activities, and school subjects below. Mark one (1) if you think the *majority of men* checked that they *liked* the interest. Mark two (2) if you think the *majority* checked that they *disliked* the interest. Note that the numbering skips lines on the answer sheet (1,2,3,4, . . . 9,10,11,12, . . . 17, etc.). *Mark your answers in agreement with the numbers.*

1. Manufacturer
9. Art galleries
17. Driving an auto
25. Algebra
33. Floorwalker
41. Photo engraver
49. Railway conductor
57. Geography

2. Musical comedy
10. Symphony concerts
18. Arithmetic
26. Literature
34. Factory worker
42. Pharmacist
50. Geology
58. Politician

3. Auctioneer
11. Auto racer
19. Talkative people
27. Physics
35. Jeweler
43. Museums
51. Real estate salesman
59. Economics

4. Auto salesman
12. Auto repairman
20. Civil Service employee
28. Dentist
36. Life insurance salesman
44. Educational movies
52. Printer
60. Vaudeville

EXHIBIT 6-1 (*Continued*)

(2) KNOWLEDGE OF WOMEN

A large and representative group of women checked whether they liked or disliked the various occupations, activities, and school subjects below. Mark one (1) if you think the majority of women checked they *liked* the interest. Mark two (2) if you think the majority checked that they *disliked* the interest. Note that the numbering skips lines as in part (1).

65. Costume designer	66. Proofreader	67. Companion to elderly person	68. Accountant

73. Bank teller	74. Magazine writer	75. Telephone operator	76. Buyer of merchandise
81. Beauty specialist	82. Interior decorator	83. Florist	84. Artist's model
89. Lawyer, criminal	90. Probation officer	91. Cashier	92. Meeting and directing people

97. Preparing dinner for guests	98. Attending lectures	99. Governor of a state	100. Typist
105. Camping	106. "True Story" magazine	107. Teacher, grade school	108. Discussions of economic affairs
113. "Good Housekeeping" magazine	114. Stenographer	115. Statistician	116. Taking responsibility
121. Teacher, commercial	122. Cooking	123. Doing research work	124. Stockbroker

(3) PERSONAL INTERESTS

The following is a list of occupations, activities, and school subjects, etc. You are to indicate whether you like or dislike each of the items. If you like the item, mark one (1) on the answer sheet. If you dislike it, mark two (2). Note that the items are numbered so that you now return to the top of the answer sheet and use the numbers left blank.

5. Manufacturer	6. Musical comedy	7. Auctioneer	8. Auto salesman, etc.

others as he has answered them for himself. While the method is simple, the clerical complications are numerous. First of all, each individual has a unique pattern: One person may give the same response for himself and others to "manufacturer" but not the same for "musical comedy"; a second person may have a different response for manufacturer but the same for musical comedy, etc. Having the respondent make his answers for himself just below the answer he made for others makes it easier to count the number of assumed similarities. In the second place, two individuals may have the same assumed similarity scores but have quite different actual similarities. For example, one person may answer "like" to manufacturer for himself and "like" for others and be right; another person may answer "dislike" to manufacturer for himself and "dislike" for others and be wrong, etc. Finally, two people may have the same assumed similarity and actual similarity scores, but be quite different in their accuracy scores. That is, one may assume similarity only on items where he is actually similar while another may assume similarity on items where he is not similar. In sum, it is necessary to deal with three related measures: assumed similarity scores, actual similarity scores, and empathic accuracy scores.

The above test measures empathy between a perceiver and a group. Empathy between a perceiver and another individual can be measured in the same way. Chance and Meaders (1960), for example, compared the answers that each student made to the Edwards Personal Preference Schedule with the answers that they thought each of two individuals had made. The inventory has more than two hundred pairs of statements like the following:

1. I like to solve puzzles and problems that other people have difficulty with.
2. I like to follow instructions and to do what is expected of me.

The respondent first answered the inventory for himself, then listened to a tape-recorded interview, and finally answered the inventory as he thought the interviewee had answered it. The score was the number of statements that the respondent answered in the same way for the interviewee as he had answered for himself.

The content of empathy measures has varied widely. Livensparger used items from the Strong Vocational Interest Blank; Chance and Meaders, from the Edwards Personal Preference Schedule; Rodgers (1959), from Gough's Adjective Check List; Dymond (1954), from the MMPI. In an entirely different area, Strayer (1960) obtained six different empathy measures for the same 70 Air Force technicians by the use of a test of knowledge, a job rating, and a sociometric rating.

Like measures of level and spread, measures of empathy have generally high reliabilities (Fiedler, 1958). Unlike measures of level and spread, however, measures of empathy have an uncertain generality. Thus, Livensparger found that a man had a highly consistent tendency to assume similarity to other men. However, this tendency had only a slight relationship to the tendency for a man to assume similarity to women. Strayer also found little relationship between the amount of similarity that his Air Force technicians assumed in one area of work with the amount that they assumed in other areas. Empathy is the product of an interaction. The amount of similarity we assume is determined by whom we are perceiving, by our personalities, and by the interaction between the two.

The People with Whom We Empathize

Identification is the process by which a person acts like another person without being encouraged or taught to do so. Children identify with their parents: A daughter feeds and cares for her doll as her mother feeds and cares for her; a son walks, talks, and thinks like his father. In a similar manner, spectators at a sport identify with the athletes and students identify with other students. The process is reciprocal: We feel, think, and act as we think others are feeling, thinking, and acting; we assume that others are feeling, thinking, and acting like us. We empathize with those with whom we identify. *Attraction* also determines empathy. The more we like a person, the more we assume that he is like us. Convincing evidence comes from a study of 17 students at the University of Michigan (Newcomb, 1956). They were all transfer students, all strangers to each other, and all residents of the same cooperative house. In return for spending five hours a week being interviewed and filling out questionnaires, they were given free room and board for the semester. The men were given no voice in the selection of roommates, but (within the limits of the university regulations) they were given complete freedom to conduct the house, including the cooking and eating arrangements, as they chose. Before their arrival, each of the 17 men filled out a questionnaire covering attitudes toward a wide range of issues: classical music, immortality, sexual morality, house rules, university regulations about driving, etc. During the semester, the men completed a variety of personality inventories, and rated themselves and each other on numerous rating scales. They also reported whom they liked and disliked. From these data, both an index of each man's liking for each of the other men and an index of his assumed similarity to each of them were calculated. Result: The greater the attraction, the greater the empathy ($r = .69$).

It is not surprising that students assumed that those they liked were like them. It is surprising that there was no relationship between attraction and *actual* similarity. A quite different study reached the same conclusion. Silkiner (1962) correlated the favorableness of a student's attitudes toward the United States with the degree of assumed similarity between his interests and those of the typical American man. Result: The more favorable, the more assumed similarity. He then correlated favorableness of attitude with actual similarity. Result: No relationship.

Generalization is a key process in empathy: When a person finds that he has some characteristics in common with another person, he tends to perceive himself as having other characteristics like that person (Stotland et al., 1961). If we are aware of a few dissimilarities, we assume many more.

A man, for example, has a few obvious similarities to other men, and assumes more; he has a few obvious dissimilarities to women, and assumes more. An American man has a few obvious similarities to other American men, and assumes many more; a foreign man has a few obvious dissimilarities to American men and assumes more dissimilarities.

Generalization works both ways: We ascribe our traits to the similar person; we also ascribe *his* traits to ourselves. Burnstein, Stotland, and Zander (1962) brought more than a hundred junior high school boys together in the school gymnasium and asked them to complete a "describe yourself questionnaire." One part of the questionnaire required them to rate their excellence in swimming, ability to hold breath under water, etc. Two weeks later, the boys were addressed in groups of a dozen by a "deep-sea diver" (one of the authors) who described his career and stressed his excellence in swimming, ability to hold his breath under water, etc. In some groups, he stressed that he was similar to the boys: He was born and raised in their rural neighborhood, went to the same school, had a father who worked in the same factory that employed most of the fathers of the boys, etc. In other groups, the diver stressed that he was dissimilar: He was born and raised in a big city, went to a large city school, had a father who was a fisherman, etc. At the end of each group meeting, the diver asked the boys to rate themselves again on their excellence in swimming, etc. Result: The boys who had heard the "low similarity" diver rated themselves about as they had two weeks before; the boys who heard the "high similarity" diver changed their ratings of themselves so that they were more like those that the diver described himself as possessing.

Familiarity is related to empathy. The longer we know a person, the more similarity to him we tend to assume. Students were brought into a room two at a time and seated at desks in such a way that they could not see each other (Bieri, 1953). Each of them took a test which pictured 24 situations with three different possible responses. Each chose the response that he would make in each situation. They were then very briefly introduced to each other and asked, even though they did not know each other very well, to fill out the test as they thought their partner had filled it out. Assumed similarity was measured by determining the number of the 24 situations in which a student picked the same response for his partner as he had picked for himself. The pairs were then given two topics to discuss for twenty minutes. Afterward, each member of the pair was asked to answer the test as he thought his partner had. Result: Higher assumed similarity after interaction.

The processes of identification, attraction, generalization, and familiarity are intimately interwoven: We identify with those we like, we like those with whom we identify, etc. The relationship, for example, between familiarity and attraction has been formulated as the Law of Propinquity: "As the frequency of interaction between two persons increases, the degree of their liking for one another increases." The law is pervasive. Beier and Stumpf (1959) started out to determine the influence of various kinds of cues on judgments of intelligence, sociability, and other personality characteristics. To do so, they presented four subjects one at a time under different conditions to over two hundred students: (1) They heard only the voices of the subjects from behind the screen; (2) they then heard the subjects and saw them making gestures but did not see their faces; (3) they heard their voices and saw them in person making the gestures; and (4) they had all of these cues and also heard the subject discuss a topic for three minutes. They rated the subjects four times: (1) with only the voice as a cue; (2) with voice and gestures; (3) with voice and gestures and face; and (4) with voice and gestures and face and discussion. Major result: The more familiar students became with a subject the more favorable their ratings became.

The Personality of the Empathizer

Chance and Meaders (1960) measured the differences in personality between those who assumed little and those who assumed a great deal of similarity to the same two individuals they heard on the same tape recordings. Results:

LOW EMPATHIZERS	HIGH EMPATHIZERS
Expressive	Inhibited
Dominating	Submissive
Independent	Dependent
Aloof	Gregarious
Cool	Warm
Aggressive	Unaggressive

The authors conclude that those who assume high similarity have a "highly developed need for social interactions although strongly tinged with dependence upon and conformity to the constraints that others impose," while those of low assumed similarity are "nonconforming, impatient with custom and authority, disinclined to plan and to accept schedules, wanting to be in the limelight, not strongly motivated toward seeking contacts with others, seeking new experiences, and preferring aggressive modes of behavior."

A similar result emerged from a different approach (Fiedler, 1961). In a series of studies, leaders were first asked to describe themselves by rating their degree of agreement with statements such as "I like good food" and to check from pairs of adjectives such as calm-exciting the one more descriptive of themselves. Each leader was then asked to use the same statements and adjectives in describing the man he thought was his best and the man he thought was his poorest worker. Next, the number of statements on which the leader assumed that each of the two workers were like himself were counted. Finally, *the difference in assumed similarity of opposites was determined.* Results: Those who assumed about the same amount of similarity to their two extreme workers were judged to be more dependent on others, more concerned about the attitude of others toward them, and more unwilling to reject unsatisfactory workers. Those who assumed much more similarity to the best than to the poorest worker were more independent, more indifferent to the attitudes of others, and readier to reject people they judged to be unsatisfactory. They were distant from people.

The aloofness of the nonempathizers may be related to childhood experiences. Stotland and Dunn (1963) measured the degree of identification of students with another student by measuring the anxiety level of the students while they were watching another student in an anxious situation. They compared the anxiety levels of first-born or only children with students who had at least one older sibling. Students with older siblings were more anxious: "The first and only born . . . react as if they only use the other person's performance level as a guide to self-evaluation and do not really 'feel with' him." They also incidentally compared the empathic anxiety of students with low and high self-esteem. Those of high self-esteem identified more with the student in trouble. "These results are reminiscent of the clinician's belief that only those who really love themselves can love others." The measurement of improvement in sensitivity during T-group training produced consistent results (Cline and Richards, 1959). Trainees rated themselves and other group members on their conceit and egotism. Those who rated themselves and were rated by others as most conceited and egotistical improved most during the training.

Empathic Accuracy

We have thus far been concerned with the amount of similarity that a perceiver assumes. Our primary interest, however, is in the accuracy of these assumptions. Three different questions are involved: How accurate is the level of similarity assumed? How accurate are the specific assumptions of similarity? What is the relationship between assumed and actual similarity?

The question of the level of empathy has been of both philosophic and psychological concern. Hume and other philosophers in the tradition of "epistemological loneliness" have viewed man as being essentially alone. They see him as capable of understanding the behavior of other men but incapable of really understanding their experiences. Following this tradition, behaviorists and psychologists have attempted to understand men through a study of their behavior alone. By contrast, some experimentalists and most clinicians assume that "after all, we are all pretty much alike" and can, therefore, best understand others by assuming that their experiences are similar to our own (Bakan, 1956):

> It should be apparent from this that when we say that we are all pretty much alike it does not mean that we must all be psychotic, nor that we must all have children, nor that we must all have had the experience of our parents dying. Not *in point of fact* need we have had these experiences. But rather in the way in which all yearning is the same, and all pain is the same, and all fantasy is the same, etc.—only in this way need we have had these experiences. And the method whereby we may become aware of the relationship between experience and behavior is through the use of systematic self-observation.

At the extreme, the behaviorist sees empathy as the source of all error; the clinician, as the source of all truth.

None of us, of course, are entirely different from or exactly the same as anyone else. The degrees of relationship can, in any given situation, be measured. For example, Livensparger (1965), who worked with the test shown in Exhibit 6-1, measured the accuracy of the level of assumptions among 57 college men and women. He first counted the number of interests that each student had answered in the same way for others as he had for himself and then counted the interests where his responses were actually the same. He then divided the total number of assumed similarity by the total number of actual similarity and multiplied by 100. If the result was 100, then the student had assumed similarity for exactly the same number of interests in which he was actually similar. One result: The average student assumed too little similarity (94 per cent). The individual variations, however, were very wide, some students having scores of less than 50 per cent and some having scores of more than 150 per cent.

The ratios of assumed to actual similarity vary with the saliency of the processes of identification, attraction, generalization, and familiarity. People identify more with their own than the opposite sex. Consistently, Livensparger found erroneously high levels of empathy with the same sex (108 per cent), erroneously low levels with the opposite sex (81 per cent). American students have more obvious similarities to and familiarity with American men than foreign students. Silkiner (1962), using a test roughly similar to that shown in Exhibit 6-1, measured the empathy levels of American and foreign and male and female students with American men. Results: For the American male students, 78 per cent, and for the foreign male students, 60 per cent; for the American women, 70 per cent, and for the foreign women, 51 per cent. All groups were more similar than they assumed. Foreign women, however, underestimated their similarity to American men by the greatest amount.

Effective training should have as one of its aims that of developing an accurate level of empathy. The problem of level seems to be most acute at the extremes: We overestimate our similarity to those that are most like us; we underestimate our similarity to those that are least like us. Experts as well as laymen suffer from the problems. Giedt (1958) had 48 clinicians judge a series of patients of varying ages, problems, and backgrounds. One conclusion: "Raters seemed particularly likely to misjudge patients whose socioeconomic and cultural status was either quite close to their own or quite distant from their own. . . . The patient whose socioeconomic and cultural position was most distant from that of the raters—a rather nomadic fellow who shared few of the high aspirations probably characteristic of most of the raters—seemed to be least well understood, and his behavior was often interpreted on the basis of an improper frame of reference. Thus reading pulp magazines and having been involved in fights as a boy—behavior which probably differed from that of the raters—was incorrectly related to impulsivity and lack of control. The patient who had a fairly high-level, managerial status had an outlook on life perhaps so close to that of the raters that they could hardly accept the possibility of serious psychopathology in him. This patient was rated far too high in adherence to reality, apparently on the assumption that no high-level person such as this could be very unrealistic."

The clinician has the most difficulty in judging those who are most or least like himself. He seems to have a similar difficulty in dealing with these extreme groups in a therapy situation. Carson and Heine (1962) had 60 clinical trainees give therapy once a week for sixteen weeks to 60 patients. Before therapy, clinicians and patients completed the Minnesota Multiphasic Personality Inventory. Patients were assigned to clinicians on the basis of their similarity or dissimilarity to them. The 60 clinician-patient pairs were divided into five groups, the first group being composed of those with the most similar profiles and the fifth group being composed of those with the least similar profiles. After the sixteen weeks, the success of therapy for each pair was independently determined. Result: Patients in the groups that were most and least like their therapists were least benefited by the therapy; patients who were moderately like their therapists (the three middle groups) were most benefited by therapy.

Level of empathic accuracy concerns the ability of the same perceiver to vary his assumed similarity from one person to another. It is measured by dividing the perceiver's assumed similarity by his actual similarity. How well in general do different perceivers of the same person adjust their level of assumed similarity to their actual similarity? This relationship between assumed and actual similarity is measured by correlating the assumed and actual similarity scores of different perceivers of the same person or group.

Some perceivers of the same person are much like him and some are quite different. How well do different perceivers recognize these differences in similarity? Bronfenbrenner et al. (1958) asked college students first to check from a list of adjectives those that described themselves and then to check those that they thought the typical student would check. From these data, assumed and actual scores were calculated and correlated. Result: .87. Silkiner (1962) repeated the study using 100 foreign and 100 American students and found a correlation of .69 for the American students and .74 for the foreign students. Conclusion: We seem to be very good at recognizing the general level of our overall similarity to other people. The conclusion as we shall see in a moment does not mean that we are equally good at recognizing specific similarities. It is as if we first see ourselves and others as unified wholes and can see much more clearly the degree of differences between these wholes than we can see the differences between specific parts of the wholes.

One might think that a perceiver who had a perfectly accurate level of empathy with a person would also have perfect empathic accuracy. That this is not necessarily correct may be illustrated by the following hypothetical response to the first four items in the test in Exhibit 6-1.

	MANUFACTURER	MUSICAL COMEDY	AUCTIONEER	AUTO SALESMAN
Responses of the perceiver	dislike	dislike	like	like
Responses that the perceiver assumes for the person	like	dislike	like	dislike
Responses of the person	dislike	like	dislike	like

In this example, the perceiver assumes he is similar to the person on two items (musical comedy and auctioneer) and is actually similar on two items (manufacturer and auto salesman) but is wrong in all of his specific assumptions about similarity and dissimilarity. The reason for introducing this example is that it is fairly true of what happens in many life situations. Both Silkiner and Bronfenbrenner found much less relationship between assumed similiarity and accuracy scores than between assumed similarity and actual similarity scores. Bronfenbrenner et al., who found a correlation of .86 between empathy and actual similarity, found only a correlation of .21 between empathy and the degree of accuracy.

The accuracy of the similiarities we assume increases with the length of acquaintanceship. In the conclusion to his intensive study of the members of a cooperative house, Newcomb (1963) states:

> Early acquaintance is characterized by a continuing process of reciprocal scanning: What kinds of things does this person view as important? Whatever they are, how does he feel about them, and also about the things I regard as important (including myself)? If the discrepancies seem not too glaring, explorative communication continues, and with it comes the possibility of changes in the scale of importance, and in attitudes toward things of varying degrees of importance. In the long run (four months, in my own investigation), attraction and association come to be relatively concentrated upon those who are perceived, usually with a considerable accuracy, as having notions similar to one's own of what is important and as having attitudes similar to one's own toward important things.

The Improvement of Empathic Accuracy

We have stressed three related aims for training in empathy: (1) improving the accuracy of the level of empathy; (2) increasing the relationship between empathy and actual similarity; and (3) improving the accuracy of specific assumptions of similarity. Traditionally, training in psychology and psychiatry has stressed the development of traits that are thought to lead to these ends. We now consider the nature of the traits and their actual relation to these aims.

THE FAILURE OF PSYCHOLOGICAL-MINDEDNESS

Gough (1954) defines psychological-mindedness as "the degree to which an individual is interested in, and responsive to, the inner needs, motives, and experiences of others." He also developed a scale for measuring the trait and showed that the scores of individuals increase as their exposure to psychology increases. Is the increase related to increased sensitivity?

Chance and Meaders (1960) measured the psychological-mindedness of 96 undergraduate men by means of the intraception scale of the Edwards Personal Preference Schedule. After the students listened to tape-recorded interviews with two men, they filled out the inventory as they thought the interviewed men had filled it out. An accuracy score for each student was obtained by counting the number of times predicted responses agreed with actual responses. The 18 most accurate students were than compared with the 18 least accurate on psychological-mindedness. Result: The most psychologically-minded had significantly less empathy. Considering this and other results, the authors concluded that the accurate judge is

> . . . a person who is active and outgoing in social relationships, who likes other people but is not markedly dependent upon them, who is ascendant but not hostile and competitive, and who is not given to intellectual reflections about his interpersonal relationships. The picture is one of an individual who finds significant satisfaction in social activities and carries on his daily life with a minimum of interpersonal or intrapersonal conflict.

The development of psychological-mindedness seems to be a dubious way of increasing empathic accuracy.

THE FAILURE OF EMPATHIC DRIVE

The training of clinical psychologists stresses the development of "therapeutic sensitivity." Abeles (1963) has defined one purpose of such training as the development of "affective complexity." To measure the success of training directed toward this end he compared the complexity of three groups: (1) 14 students in prepracticum training; (2) 15 students who had finished the prepracticum and begun the practicum; and (3) 16 students who had completed the practicum. Affective complexity was measured by scoring Thematic Apperception Test responses according to the following scale:

1 MINUS MONOTONIC NEGATIVE AFFECT: Predominant mood is negative, painful, depressed. Feelings or attitudes focus on negative aspects of event or person. No ambivalence or positive affect expressed.

ZERO AFFECT INHIBITION: No affect or feeling expressed in story. Largely descriptive with no indication of emotional involvement.

1 PLUS MONOTONIC POSITIVE AFFECT: Affect expressed pleasant, positive, focus on feelings or attitudes are entirely pleasurable. No ambivalence of negative affect expressed. Affect is simple, nonoffensive.

2 PLUS   AMBIVALENT AFFECT: Affects with dual, conflicting qualities of attrition-avoidance, but with no conflict resolution
evidenced.

3 PLUS   AMBIVALENT AFFECT WITH CONTROLLED RESOLUTION INDI-
CATED: The most adaptive and efficiently complex pattern
in which there is flexibility of thought, sensitivity to intri-
cate objects relationships. Differences accepted as non-
threatening, ability to respond to rather than rebel against
affect complexities.

A high correlation (.73) between these TAT scores and rankings
by instructors who knew the students indicate that the scores were valid.
While there are some reservations regarding the experimental design, the
advanced students did have higher affective complexity scores than the
beginning students.

Are increases in affective complexity related to increases in sensitivity
to the client? Abeles made no effort to answer this question, but the
results of Mullin (1962) have some bearing on it. He developed a projective test of *empathic drive,* i.e., the tendency of people to orient themselves toward the inner states and feelings of people. He first had students
in a pilot study look at five-minute silent films of six different people being
interviewed. At the end of each film he asked the students to write "as
lifelike a picture of the person as you can." He then classified each sentence of each student's description into one of three categories: (1) physical ("is wearing a coat," "has dark features," "is wearing glasses," etc.) ;
(2) sociological ("is unmarried," "is looking for work," "could be retired
school teacher," etc.) ; (3) psychological ("is unsure of himself," "loves
to gossip," "does not trust the interviewer," "worries a lot," etc. The
students varied widely and consistently: the correlation between the average number of psychological sentences they used in describing one person
and the average number they used in describing another person was .79.

Based on the responses given in the pilot study, Mullin then developed an objective test consisting of 90 statements, 30 for each of three
film subjects (Exhibit 6-2). The three alternatives were selected from
statements made by the students in the pilot study, the underlined ones
being those classified as psychological. The test is reliable, correlations
for different college groups ranging from .82 to .86. That is, the tendency
of students to choose the "psychological" statements remained remarkably
constant from statement to statement and from person to person.

Is the strength of the empathic drive related to accuracy? Mullin
correlated scores on his test to a wide variety of measures of observational,
group, and interpersonal accuracy. The overall result: .00. Scores were,
however, related to some personality traits: submissiveness, pessimism,
and psychological distance from people. Higher scorers were also younger.

EXHIBIT 6-2   *A Projective Test of Empathic Drive*
(Adapted from Mullin, 1962)

Directions: This is a study of the impressions people make on others. You will see three people in silent movies. *Try to form as lifelike an impression of each as you can.* The first will be Mrs. P.; the second, Mr. W.; and the third, Mrs. N. As each film is finished the camera will be stopped. Then, in each of the groups of statements numbered below, *pick the one that is like your impression of the person.*

THE CASE OF MRS. P.

1. (a) *is sincere*   (b) wearing a coat   (c) fairly attractive
2. (a) is about forty years old   (b) talkative   (c) *self-satisfied*
3. (a) moistens her lips   (b) *is glad to leave*   (c) experienced with small groups
4. (a) *feels inadequate*   (b) is facially expressive   (c) average looking
5. (a) considers the interview serious   (b) *is gregarious*   (c) shows signs of amusement
6. (a) is a typical housewife   (b) has family problems   (c) *is intelligent*
7. (a) is sitting straight   (b) *enjoying herself*   (c) a good sport
8. (a) is a modest dresser   (b) active in the community   (c) *uncertain of her answers*
9. (a) *is very friendly*   (b) left the interview feeling very satisfied   (c) sitting stiffly
10. (a) is between thirty-five and forty years old   (b) *an emotionally stable person*   (c) looking for a job

It seems that the benefits of an increased empathic drive, if any, are balanced by a tendency to project.

The power of projection in our judgments of inner states of others is suggested by a study relating the ratings of autobiographies of graduate students to their predictions about people (Weingarten, 1949). The autobiographies were read and rated for tension in three major areas: the self, the family situation, and the social environment. The students were then given a series of statements such as "D. daydreams a great deal of the time," and asked to indicate for each statement the most likely explanation of the behavior. The explanations of the students were then related to their own tension areas. Conclusions:

1. An individual's perception of other people's problems is directly influenced by his own emotional adjustment.
2. An individual sees more problems in those areas in which he is most insecure himself.

SENSITIVITY TRAINING

The goals of Sensitivity Training are numerous and variable. They include increasing the ability to perceive what is actually going on in a social situation, skill in assessing ongoing situations, and the ability to intervene effectively in ongoing situations in such a way as to maximize personal and group effectiveness and satisfaction. They at least implicitly include the development of psychological-mindedness and empathic drive.

The procedures of Sensitivity Training involve a "laboratory" composed of 30 to 150 people, meeting in a conference setting for two or three weeks. The core experience is ordinarily a training group which meets for thirty to forty hours, carrying on a study of its own processes. Most laboratories also involve a wide range of other activities: lectures and demonstrations reviewing material from the social sciences, consultation on back-home problems, and planned exercises. The exercises may range from replications of classic experiments in social psychology to full-scale organizational simulation designs that continue for a day or two.

To determine whether training achieves all or any of its goals is extraordinarily difficult (Miles, 1960):

> The persons appearing for human relations training are highly self-selected, and it is excessively difficult to get comparable pools of subjects to serve as members of control groups. Ordinarily the N in any particular training laboratory is relatively small. Where training laboratories are composed of persons from widely spread geographical areas, getting accurate follow-up measures is difficult; where laboratories are held with members of an intact organization, it is almost impossible to separate the presumed outcomes of the laboratory from organizational growth factors.

In an effort to solve these problems, Miles used 34 elementary school principals attending a two-week training laboratory at Bethel, Maine, during August of 1958. Each principal was matched with another principal who did not attend the conference. In addition, each participating principal gave names of six to eight associates on the job who could describe his job behavior. Results: There was no change in either the experimental or control group in a leadership behavior scale given before and after training. There was a change in both the experimental and control groups in their participation habits as measured by a group participation scale. There were significant changes in the experimental but not in the control group in the way they perceived themselves: "listens more," "communicates better," "shares decisions more," "gives help to teachers," etc. However, there was no relation between the amount of this change and the initial expressed desire for improvement. "If anything the relationship was inverse . . . a high wish to change in this sample was a kind of defensive protestation." Ego, strength, flexibility, and need for affiliation were not related to changes at the laboratory or back home although the experimenters assumed they would be.

Conclusions from such a complex study can only be tentative. The results, however, are consistent with the interpretation that the trainees which he is a part, and in his ability to differentiate between the important individuals in his life. Disturbed children do not understand their parents; disturbed students do not understand their teachers; disturbed workers do not understand their bosses; unhappy couples do not understand each other; and neurotics understand neither themselves nor other people.

The increase of client sensitivity as a goal of therapy has much to commend it. It focuses upon the person with the problem: the client. It is uncomplicated by the ethical and value conflicts that plague other goals of therapy, for teaching a person to understand others is not essentially different in this respect from teaching him to read or write. It suggests ways that the therapist might go about achieving this end. Above all, it suggests ways of giving objective feedback to clients and ways of measuring the success of therapy. The child who predicts the responses of his parents more accurately after therapy than before has achieved a kind of success. The couples who can predict each other's behavior more accurately after marital counseling have also achieved some success. And the neurotic who can predict more accurately what others think of themselves and of him also suggests that the treatment has been successful.

Sensitivity Training

The philosopher Whitehead in a statement in *The Aims of Education* (1929) said:

> In the history of education, the most striking phenomenon is that schools of learning, which at one epoch are alive with the ferment of genius, in a succeeding generation exhibit merely pedantry and routine. The reason is that they are overladen with inert ideas. Education with inert ideas is not only useless: it is, above all things, harmful—*Corruptio optimi, pessima.* Except at rare intervals of intellectual ferment, education in the past has been radically infected with inert ideas. That is the reason why uneducated clever women, who have seen much of the world, are in middle life so much the most cultured part of the community. They have been saved from this horrible burden of inert ideas. Every intellectual revolution which has ever stirred humanity into greatness has been a passionate protest against inert ideas.

Sensitivity Training with its stress upon the trainee rather than the trainer, upon the process rather than the content of training, and upon emotional rather than conceptual learning seems to be one "passionate protest against inert ideas." Its mushrooming influence suggests that it has also stirred at least some of humanity.

The heart of Sensitivity Training is the T group. A T group (for training group) starts as an unstructured group in which individuals participate as learners. The content of the training is the behavior of the members of the group as they struggle to create a miniature society within their group and to support one another's learning within that society. Each member learns about his own motives, feelings, and strategies in dealing with other persons; of the reactions he produces in others as he interacts with them; and to understand others as individuals and as cooperative members of a group.

As in psychotherapy groups, T groups are concerned with increasing the sensitivity of the members to themselves and to others. Both types of groups are unstructured at the beginning and the agenda of each meeting grows out of the members' own functioning. Unlike therapy groups, T groups are not composed of patients seeking relief from distress but of normal persons trying to learn new skills. Unlike therapy groups, T groups do not stress the unlearning of old and inadequate ways of behaving but of learning new and better ways. And unlike therapy groups, T groups do not focus upon the individual and his problems but upon the group and its problems in functioning effectively. The attitudes of individual members are a subject of concern only in relation to their effects on the functioning of the group.

In the T group, as in the classroom, the stress is upon learning, not upon gratifying members or upon producing objective changes in the environment. Like the teacher, the trainer meets resistance to learning, tries to develop group norms which support learning, and is concerned about the consistency, scope, and permanence of what individuals learn. In contrast to the teacher, the trainer deals with adults rather than with children, plays a less central and less differentiated role, and stresses learning about the here-and-now rather than about the there-and-then. The T group is much less stable, its members seldom meeting as a group for more than forty hours while many of the members of a sixth-grade classroom may have been together for more than five thousand hours.

A T group is concerned with sensitivity as a way of increasing group effectiveness; we are concerned with the T group as a way of increasing sensitivity. How effective is it for this purpose? Gibb (1952) divided 140 college students into five groups. Subjects in all groups were given pre- and posttests designed to measure their first-person accuracy (their ability to predict how others would rate their likeability, sociability, and adjustment). Members of Group A shared a T-group experience and were given continual training in role playing and individual knowledge of all pretraining test scores. Group B shared a T-group experience and was told about pretraining test scores but received no training in role playing. Group C shared a T-group experience but was given no role playing or feedback. Groups D and E did not participate in a T group but differed in that Group D received knowledge of pretest results and Group E did not. Results: "The significant difference between Group C and Group E indicated that the training, even without role playing and knowledge of results, improved self-insight . . . . The significant improvement of Group A (role-playing group) over Group B (all aspects of training but no role playing) adds a significant increment to the training methods we are using."

Such studies are few and the general effectiveness of the T group as a way of increasing sensitivity is as yet uncertain. It is, however, quite certain that there are wide individual differences in the benefits derived from T-group experience. Stock (1964, p. 434) summarizes the research in this manner:

> What the individual is like when he comes to the laboratory seems to have a great deal to do with the learnings he takes away with him. In separate studies, Stock and Mathis suggest that conflict or some internal awareness of lack of fit or consistency have something to do with readiness for learning. But Watson et al. suggest that there is some ceiling on this: highly anxious persons learn little. Consistent with this, Harrison has hypothesized that individuals so threatened by confrontation with dissonance that they must defend against it with rejection of the laboratory, distortion, and so on, are likely to close themselves off from opportunities to learn. Miles, too, found that threat-oriented individuals were less receptive to feedback of certain kinds. Mathis suggests that tendencies toward pairing and fight make for readiness to learn, while tendencies toward dependency and flight work against learning. This seems consistent with some of the findings of Watson et al. that responsive, outgoing persons are more likely to apply laboratory learnings. Miles found that the personality characteristics of ego strength, flexibility, and need-affiliation are relevant in that they facilitated unfreezing, involvement, and the reception of feedback, and these in turn influenced learning.

Individual sensitivity in the T group is viewed as one means to an end: the increase of group effectiveness. It might better be viewed as an end in itself. Even if we assume that the T-group method is best for increasing group effectiveness, it does not follow that it is best for increasing sensitivity. In fact, it seems best for only some individuals in only some phases of their training. If sensitivity were singled out as a separate goal with its own special training program, the success of the overall program might well be enhanced.

Concentrating on sensitivity would make training evaluations more precise. In the long run, this may be the greatest advantage of the concentration. From its beginning the T-group movement has had a research orientation. The multiplicity of its aims, however, has made evaluation difficult. Considering its goals one at a time instead of all at once may be an answer to these difficulties. Sensitivity Training has a more flexible and innovative spirit than either clinical or academic training. The spirit makes it likely that our knowledge of how to increase sensitivity will be most advanced in the future by new programs and research in the area of Sensitivity Training.

The Teaching of Psychology

The President of the Division on the Teaching of Psychology of the American Psychological Association recently commented (MacLeod, 1965, p. 345):

> In the 4-year curriculum which has become more or less standard throughout the country a student who takes a particular course is expected to devote to it from one-fifth to one-quarter of his working time. The time devoted to his major subjects usually adds up to anywhere from 40% to 60% of the 4-year period. This is a formidable amount of time, time which conceivably might have been spent more profitably on something else. It is a disturbing thought. I am sure that at the end of a lecture hour you have often asked yourself, as I have more often than I like to admit: Was it really worthwhile? One hour each from 150 students; 150 hours of precious adolescent time; at 8 hours a day, the equivalent of almost 20 working days. It ought to be a pretty good lecture to justify that kind of investment. Not long ago I overheard one student calling to another, evidently with some ulterior motive: "Hey, Sally, have you a dead hour at 11:00?" Answer: "Have I a dead hour! I have psychology." Students are usually charitable. They condemn us when we are unfair or unsufferably dull, but are willing to believe that with a better teacher the course would have been worthwhile. Occasionally, however, they ask the question which we ought to be asking ourselves: not just, Was this a good lecture? but, Was this course worth teaching? or even, Does psychology as a subject really deserve its present place in the curriculum?

The experimental method is the natural way for psychologists to try to answer such questions. In 1946, the present author was impressed by the following paragraph in *The Background for College Teaching* by Luella Cole (1940, p. 509):

> Any good instructor is continually trying new procedures. With very little more time and effort he could find out objectively if the changes he makes are effective. As it is, he usually has only his own impressions to go by in estimating the worth of any technique. This kind of investigation is especially vital to the teaching profession, and only teachers can carry it on. The trouble is not that college teachers fail to experiment

Chapter Seven

OBSERVATION

NOTHING IS MORE obvious than that our understanding of a person depends on how well we observe him. Nothing has been more obviously neglected by psychologists. The value of being a good observer is often extolled; training programs for developing observational skills are occasionally instituted; but research on what it takes to be a good observer is almost nonexistent. Neither Harris (1962) nor Bruni (1963) was able to locate a *single* study directly concerned with the problem. With this handicap, we now consider the nature of observation, the measurement of observational accuracy, the causes of differences in it, and ways of training people to improve their accuracy.

The Nature of Observation

Common sense views observation as a quite passive affair: the eye is a motion-picture camera; the ear, a tape recorder. What we see a person do and hear him say is transcribed on the slate of our awareness. The records are then sorted, edited, and evaluated. However, the more informed we become, the less the eye and ear seem to be like a camera and a recorder. They select what they see and hear. They also scan, peek, watch, neglect, scrutinize—and distort. We observe what we want to observe. McClelland and Atkinson (1948) had 108 candidates for submarine training look at ambiguous stimuli projected on a dimly lit screen. They were told what to look for: "Three objects on a table," or "All of the people in the picture are enjoying themselves. What are they doing?" Of the sailors 44 took the test one hour after eating; 24 took it four hours after eating; and 40 took it sixteen hours after eating. The hungrier the sailor, the more food-related objects he reported.

We observe what we expect to observe. Siipola (1935) flashed on a screen for a tenth of a second such nonsense syllables as "chack," "sael," and "dack." Each of 180 subjects wrote down what he thought the words were. Half of them were told in advance that the words to appear would have to do with animals or birds; the other half was told that the words would have to do with travel or transportation. The first group gave animal or bird responses 63 per cent of the time: "chick," "seal," "duck," etc. The second group gave travel or transportation responses 74 per cent of the time: "check," "sail," "deck," etc.

We observe what we have learned to observe. Bruner and Postman (1949) quickly flashed playing cards before subjects and asked them to name the cards. Some of the cards were especially manufactured to reverse the usual relation between color and suit: a black six of hearts, a red four of spades. Most persons saw what they had previously learned to see: a six of spades and a four of hearts. In another experiment, Bruner, Postman, and Rodrigues (1951) cut a lemon, a carrot, and a tomato from the same sheet of paper. Subjects looked at each piece and then turned around and set a color wheel to match the color of the paper. When the paper was identified as a lemon, the matching color was yellower; when the paper was identified as a tomato, the matching color was redder.

What we are observing can change without our knowing it. Two photographs, each of a different face, were mounted in a stereoscope so that subjects saw one with the left eye and the other with the right eye at the same time (Engel, 1961). At first, the observer saw just one of the faces with normal illumination. Next, he was given the first face normally lit, with the second face under very low illumination. The procedure was repeated with slight increases in light on the second face until the observer was seeing both faces with normal lighting. At each step he was asked whether any change had taken place in what he saw. Most reported that they saw no change. The light on the first face was then reduced by small steps to zero. At this point, the observer was looking at the quite different second face. Observers still continued to report that they were looking at the same face.

Observation is not a passive process; it is an interaction between the observer and the observed comparable to the interaction between a batter and a pitcher (Ittelson and Cantril, 1954, pp. 3-4):

> We cannot have a batter without a pitcher. It is true that someone can throw a ball up in the air and hit it with a bat, but his relationship to the batter in the baseball game is very slight. Similarly, there is no pitcher without a batter. The pitcher in the bull-pen is by no means the same as the pitcher in the game. But providing a pitcher for a batter is still not enough for us to be able to define and study our batter. The batter we are interested in does not exist outside of a baseball game, so that in order to study him completely we need not only pitcher, but catcher, fielders, teammates, officials, fans, and the rules of the game.

Our batter, as we see him in this complex transaction, simply does not exist anywhere else independent of the transaction. The batter is what he is because of the baseball game in which he participates and, in turn, the baseball game itself is what it is because of the batter. Each one owes its existence to the fact of active participation with and through the other. If we change either one, we change the other.

The interactional approach describes what goes on during observation more adequately than the passive approach. The research that documents this does not, however, provide any useful ideas about observational accuracy. We rarely observe people for a tenth of a second or see a different person with each eye. How accurate are our observations of others and what influences our accuracy? The first step toward an answer is to measure observational accuracy.

The Measurement of Observational Accuracy

Hit on the back of the head, we *sense* blinding flashes of light and color. Hit in a slightly different place, we *perceive* stars and butterflies. Sensation is the registration of stimuli in the brain. Perception is an awareness of objects, qualities, or relationships by way of these sensations: We sense heat, but perceive fire; we sense loudness, but perceive a drum; and we sense sourness, but perceive vinegar. Perception is the interpretation of sensations, the prediction of a substance from sensory clues. We are so used to predicting the substance from its sensory shadow that we normally feel that the shadow *is* the substance: We do not see green, but a pea; we do not hear high-pitched sounds, but a child; we do not smell smoke, but a cigar. Our observations, outside the laboratory, are not reports of sensations but of perceptions, i.e., they are interpretations of sensations.

Our observations of people are generally not even a report of perceptions, but of inferences based on perceptions. When Betty perceives that Albert has smiled and offered her a chair, she infers that he likes her. Our common human experiences create so many similar situations in which an inference based on a perception is accurate that inferences dominate everyone's thinking about people. They also dominate the thinking of psychologists about the observation of people. A study by King et al. (1952) is entitled "Experimental Analysis of the Reliability of Observations of Social Behavior." The study, however, is concerned with the reliability of inferences about the sociability, cooperativeness, aggressiveness, etc. of children based on what the children said and did during an interview.

Observational accuracy is not the accuracy of inferences based on perceptions, but the accuracy of the perceptions themselves: Did Mary wear a ring, use lipstick, have black hair, say her husband worked in a factory? Psychologists have long known how inaccurate such perceptions may be. They have only recently, however, become interested in the everyday implications of perceptual accuracy. Nichols and Stevens (1957), authors of *Are You Listening?*, state in their introduction: "Incredible as it may seem when we think about it, this book, to our knowledge, is the first close analysis ever made of the oldest, the most used, and the most important element of interpersonal communication—listening."

Most tests of perceptual accuracy have been developed for a specific research and have no general usefulness. Harvard students, for example, with varying degrees of prejudice against Jews, were shown photographs of Jews and non-Jews to determine how accurately they could identify the two groups (Lindzey and Rogolsky, 1950). The purpose was to determine whether the prejudiced were more accurate at this particular kind of observation. They were: "The bigot . . . is particularly sensitive or *vigilant* to stimuli that will permit the correct identification of the Jew and non-Jew."

A study of military leadership used a more comprehensive test of accuracy (Showel, 1960). Squad leaders were asked the following questions about each of the ten infantry trainees under them:

1. What is his first name?
2. Has he been on KP during the past week?
3. Has he been on sick call during the past week?
4. Has he had a pass during the past week?
5. What is his rifle qualification score?
6. How many years of schooling has he completed?
7. What was his job before entering the army?
8. What is his principal hobby or interest?
9. What is his ambition for a future civilian career?

The squad leaders answered similar questions for their trainee sergeant and trainee platoon guide. The correctness of their answers was determined by comparing them with the answers actually given by the trainees, the sergeant, and the guide. The accuracy score was the total number of correct answers. The leaders with the highest accuracy score, incidentally, were the best leaders as judged by (1) ratings by their trainees; (2) rating by the sergeant; (3) rating by the platoon leader; and (4) score on a standardized leader reaction test.

Standard listening comprehension tests have been developed that follow the format of reading comprehension tests. Hartlage (1963), for example, tested the listening comprehension of blind and sighted high school students by playing recorded prose selections to them. Intelligence

test scores were highly related to listening scores. There was no difference, however, between blind and sighted students in listening ability.
Brown (1962) used the Educational Testing Service Test of Listening
to verify the hunch that good listeners would imitate the breathing pattern of the speaker. They did not. However, people did have different
breathing patterns when they were listening from when they were not.

Harris (1962) made the first effort to develop a standard test for
measuring accuracy in observing people. He used six brief filmed interviews, three of men and three of women. The camera is stopped at the
end of each interview and the respondent answers 30 selected true-false
statements about the interviewee: "Her fingernails were polished red,"
"She ran her finger along the edge of the table," "She said she loses
her temper when tired and nervous," "She said she can't remember faces
very well," etc. The test takes less than an hour to complete and has
a fairly adequate reliability ($r = .67$).

Bruni (1963) used the same filmed interviews as Harris. He developed a similar test that yields separate scores for the observation of physical appearance and of conversation and for the observation of men and
of women. The test for men had the following instructions:

> You are going to see five-minute filmed interviews with three men: Mr.
> G., Mr. W., and Mr. Z. When the film is over you will be asked to
> answer questions about what they looked like, what they did, and what
> they said. The statements in the test are of the following kinds:
>
> > He had a red hat.
> > He smiled frequently.
> > He said he liked to play chess.
>
> On the separate answer sheet:
>
> > Mark "1" if you think the correct answer is Mr. G. (the man in the
> > first interview).
> > Mark "2" if you think the correct answer is Mr. W. (the man in the
> > second interview).
> > Mark "3" if you think the correct answer is Mr. Z. (the man in the
> > third interview).
> > Mark "4" if you think the statement applies to none of the three men.

Students who took the test were quite consistent in their accuracy.
The overall reliability of the test was .74, but the conversation subtest
was considerably more reliable than the appearance test (.73 versus .49).
Students were also quite stable in their scores. Correlations between scores
for the same students on the same test taken eight weeks apart was .69.
Accuracy of listening scores was more stable than accuracy in observing
appearance (.70 versus .55). However, looking and listening accuracy
were related (.40).

Even among those of high intelligence, it seems, there are large and consistent differences in the ability to observe people accurately, particularly in the ability to listen accurately. The differences can be measured conveniently and response accuracy can be checked against an impeccable criterion—what the person actually looked like, did, and said.

Sex and Accuracy

Good observers are good judges. Neither Harris nor Bruni, however, found any relationship between observation and a wide variety of tests of achievement, intelligence, and personality. Bruni concluded: "The major finding in regard to personality and observational accuracy was that personality traits have little if any relationship to observation." He did find that women were superior observers.

Whether women make more accurate predictions about people than men is still doubtful. Allport (1937) gave the following persuasive but fictional case of female superiority:

> Returning home from a dinner party her husband perhaps reports as the extent of his observation that the hostess looked rather pretty in her new green dress. Whereupon the wife may add that the dress was not new, that it was formerly white, and that it had been lengthened with tulle to bring it into style; furthermore, that the hostess is worried about money-matters and about her husband's drinking, that she is having trouble with the new maid, that she has dyed her hair, and that she is something of a flirt, but nevertheless jealous of her husband's stenographer, and all things considered, that it would not be surprising if there were a divorce in the family within the year.

Nonfiction is less persuasive, for the typical study has shown only a slight female superiority. The best controlled study, however, gives a decided edge to the women. Trumbo (1955) carefully matched women with men having the same intelligence, academic record, and anxiety scores and then gave them a written test of sensitivity. The women were superior in every comparison.

Women *are* superior observers. Not only did Bruni find them superior, but studies by Kaess and Witryol (1955) showed a striking superiority in favor of women. In the most recent study Witryol and Kaess, 1957), women were superior to men on three different observational tasks. Two of these tasks required the recall of names associated with photographs. In the third task, five men and five women at a time were given aliases and assigned to a group in which the experimenter conducted a one-minute "sidewalk interview" with each of them. In every interview the interviewee spoke his alias at least once. Later, in the test situation, the ten aliases were written on the blackboard, the participants were asked to stand up one at a time, and the members of the group tried to match the person with the correct alias. Again, the women were superior.

Why were the women superior? Not because the women were more intelligent, for the men and women had the same average intelligence (108 on the Modified Alpha Examination Form). Not because the women had better rote memories, for their performance on a test of number memory was the same. The authors conclude: "Our tentative explanation for the consistent female superiority . . . is found in the emphasis upon greater social facility for the female sex role with the concomitant development of better skills." The superiority of women is due to their greater interest in observing people.

Whether we are men *or* women, the kind of interest we have in a person largely determines what we observe about him and how well we observe it. Motivation seems to be the key to observational accuracy.

The Ways We Look at People

Our preoccupation with sensitivity might suggest that a typical perceiver looks at a person with the dispassionate curiosity of a mechanic looking at a motor, that he is driven to find out what "makes him tick." Nothing seems further from the truth. We look at another person from the point of view of our own hopes and our own interests. It is closer to the truth to say that we strive to observe as *little* as we can about a person—and still get from him what we want. Our thoughts are dominated by such questions as: What can he do for me? What can he do for us? It is only rarely that the question becomes: What does he think of himself, why does he think so, and how is he likely to think and behave in the future?

WHAT CAN HE DO FOR ME?

We often see people in order to get something from them. When we do, we are interested in the answers to questions like the following: Can he give me what I want? Does he like me well enough to give me what I want? Is he able to and will he give me dependable information about what I want and cooperate with me in using it? How much is he like me? The last is most basic, for those who are like us tend both to like and to cooperate with us.

People who like us are more likely to satisfy our needs for food and shelter, for safety, for belonging, for status and self-esteem, and for self-fulfillment. We, therefore, like people to like us. Consequently, our relationships are pervaded by efforts to get others to like us. Whether we think we have succeeded has a strong influence on all our judgments of them.

"Warm" people like people; "cold" people do not. When a person acts warmly toward us, we react quite differently from when he acts coldly. Eight graduate students were asked to give the Rotter Incomplete Blank to two attractive girls and to interpret the results (Masling, 1957). Unknown to the students, the girls were asked to act warmly in half of the examinations, coldly in the other half. The girls were also instructed in how to act warmly ("act interested in both the test situation and the examiner, make him feel comfortable and accepted") and how to act coldly ("be formal, disinterested, make him feel awkward and incompetent"). The Rotter test consists of a series of incomplete sentences like the following:

I feel . . .
Back home . . .
The best . . .

The personality diagnoses from the test are based on the answers given in completing the sentences. To make the answers constant, the two girls memorized the same answers and repeated them when the students gave them the test ("I feel *depressed*," "Back home *in Indiana*," and "The best *time is right now*"). The following is a typical interpretative sketch of the same girl making the same response when she was warm to a student and when she was cold:

Girl is Warm:
She feels part of the family group . . . enjoys school very much . . . seems to be very conscientious and recognizes deficiencies within herself which she is trying to remedy . . . positively oriented toward the future . . . sensitive, introspective . . . likes people.
Girl is Cold:
She has little insight or definition of her problem . . . frequently expresses considerable tension . . . goes on crying jags and feels sorry for herself . . . feels depressed . . . compulsively sets exacting standards for herself . . . lack of sympathy for others . . . uncomfortable in strongly affective situations and solves her problems by ignoring them and denying their existence.

In general, the author concluded, ". . . when the present subjects acted warm to an examiner, more positive statements were made about them than when they acted cold." The differences occurred in the face of the fact that the students were trained to be objective, were in a professional situation, and were interpreting the results of a semiobjective test.

The same person acting in the same way is judged differently when he is given a warm rather than a cold reputation. Three classes at the Massachusetts Institute of Technology were told that their regular instructor would not be able to attend and that a substitute would conduct the class (Kelley, 1950). They were also told: "He is 26 years old, a veteran and married. People who know him consider him to be a rather (_____) person, industrious, critical, practical and determined." In some classes, the blank was filled in with the word "cold"; in others, with the word "warm," although it was the same instructor. Results: Less than a third of the students participated in class discussion when the instructor was described as cold; almost two-thirds participated when he was described as warm. After class, the warm instructor was rated by the students as more sociable, considerate, informal, and humorous.

Even the words "warm" and "cold" associated with, but not describing, a person seem to influence our judgments. Cofer and Dunn (1952) first had a group of 15 students learn a list of words beginning: "Between, present, *cold, . . .* and then had them rate 12 people from their photographs on 11 different traits. Another group of 15 students followed exactly the same procedure except that "warm" was substituted for "cold" in the list. The group that had learned the "warm" list rated the people in the photographs as more altruistic, less restrained, more humane, more humorous, and more good-natured.

We find out no more about people than we want to find out. If we really only want to find out if people like us, we can observe evidences of our success or failure: friendliness and supportiveness or unfriendliness and rejection. If we want information, we are sensitive to evidences of frankness, objectivity, and reliability. If we want people to do something for us, we are sensitive to signs of cooperativeness, dependability, and willingness to work (Jones and Thibaut, 1958). If we learn that people are unfriendly, secretive, or undependable, we may have learned all that we want to know. Such knowledge may answer our question. It is, however, of little help in understanding how a person will think, feel, and behave in situations that have no relation to us.

WHAT CAN HE DO FOR US?

We are social animals, and the satisfaction of our needs often comes through social channels. Our interest in a person, therefore, is often directed toward finding the answers to social questions: Is he helping or harming us? Does he like or dislike us? Is he like us or different from us? When a person is a leader, such questions are inevitable. A function of the dominant person is to determine how well a subordinate meets the social norms that apply: Is the child as obedient as he should be? Is the student learning at a satisfactory rate? Is the worker fulfilling the duties of his job? Does the applicant meet the job requirements? If so, the child is given his allowance; the student, his A; the worker, his raise; and the applicant, the job. The behavior of the person in a dominant role is constrained by the social norms: The inadequate worker must be removed; the neurotic sailor must be given shore duty; and the drunken driver must be arrested. To fulfill his role, the dominant person need only observe enough about another person to enable him to match him to the relevant norms.

The role of the psychotherapist requires that he see his client as he is, objectively and actually, rather than as he would like the client to be. Still, he is a representative of a trained elite with whom, because of his reputation, his clients tend to assume a subordinate role. Consequently, it is easy for him to assume a social orientation, i.e., to see his role as determining how "normal" his client is and applying the appropriate sanctions he has learned in his professional training. One of the patients of Trigant Burrow (1927) questioned his sincerity and asked him to change positions with him: he would take the chair of the therapist and the doctor would take the position of the patient. In the process, Burrow gained an insight into the professionalism that had crept into his therapeutic attitudes: "The analysis henceforth consisted in the reciprocal effort of each of us to recognize within himself his attitude of authoritarianism and autocracy toward the other."

The therapist may also adopt a self-orientation and seek to satisfy his own needs in the relationship by trying to convert the client to his own values. The warning of Freud was not without reason: "The patient should be educated to liberate and fulfill his own nature, not to resemble ourselves."

WHAT IS HE REALLY LIKE?

To most fully understand another person, we must view life from his point of view. It is his interest, his values, and his hopes that lead to an understanding of him—not our own. The questions are: What is he like? What is he experiencing? Why is he the way he is? The answers are best obtained by attending to him, noting what he looks like, listening to what he says, and thinking about him. The necessity of this approach for understanding another person is as obvious as it is rare. We are seldom that much interested.

What can he do for me? What can he do for us? What is he really like? The dominant question is, in part, determined by the social role we are playing. Consider the different orientations that a person might have as a spectator, a jury member, or a court-appointed psychiatrist at the trial of an alleged murderer. As a spectator he might well say to himself: "I wouldn't want to meet him in a dark alley," or "He looks like a clean-cut fellow, the kind of person I'd like to know." As a jury member, he is more likely to be preoccupied with the questions: "Did he or did he not kill the person? If he did, did he do it in a way that fits the legal definition of murder?" As a psychiatrist, questions like these might preoccupy him: "What is the alleged murderer really like? How influential was his unstable home environment in determining what he did? How is he likely to think and behave in the future?"

The Improvement of Observational Accuracy

Observational accuracy is the most basic component of sensitivity; it is also the easiest on which to show dramatic improvement. Kepes (1965) gave the Bruni film test at the beginning of training and again eight weeks later to students participating in a program designed to improve their accuracy. They made very large improvements in the accuracy of their observations of the appearance, actions, and comments of the six interviewees in the film. So did a control group that did not have the training. Members of both groups, however, were given their scores of the first test and told that they would be tested again. The motivation and knowledge provided by the feedback was the major element accounting for their improvement. Conclusion: Most of us most of the time operate far below our actual capacity for observing.

We observe what we are interested in observing about a person. Even when our role would seem to demand accurate observation, however, we are often negligent. The major purpose of the employment interviewer is to find out about a candidate. An obvious necessity for fulfilling this purpose would seem to be to listen to the candidate. Typically, interviewers do not. Daniels and Otis (1950) recorded a sample of 60 employment interviews from eight companies. The average interview lasted ten minutes, the interviewee talking for one-third of the time and the interviewer talking for two-thirds. The humorous cartoon of the bored client listening to the childhood experiences of his therapist suggests that employment interviewers are not the only violators of the listening principle.

PRACTICE IN PLAYING THE OBSERVER ROLE

It seems easy for us to shift from one role to another in observing. Naval Air Cadets heard a recorded interview between a psychologist and an ex-prisoner of war who had signed several communistic statements (Jones and deCharms, 1957). Cadets in one group were asked to imagine whether they would like the prisoner as a friend; in another group, they were to imagine they were members of a judicial board of inquiry empowered to study the case and to decide what the formal charges should be; and in a third group, they were to imagine they were members of a medical-psychological board of review empowered to find out why the prisoner did what he did. The varying sets produced strikingly different pictures of the prisoner.

The role we take not only influences the kinds of inferences we make but also their accuracy. Lundy (1956) had students fill out the Allport-Vernon scale of values. Two weeks later each student met with two other students and discussed a topic for five minutes with each of them. Before and after each discussion the students filled out the scale as they thought their partners had filled it out. With one partner the student was instructed to focus his attention upon himself; with the other, to focus attention upon his partner. Results: When the student focused upon himself his empathy increased and his accuracy decreased; when he focused upon the other student his empathy decreased and his accuracy increased. Conclusion:

> Therapists who, by their training, concentrate upon themselves and what they have to say may succeed only in projecting their own ideas upon the patient. Therapists trained to pay attention to their patients may be better able to understand the particular patient being treated.
>
> Patients, by the same token, may become more accurate and less projective in their perceptions of other people if they can be brought around to paying attention to other people instead of to themselves.

Improving a person's skill in playing the role of observer is not as easy as the above results might suggest. Maier, Hoffman, and Lansky (1960) evaluated the effectiveness of a training program designed to improve both listening skill and skill in getting people to "open up." Three psychology classes were used. Group 1 heard a series of lectures on causation and attitudes as they influence group behavior. Group 2 heard the same lectures as group 1 as well as additional lectures on democratic leadership. The group 2 students also participated in weekly role-playing sessions. Group 3 had all the training given to groups 1 and 2. In addition, group 3 had lectures on nondirective counseling and special sessions of practice in reflecting feeling.

The criterion of success was the quality of performance in a role-playing scene at the end of training. Each student was asked to play the role of Mr. Jones, a personnel manager interviewing Mr. Smith. The following information was given to Mr. Jones (Maier et al., 1960):

> You have a persistent problem with Mr. Smith, the manager of a large office group in the company. He objects to older employees and refuses to accept transfers. . . . You can't understand Smith's position and, therefore, you have decided to talk to him to see if you can't give them a better deal. Here are some things you should know about the behavior of the older girls.

There followed a list of 10 facts about the older girls. Some were favorable (absences lower, less tardiness), some were ambiguous, and some were unfavorable (more time in rest rooms, less willing to do unpleasant jobs). The measure of listening skill was the number of these facts introduced into the interview by the trainee. The lower the number the better the score, since it was assumed that the fewer the facts the trainee introduced, the more he was listening to what Mr. Smith said. Conversely, the greater the number of facts introduced by Mr. Smith, the better the trainee was rated in the skill of getting people to open up.

Results: The training given group 3 was more effective in improving skill in listening; that given group 2, next; and that given group 1, least effective. The average number of facts introduced by group 3 was only 27 per cent of the 10 facts available; by group 2 members, 35 per cent; and by group 1 members, 41 per cent. However, the impact even of the third group's training was small in spite of the time devoted to the development of the quite specific skills of listening and getting people to open up. The authors concluded (Maier et al., 1960):

> The implication of these results for the amount and type of training received by supervisors and executives in the typical industrial training course in human relations is obvious. Training is a slow process of re-orientation and of the accumulation of new concepts, attitudes, and skills. . . . We conclude that where management is seriously interested in training supervisory personnel in effective human relations, they must expect to invest considerably more time than is presently customary.

THE RECORDING OF OBSERVATIONS

The sooner we record our observations, the more details we will remember. Three groups of four persons recorded their observations of people they had interviewed (Symonds and Dietrich, 1941). The first group recorded their impressions immediately; the second, after two days; and the third, after seven days. The interviews recorded immediately were far more complete. If we do not record immediately, we remember what seems meaningful and forget the meaningless. Unfortunately, what seems meaningful may not be. Worse, our quest for meaning causes us to select and twist our observations. If we do not record, we also forget much that is meaningful. For example, nothing is more meaningful to supervisors than effective performances by their subordinates. However, they forget such performances. Supervisors of the Delco-Remy Division of General Motors recorded incidents of effective performances among their men after different intervals: 25 recorded them daily; 25 recorded them every two days, and 25 recorded them each week (Flanagan and Burns, 1962). The following incidental is typical:

> I observed an employee looking through the scrap tub. Shortly after, he came to me stating that someone had thrown a large piece of cast-iron piston into the scrap tub. We salvaged this piston and a short time later used the piece to make a pully for a very urgently needed job.

The supervisors who kept daily records reported twice as many incidents as those who kept biweekly ones. Electric recordings provide a complete record. A comparison of written reports with electric recordings showed that the former omitted over half of the facts (Covner, 1942). Of the facts that were written, the most common error was to change the order in which things were said so that the implication was given that one statement lead to another when actually it did not. Unfortunately, making recordings is sometimes impossible and making typescripts of recordings is always burdensome.

Jottings are a good solution for the recording problem in many situations. They take little time, they keep ideas and acts in sequence, and they serve as a useful reminder of details. The supervisors at Delco-Remy were trained to jot down incidents of effective and ineffective behavior like these for John Henry: "$1/14$. Needed ladder" and "Good decision on bolts." Later these jottings recalled to the supervisor that "Henry had to get ladder to reach raw stock near machine so that time was wasted getting and returning the ladder" and "Henry quickly decided on the best size of bolts to use on new part." In this study, the average supervisor spent only 5 minutes each day making such jottings.

TRAINING IN WHAT AND WHEN TO OBSERVE

Observation is selective, for we usually can attend to only a part of what a person is saying and doing. What we should attend to is often quite apparent. A supervisor, for instance, is primarily interested in those things that bear most directly upon an employee's performance. When our objective is to understand another person as fully and as accurately as possible, the problem of what to observe and when to observe becomes acute. What are the most important things to observe in order to obtain the best understanding of a person? Knowledge about the answer to this question is very incomplete, and fads sometimes conflict with expert opinion.

Is it best for the observer to make a habit of concentrating on cues that reveal the person's attitude toward the observer (first person), the person's attitude toward himself (second person), or another person's attitude toward the person (third person), or on nonpersonal cues that reveal what he really is? To answer the question, Linden (1965) developed the projective test, part of which is shown in Exhibit 7-1. Each of the 52 cases in the test requires the respondent to choose among first-person, second-person, third-person, and nonpersonal orientation. Scores

EXHIBIT 7-1   *Human Relations Scale*
(Linden, 1965)

This is a scale measuring beliefs about how people react in different situations. There are no right or wrong answers. In many cases it may be difficult to choose an answer, but please mark a choice for each one.

THE CASE OF BOB

Bob is a senior majoring in math and plans to go to graduate school next year. His math teacher, Mr. Lewis, is retiring. How does Bob feel about this bit of news?

1. "Mr. Lewis thinks I have a lot of ability in math." (first person)
2. "He thinks he can't convey the material as well now." (second person)
3. "Students will be happy to hear this; they thought him too hard." (third person)
4. "It's best for all that he retire now." (nonpersonal)

THE CASE OF ELLEN

Ellen has been dating a boy steadily for three months. They are both freshmen and have decided to stop seeing each other for a while. How does Ellen feel?

1. "I hope he still likes me as much even though we're not dating."
2. "I wonder how he feels about it."
3. "I wonder if his friends think he was the one hurt."
4. "It's best for both of us because we're too young to get serious."

THE CASE OF MR. MOORE

Alan Moore is in the market for a new car. He is deciding between a Lincoln and a Cadillac. What might he be thinking as he is talking to one of the salesmen?

1. "I wonder if he thinks I'm an easy customer to sell."
2. "He thinks he's a pretty good salesman."
3. "I've heard he's a well-respected salesman."
4. "He is thoroughly familiar with his product."

on each of the four scales measuring habitual attitudes toward people were correlated with measures of personality and predictive accuracy.

Results: Neither the first-person nor nonpersonal scores were related to accuracy but were related to personality, the high scorers on the first-person scale reporting themselves as excitable and irritable; high scorers on the nonpersonal scale, as calm and amiable. The only relationship with the second-person scale (What does he think of himself?) was with observation—high scorers were less observant than low scorers. High scorers on the third-person scale described themselves as more tough-minded and skeptical. They were also significantly more accurate in their predictions than the low scorers. Conclusion: Contrary to popular opinion (but consistent with the findings regarding psychological-mindedness and empathic drive), high scorers on the second-person scale were poor observers. On the other hand, those who viewed persons as they thought they would be seen by others were more accurate in their judgments. Perhaps this orientation filters out the projective tendencies arising from trying to figure out what the person is thinking of himself.

Giedt (1955, 1958) recorded interviews with four patients in order "to study the sorts of observations that aid the clinician in making accurate judgments of a patient's personality." The interviews were presented as silent films, written transcripts, sound recordings, or complete sound films to 48 psychiatrists, social workers, and psychologists. These professionals made ratings of the personality characteristics and predicted the responses to incomplete sentences of the interviewed patients. The results lead to conclusions of the following sort.

Read before you listen; listen before you look. The experts were able to predict as accurately from seeing a transcript of the interview as from seeing a film of the interview. In fact, at least some of the judges were misled by seeing the dress, appearance, and facial expressions of the patients. It was hard for the observers to pick up appropriate expressive movements and correctly interpret their meaning—noting that a person had a "rigid face" led to overestimates of a patient's rigidity; noting that a person had "an intent look" was a poor indicator of anxiety. Furthermore, impressions from appearances seem to dominate impressions from more objective sources. For example, observers often listed the right cues for making a correct judgment but would then say things like "But he didn't seem anxious," and shift to a wrong prediction.

The results suggest that first reading about the person, then listening to him, and finally seeing him would use cues from all sources in the most effective manner. In any case, a practical matter is involved, for it is generally much easier and cheaper to obtain a written record than to conduct a personal interview. If the former is just as good or maybe better, then it should be preferred (Giedt, 1955):

Often at considerable expense and inconvenience to both applicant and employer, a personal interview is arranged. If the results obtained in this study hold for the assessment of employees, then it might be possible for an applicant to be interviewed by telephone or for him to submit either a sound recording or a written protocol of an interview conducted by some recognized local interviewer.

Stick to what the person says about himself. The interviewers inevitably made inferences about a person from what he said about himself. Some of these were correct. On the whole, however, the interviewers made too many and too speculative inferences and wandered too far from what the person had said. Incorrect inferences of anxiety, for instance, were made because a patient moved around in his chair and smoked a lot. Incorrect inferences about dependency were made because a patient lapsed into silence, made lengthy responses to questions, or was "acting like a little boy before a parent figure." Incorrect inferences were also made by totally ignoring what the patient said about himself. A patient, for example, was rated low in anxiety even though he said he was so anxious that he could not work or needed hospitalization. A related kind of error grew out of the tendency of interviewers to believe "in the almost magical power of confession and catharsis." That is, the interviewers tended to underestimate a patient on undesirable feelings or traits that he confessed. An incorrect rating of high friendliness was justified on the basis that a patient "expressed dislike of father with embarrassment." A too-low rating on impulsiveness for a patient was justified on the basis that the patient reported feeling guilty about his impulsiveness and had resolved to do better in the future. A too-high rating on warmth for a patient was justified because the patient was "able to express hostility in the interview." In general, the raters were more accurate when they based their judgments "directly on what the patient said as to his feelings, preferences, or past behavior. When the observers tried to use more devious interpretations or to infer from direct behavior, they tended to err" (Giedt, 1955).

Use explicit rather than implicit theories. Interviewers made inferences about patients from their observations on the relationship of traits. Some correctly inferred high intelligence from the patient's good grooming and alertness; anxiety, from the way he averted his eyes or touched his face; hostility, from his habit of cleaning his nose and fingernails; and independence, from his social poise during the interview. Some incorrectly inferred overdependency from a patient's asking others to help him; high intelligence, from high anxiety; and low hostility, from the fact that a patient confessed to having hostile feelings.

Correct or incorrect, the inferences of the interviews were based upon implicit theories. The more explicit the theories that an observer uses, the more accurate his judgments are likely to be and to become. An explicit theory may be as wrong as an implicit one. However, the errors of the former may be discovered, while the errors of the latter will not be. The more often a theory is tested and modified, the more adequate it becomes. The life sciences are largely devoted to making explicit theories about how people behave and testing and modifying them. As we shall see in the next chapter, perceivers who use such explicit theories in judging people are almost always more accurate than those who use implicit theories based on their "intuition."

Part Four

THE PERSON

Chapter Eight

STEREOTYPES

IN THE LAST TWO sections we emphasized the perceiver and the processes by which he perceives others. We now focus upon the person being perceived. In some ways he is like other people and in some ways he is different. Our concern in this chapter is with the ways in which he is like others, with stereotypes and their accuracy.

The Nature of Stereotypes

In 1798, a London paper announced that "the celebrated Didot, the French printer, with a German, named Herman, have announced a new discovery in printing which they term stereotype." The process involved printing from a plate of type metal cast from a set of type instead of from the type itself. Gradually, the term came to be used in a more figurative sense to mean "something continued or constantly repeated without change." Before 1900, for example, psychiatrists were referring to the highly repetitive motions of the arm or body by patients as "stereotyped movements." Now, the term means "something conforming to a fixed or general pattern and lacking individual distinguishing marks or qualities, especially a standardized mental picture" representing a judgment of a group.

For printers, the use of stereotypes was a step forward. Until recently, social scientists viewed the stereotyping of persons as a step backward. A growing body of evidence, however, shows that we all make heavy use of stereotypes. Furthermore, we often make better judgments when we stick to our stereotypes than when we do not. A group of student judges was told only the general category of a series of students: undergraduate male education major, graduate female art student, etc. They then filled out an interest inventory as they thought each student had filled it out. Next the judges observed each student as he described

133

the room he was in, made a drawing at the blackboard, and engaged in several other expressive acts. After seeing each student, the judges again filled out the interest inventory as they thought the student had filled it out. The accuracy of the before-and-after predictions was compared. They were *more* accurate before than after. The judges made better predictions on the basis of their stereotypes alone than they did on the basis of their stereotypes plus their personal observations (Stone Leavitt, and Gage, 1957).

The findings of Stelmachers and McHugh (1964) amplify the conclusion. They had 42 experts predict 171 responses to the Minnesota Multiphasic Personality Inventory that each of four persons would make: (1) a normal female teen-age college sophomore; (2) an elderly female patient with a very extensive medical and psychiatric history; (3) an adult male psychiatric patient with a diagnosis of "depressive reaction"; and (4) an unemployed teen-age boy who had both a lengthy criminal record and a psychiatric history as well as being a practicing homosexual. Before making their predictions, the experts were given different kinds and amounts of information about the four people. The first group was told only the age and sex of the four persons whose responses they were predicting. The second group was told only the education and occupation of the four persons. The third group was given only a "differentiating stereotype," i.e., for subject 1, "a well-adjusted normal"; subject 2, "person with long-standing, chronic illness"; subject 3, "psychiatric patient"; and subject 4, "delinquent." The fourth group was given all the stereotype information about each subject: age, sex, education, occupation, and differentiating stereotype. The fifth group was given three personal descriptions for each subject written by intimates of the subjects. The sixth group was given the five personality traits which intimates agreed were most descriptive of a subject. The seventh and final group was given the most complete information, including the subject's answers to a biographical questionnaire, an interest and activities questionnaire, and a sentence completions test as well as history material collected from hospital charts and interviews. The accuracy of the predictions made by judges from each of these kinds of information was then compared.

Predictions based on stereotypes were surprisingly accurate. For example, judges who were given only the differential stereotype (well-adjusted normal, etc.) were *more* accurate than those judges who had the personal descriptions by friends or the judges who had the traits which friends thought were most descriptive of the subjects. Only the judges who had the most complete information (group 7) were more accurate than the differential stereotype group.

These results incompletely state the case for stereotypes, for the stereotype judges had only their impressions of how the typical well-adjusted normal or delinquent would answer the 171 statements. Undoubtedly, some judges had more *accurate* stereotypes than others. Suppose the judges had an entirely accurate stereotype, i.e., knew how typical subjects answered each of the questions. How would their scores then compare with the experts? The handbook of the MMPI gives the percentages of college girls, adult females, and adult males making a "true" response to each question in the test. It was assumed that the responses of the college girl would be the same as those of the majority of college girls; of the homosexual delinquent, the same as the majority of adult males, etc. The accuracy of these assumptions was then determined by comparing each subject's actual responses with these typical responses. Finally, these stereotype accuracy scores were compared with the scores of the experts. In three out of four cases, the stereotype scores were much more accurate than the scores of the experts. Conclusion:

> Psychologists would do well studying the base rates of various types of behavior in as many separate populations as is practicable. Apparently even a very approximate matching on a very few variables between subject and population can lead to a significant improvement in predictive accuracy if the population norms are known to the judge. For most pieces of behavior assumed to be relevant in personality assessment, such norms are not available. Therefore, it seems that the establishment of them for a select number of broadly defined populations could be beneficial to the clinicians' performance in the area of behavior prediction.

Do all perceivers use stereotypes in making their judgments of people? They do. Can stereotypes be helpful in improving accuracy? They can. The critical question is: How accurate is a particular perceiver's stereotype of a particular group and how can accuracy be improved? The answer to the first part of the question is a problem of measurement.

The Measurement of Stereotype Accuracy

The number of groups about whom we may have stereotypes is countless. The two studies mentioned in the previous section include only a few of the possible ones: undergraduate male education major, graduate female art student, women, men, young people, old people, well-adjusted normal people, psychiatric patients, delinquents, etc. The groups may range from broad to narrow—from men in general to men in the United States, to male psychologists in the United States, to male experimental psychologists in the United States, to older male experimental psychologists in New York, etc. Problems of reliability, validity, and generality appear in the measurement of stereotype accuracy as in the measurement of everything else. The stereotype-accuracy scales developed by Johnson (1963) attempted to solve measurement problems raised by earlier efforts.

Johnson's test consists of four subtests: men versus women, young men versus old men, psychologists versus men in general, and unskilled versus professional men. The form of each of the subtests is the same as the unskilled versus professional men scale shown in Exhibit 8-1. As the form requires the respondent to match each interest to either the upper or the lower status occupational group, the influences of level and spread are eliminated. The form reduces the likelihood that responses will be made on the basis of assumed similarity by using the *differences*

EXHIBIT 8-1 *Test of Stereotype Accuracy in Judging the Differences between Unskilled and Professional Workers*

Directions: Circle "U" if you think *more unskilled workers* than professional and executive workers like the interest; circle "P" if you think *more professional and executive workers* like the interest.

U	*P*	1. Physics	*U*	P	28. Opportunity to understand just how one's superior expects work to be done
U	*P*	2. History			
U	P	3. Boxing			
U	P	4. Physical training			
U	P	5. Detective stories	U	*P*	29. Work for yourself
U	*P*	6. Mathematics	U	*P*	30. Freedom in working out one's own methods of doing the work
U	P	7. Climbing along edge of precipice			
U	*P*	8. Golf	U	*P*	31. Great variety of work
U	P	9. Agriculture	*U*	P	32. Giving "first aid" assistance
U	*P*	10. Musical comedy			
U	*P*	11. "New Republic"	U	*P*	33. Adjusting difficulties of others
U	P	12. Typist			
U	P	13. Office clerk	U	P	34. People who always agree with you
U	P	14. Lawyer, criminal			
U	*P*	15. Lawyer, corporation	*U*	P	35. People who chew gum
U	*P*	16. Secret service man	U	*P*	36. Thrifty people
U	*P*	17. Manufacturer	*U*	P	37. Nervous people
U	*P*	18. Sales manager	U	*P*	38. Conservative people
U	*P*	19. Scientific research worker	*U*	P	39. People who talk very slowly
U	P	20. Electrical engineer			
U	*P*	21. Advertiser	U	P	40. People with gold teeth
U	P	22. Draftsman	U	*P*	41. Energetic people
U	P	23. Repairing a clock	U	*P*	42. President of a club
U	*P*	24. Magazine writer	*U*	P	43. Pet monkeys
U	*P*	25. Editor	*U*	P	44. J. J. Pershing, soldier
U	P	26. Repairing electrical wiring	U	*P*	45. John Wanamaker, merchant
U	P	27. Definite salary			

between groups. It also assures that the respondent is judging only these two *particular* groups. The correct answers in all cases are based on data collected in standardizing the Strong Vocational Interest Blank.

Earlier measures of stereotype accuracy have failed to eliminate the influence of level and spread components. In May, 1941, Wallen (1943), for example, asked 237 women at a Midwestern college to make the following estimates:

1. The percentage of women on the campus who believe that the U.S. will be at war by mid-summer of this year
2. The percentage in favor of the Selective Service Act as it is now operating
3. The percentage in favor of the St. Lawrence Seaway Project

The same women also stated their own beliefs about the questions. The accuracy of a woman's estimate was measured by comparing the actual percentages with the percentages she thought would be answered in that way. This method does not separate the influences of level and spread accuracy from stereotype accuracy. That is, a girl may have obtained a low score because she was ignorant of what the other girls felt about the issues; she may also have obtained a low score, even though she knew how the girls felt, because she habitually rates too low or too high on everything. The influence of level and spread would have been eliminated if the girls had been asked to indicate to which of the three questions most students would have answered "yes."

Other ambiguities appear in Wallen's method of measurement. Since the students judged the opinions of a group to which they themselves belong, the tendency to assume similarity was probably exaggerated. There is also no way of telling whether a student's accuracy was a measure of her understanding of this particular group of college women or of people in general in the United States at the time. In brief, what seemed to be a measure of stereotype accuracy of a particular college group may have been a measure of level accuracy in relation to all people.

A measure of group sensitivity by Travers (1943) used the same method as Wallen and is subject to the same criticisms: (1) failure to eliminate the influences of level and spread; (2) failure to minimize the influence of empathy; and (3) failure to eliminate the possibility that an apparent measure of knowledge of a particular group was not actually knowledge of a much larger group. Travers tested 31 students in a general psychology class at the end of the eighth week of the course. The test consisted of two parts: a vocabulary test and a general information test. The vocabulary test consisted of 12 words of graded difficulty: (space, pact, chortle, etc.). The information test included 12 questions

like "The population of the United States is about _____ millions."
After each student completed the test, he indicated the percentage of
the class that he thought would get each item in the test correct. Result:
Accuracy in estimating the vocabulary knowledge of the group was only
slightly related to accuracy in estimating informational knowledge
($r = .35$). A student, incidentally, tended to assume that his knowledge
was similar to the group's knowledge: the higher his own knowledge,
the larger percentage of the group he assumed had gotten the questions
correct.

Zavala (1960) eliminated the influences of level and spread by substituting a ranking for a rating procedure. The instructions for his test
were as follows: "Undergraduate men in a Midwestern university were
asked whether they liked or disliked each of a large number of different
occupations, school subjects, amusements and kinds of people. Mark the
one of the four in each of the following groups that you think was liked
by the most students." The questions in the test were of the following
type:

1. (*a*) artist   (*b*) army officer   (*c*) author of a novel   (*d*) pharmacist

In this form, the respondent does not indicate what per cent of college
men said they had a particular interest; he indicates which of four interests would rank first. While the test eliminates the influences of level
and spread, it does not let us know whether the men who got the highest
scores did so because they understood college men or because they understood men in general. Johnson's test overcame this difficulty by having
the respondent estimate the difference between groups.

Is stereotype accuracy a general trait? That is, does the perceiver
who understands one group well tend to understand other groups? One
virtue of Johnson's approach is that it can give an answer to this question
unclouded by either perceiver habits or the influence of knowledge of
a more general group or of a more specific one. He found that his subtests
were quite reliable: perceivers varied widely and consistently in their
accuracy on each of the tests. Were those who were good judges of sex
differences also good judges of age differences, of differences between
psychologists and nonpsychologists, and of differences between unskilled
and professional workers? No. The median correlation between scores
on the subtest was only .21 and the largest was .30. Both Zavala (1960)
and Silkiner (1962) reached a similar conclusion.

There is no royal road to stereotype accuracy. That a perceiver
knows a great deal about one group tells us little about his knowledge
of other groups, even when the groups are as broad and as well known
as men versus women, young versus old men. The more specialized the
groups, the more obvious the conclusion becomes. Why should people
who understand Australians understand Mexicans? Why should people

who understand engineers understand morticians? Why should people who understand clerks in an insurance company understand coal miners in Kentucky? Some individuals understand many groups well and are adept at learning about new groups. On the whole, however, stereotype accuracy is specific.

Stereotype Accuracy and Leadership

Good leaders are good observers of the individuals they lead (Showel, 1960). Do they also know the attitudes of the groups they lead? Studies disagree (Campbell, 1955), but they have been entangled in a web of methodological problems. They have determined whether a person is a leader or not a leader rather than whether he is a good or a bad leader. The measures of leadership have been confused with those of group knowledge, and the influence of stereotypes has not been separated from the influences of level and spread.

Johnson (1963) surmounted these problems. As a measure of general stereotype accuracy, he used the total scores on his four subtests (men versus women, young versus old, psychologists versus nonpsychologist, and workers versus executives). As a measure of constructive leadership attitudes, he used the forced-choice leadership questionnaire developed by Dore (1960). The questionnaire has the following instructions: "In each question there are two statements of things that a leader can do. Choose the one that you feel it is *more important* for him to do." The first of the two scales which measures consideration for others has choices like the following:

1a. *To create a pleasant work atmosphere*
 b. To speak in a manner not to be questioned
2a. *To let worker take time out from the monotony*
 b. To give detailed instructions on just the way to do each job

The second scale, which measures the importance attached to the leader's role in organizing group activities, has choices like the following:

1a. *To teach his workers new things*
 b. To work along with the men as much as possible
2a. *To carefully schedule the work of his men*
 b. To work hard himself

Johnson related the stereotype-accuracy scores of more than a hundred men to scores on the two scales as well as to a wide variety of demographic, personality and aptitude measures. High scorers were somewhat older, more intelligent, better listeners, and more open-minded. However, the largest difference between good and poor stereotypes was in leadership attitudes. Though scores on the two scales are unrelated to each other, scores on both were significantly related to stereotype accuracy. Conclusion: Those who are most considerate and most concerned about effective group organization are best informed about the interests of these groups.

The Social Sciences as a Source of Accurate Stereotypes

Social scientists have tended to view all stereotypes as always inaccurate and always accompanied by prejudice, dislike, and disapproval of the members of the group involved. The facts do not fit the view: people can have more favorable but less accurate stereotypes; less favorable but more accurate ones. Jews, for example, judge other Jews as brighter than non-Jews and avoid identifying a Jew as a Jew if he is not likeable (Toch, Rabin, & Wilkins, 1962). On the other hand, people prejudiced against Jews identify them more accurately because "people who are unprejudiced are less sensitive to the identity of those with whom they deal. . . . The question of racial identity is of small importance to the person free from prejudice. Yet it is of considerable importance to the bigot, and for this reason the bigot apparently learns to observe and interpret both facial features and expressive behavior so that he can more swiftly spot his 'enemy' " (Allport and Kramer, 1946).

It is part of the business of social scientists to discover accurate stereotypes: the differences between the typical man and the typical woman, the typical Negro and the typical white, the typical lower-class and the typical upper-class citizen, the typical neurotic and the typical normal person, the typical two-year-old and the typical four-year-old, the typical moronic and the typical bright person, the typical Japanese and the typical American etc. The experimental- and control-group design is an incisive way of establishing accurate stereotypes.

The problem is to present the known facts about groups in a way that will actually improve the student's judgments of persons. It is hard to present the facts in such a way. Johnson and Terman (1935) in their search for accurate stereotypes compared 100 happily married couples with 100 unhappily married and 100 divorced couples. All completed an extensive battery of personality tests. Couples and friends of the couples rated the happiness of the marriage. How could the facts gathered about the differences between these groups be used to improve judgments of people about to be married or already married? The beginning of an answer would be to determine how accurate are the differential stereotypes the student already has. Close (1963) developed a test of

EXHIBIT 8-2 *Test of Stereotype Accuracy in Judging the Differences between Happily Married, Unhappily Married, and Divorced Men*

Directions: The following test investigates your knowledge of the different interests and traits of happily married, unhappily married, and divorced men. The correct answers are based on a comparison of the replies of carefully selected groups of happily married, unhappily married, and divorced men.
    Circle:
    "H" If you think the responses of more *Happily Married Men* than unhappily married or divorced men fit the statement.
    "U" If you think the responses of more *Unhappily Married Men* than happily married or divorced men fit the statement.
    "D" If you think the responses of more *Divorced Men* than happily married or unhappily married men fit the statement.

H	U	D	1. Enjoy teaching adults
H	U	*D*	2. Most likely to avoid dictatorial or bossy people
H	*U*	D	3. Dislike educational movies
H	U	*D*	4. More apt to like the occupation of novelist
H	*U*	D	5. Views self as a radical, while actually conservative in nature
H	U	D	6. Enjoy household pets
H	*U*	D	7. Most likely to have difficulty in making up their minds
H	U	D	8. Like cautious people
H	U	*D*	9. Best able to compete in a game against an opponent of superior ability
H	U	D	10. More apt to like religious people
H	*U*	D	11. Care least for the occupation of teaching
H	U	*D*	12. More often willing to take chances
H	*U*	D	13. Least often take the lead to enliven a dull party
H	U	*D*	14. Like the occupation of stockbroker
H	U	*D*	15. Prefer commission to definite salary
H	*U*	D	16. Care least for symphony concerts
H	*U*	D	17. Prefer outside work
H	U	D	18. Most tolerant of sick people
H	U	*D*	19. Most often seek someone for cheer when feeling low
H	U	D	20. Most likely to solicit funds for a cause of interest
H	U	D	21. Place the most emphasis on quality of work
H	U	D	22. Prefer developing plans to executing them
H	U	*D*	23. More apt to like playing poker
H	U	D	24. Most meticulous and methodical in work
H	U	*D*	25. Like the occupation of criminal lawyer
H	*U*	D	26. Most neurotic
H	*U*	D	27. Seldom become excited
H	U	*D*	28. Like fashionably dressed people
H	U	D	29. Are seldom asked for advice
H	U	D	30. Prefer to spend a night at home

stereotype accuracy based on the findings of Johnson and Terman that included 60 statements about men and 60 about women. The directions for the test and 30 of the statements for men are shown in Exhibit 8-2. The correct answers are italicized.

How could stereotype accuracy be improved? Feedback to students would be some help. Alone, however, feedback leaves the student to form his own generalizations. Johnson and Terman provided these generalizations. They found that the typical happily married man is the most kindly and tolerant and the least neurotic. He is more amiable and cautious, and less touchy, grouchy, irritable, and critical. He is not very sociable, preferring to spend his evenings at home. The unhappily married man has neither the self-discipline nor the amiability for marriage, nor the aggressive qualities which would enable him to break up the marriage. He rebels at orders and dislikes being told how to do things. The divorced man is self-confident, self-sufficient, self-willed, and self-centered. Compared to the married man, he is more radical in his attitudes, more gregarious, and more interested in art and literature.

Psychologists have learned, sometimes painfully, that students can often quickly obtain a verbal mastery of a generalization and yet show no signs of being able to apply it. The ultimate aim in stereotype-accuracy training is to improve the trainee's ability to understand the people he meets in everyday life. The first step in this direction may be to improve the trainee's performance on a criterion such as that shown in Exhibit 8-2. However, the first step is not the top of the stairs.

The Improvement of Stereotype Accuracy

We learn about groups from everyday experience with them: about men from men, about women from women, etc. The returns from experience, however, seem to diminish rapidly—a little experience helps, but a great deal of experience helps little, if any, more. Oakes and Corsini (1961) compared the accuracy with which students after one and after thirty-six hours in an instructor's class could describe the instructor as he had described himself.

The students did rather well after one class (a median correlation of .54 between the way students thought the instructor had sorted adjectives to describe himself and the way he actually had). They did only slightly better after thirty-six hours ($r = .63$). They compared this result with the results obtained by husbands and wives attempting to describe each other in the same way on the same test. Result: "Exposure to an instructor in a classroom for 36 hours seems to result in an average accuracy of perception of his self comparable to the average perceptiveness of a mate's self attained through six years of exposure in marriage."

A comparison of foreign and American students produced consistent results (Silkiner, 1962). American students had more accurate stereotypes of men than the foreign students did. However, the months of the foreign student's stay in the United States had no relation to his accuracy score. In a similar vein, the number of psychology courses taken had no relation to a student's accuracy in predicting the interests of psychologists (Johnson, 1963).

Students who had interviewed faculty members about their attitudes toward a university magazine did no better in predicting attitudes than students who had not (Olmsted, 1962). Twenty students were told that a survey of attitudes of 400 faculty members toward their university magazine had been conducted. They were shown the questionnaire form and asked to estimate what percentage of the surveyed group had answered the questions in various ways. A second group of students made the same estimates. Each of these students, however, had the experience of actually interviewing 15 of the faculty members who completed the survey. The experience did them no good, for they made the same average error as those without the experience.

THE FAILURE OF LECTURES

Raw experience with members of a group seems to have only a slight and uncertain influence upon the accuracy of knowledge of that group. How about lectures where the salient characteristics of a group are pointed out? At the beginning of a second course in psychology, the author gave 72 students the test measuring accuracy of knowledge of the differences between the interests of psychologists and of men in general (Exhibit 8-3). The mean score was 37, the range was wide, and the reliability of the test was fairly good ($r = .70$). For the next six meetings he lectured on psychologists: their education, their places of work, the kinds of problems they worked on, their methods of solving the problems. The test was administered again. Result: No improvement.

The results suggest that stereotypes are easily formed and highly resistant to change. The suggestion is supported by the following anecdote (Lamming, 1960):

> I would recall an episode on a ship which had brought a number of West Indians to Britain. I was talking to a Trinidadian civil servant who had come "to take something called a Devonshire course." A man about forty to forty-five, intelligent enough to be in the senior grade of the Trinidad Civil Service, which is by no means backward, a man of some substance among his own class of people. We were talking in a general way about life among the emigrants. The ship was now steady; the tugs were coming along side. Suddenly there was consternation in the Trinidadian's expression.
>
> "But . . . but," he said, "look down there."
>
> I looked, and since I had lived six years in England I failed to

Exhibit 8-3 *A Test of Stereotype Accuracy in Judging the Differences between Psychologists and Men in General*

Directions: How do the interests of psychologists differ from those of other men? To answer the question, several hundred male psychologists and several thousand other business and professional men checked whether they would "like" each of many different occupations, amusements, activities, and kinds of people.

A higher percentage of the psychologists liked some interests. For example, 41 per cent of the psychologists said they would like to be the "author of a novel"; only 32 per cent of men in general expressed such a liking. A *lower* percentage of the psychologists liked some interests. For example, only 29 per cent of the psychologists said they would like to be a "sales manager," whereas 37 per cent of men in general expressed a liking for this occupation. Below, mark "1" if you think a *higher* percentage of psychologists than men in general liked the interest; mark "2" if you think a *lower* percentage of psychologists liked the interest.

1. Actor*	31. Chess*
2. Artist*	32. Solving mechanical puzzles*
3. Astronomer*	33. Travel movies
4. Corporation lawyer	34. Fishing
5. Manufacturer	35. Making a speech*
6. Athletic director	36. Teaching adults*
7. Chemist*	37. Taking responsibility
8. Cashier in bank	38. Doing research work*
9. Editor*	39. Writing reports*
10. Foreign correspondent*	40. Regular hours of work
11. Inventor*	41. Developing business systems
12. Magazine writer*	42. Saving money
13. Office manager	43. Conservative people
14. Orchestra conductor*	44. Energetic people
15. Physician*	45. People who are natural leaders
16. Poet*	46. People who make fortunes in business
17. Rancher	47. Thrifty people
18. Sculptor*	48. Religious people
19. Statistician*	49. Socialists*
20. Surgeon*	50. Independents in politics*
21. Wholesaler	51. People who talk about themselves*
22. Geometry*	52. Carelessly dressed people*
23. Algebra*	53. Absent-minded people*
24. Physical training	54. Outside work
25. Physiology*	55. Physical activity
26. Literature*	56. Usually drive myself steadily*
27. Hunting	57. Have more than my share of novel ideas*
28. Symphony concerts*	58. My feelings are easily hurt
29. Sporting pages	59. My advice is sought by many*
30. Golf	60. Put drive into the organization

* The correct answer for these items is 1; for the others, 2.

see anything of particular significance. I asked him what he had seen: and then I realized what was happening.

"*They* do that kind of work, too?" he asked. He meant the white hands and faces on the tug. In spite of films, in spite of reading Dickens—for he would have had to at the school which trained him for the Civil Service—in spite of all this received information, this man had never really felt, as a possibility and a fact, the existence of the English worker. This sudden bewilderment had sprung from his *idea* of England; and one element in that idea was that he had never seen an Englishman working with his hands in the streets of Port of Spain.

The firmness with which stereotypes may become fixed is indicated by studies of the stereotypes that union and management leaders have of each other. The typical manager thinks of union leaders as "dishonest, unscrupulous, greedy, emotional, and egotistical." Union leaders, on the other hand, see managers as "unintelligent, stubborn, arrogant, and hypocritical" (Bakke, 1946). The same photograph and thumbnail sketch of a man were shown to union officials and company executives (Haire, 1955). When the picture was labeled "secretary-treasurer of his union," the unionists rated him as conscientious, honest, and responsible; the executives did not. When the picture was labeled "local manager of a small plant which is a branch of a large manufacturing concern," the executives rated him as conscientious, honest, and responsible; the union leaders did not. Stereotypes of this sort are not likely to be changed by an informative lecture.

TRAINING IN THE CORRECT USE OF STEREOTYPES

All people use stereotypes. Since they do, one step toward accuracy would be to practice organizing and using stereotypes effectively. One error is to judge a person on the basis of just one of the many groups to which he belongs (Negro, Jew, man, woman, college student, etc.). Brief practice in a technique for systematically using a person's multigroup memberships in judging him resulted in significant improvement (Wakeley, 1961). Since the study is one of the rare efforts to evaluate the effectiveness of different training methods, we consider the study in some detail. The study compared the effectiveness of different methods of improving sensitivity. The six methods were (1) *Pooling:* "Use the information which you have about people whom you know well when you are making judgments about people whom you know less well"; (2) *Observing the self:* "Pay attention to yourself"; (3) *Observing others:* "Pay attention to the other person"; (4) *Individual differences:* "Everyone is different from everyone else"; (5) *Recording-rating:* "Avoid level and spread errors"; and (6) *Combination* of the above methods.

Only the pooling method produced significant improvement. Part of the ten-minute instructions given the trainees using the pooling method follows:

> In the course of your living you have obtained a great deal of information about many people. The pooling principle simply suggests that you use this information when making inferences about a person with whom you have had little contact. When you are attempting to make inferences about a person whom you do not know well, one of the things which you can do is to form a pool of people whom you do know well who are like the unknown person. You take what you do know about the person, form a pool of people you know well, and then make your predictions or judgments based on the pool. The important things to remember in making these pools are to use people you know well and to use all of the information you have about the person you are trying to judge. You may form a pool that leads to wrong predictions if you use just one piece of information about the person, such as, his skin color, his religious preferences or any other single piece of information. You may also form some pools that lead to wrong predictions if you use people whom you do not know well.

Essentially, these pooling instructions advised the trainees to (1) observe the groups to which the individual belongs, as, for example, "a young Catholic mother with an eighth-grade education whose husband is a carpenter"; (2) pick from people that you know well those that most closely match this person; and (3) assume that the person will think, feel, and behave as the average person in this matched pool would think, feel, and behave.

Each of the six groups of 20 members met for three hours. Only one hour, however, was devoted to instruction and practice. The first and last hours were devoted to taking a film test of sensitivity. During the hour of training the trainees were not only told about the principle they were to use, but were also given about forty-five minutes of practice in applying it with feedback. A control group had no training but took the pretest and the endtest. Only the "pooling" group made significant improvement over their initial performance and over the control group. In a follow-up study, older businessmen made similar improvements using the same method.

THE PROGRAMMED LEARNING OF STEREOTYPES

The ideal way to learn a stereotype would be through a learning program that systematically applied learning principles to the process of learning about a particular group so that the trainee quickly and completely mastered it. A list of the things the programmer wants the trainee to be, to say, or to do at the end of the program is called a *specification of the terminal behavior for the program*. A specification of both the initial behavior and the terminal behavior tells the programmer what skills the program must teach. His task is to change the trainee's initial behavior until it matches the terminal behavior. In stereotype training the task would be to increase the trainee's knowledge of a particular group. No such programs exist.

The value that such programs may have is illustrated by the experience of IBM in another area. The company has a central training center where employees from all parts of the company are sent for instruction (Hughes and McNamara, 1961). One course given at the center is a sixteen-week course for computer servicemen concerning the IBM 7070 data-process system. In March, 1960, an instructor in the course and a psychologist began preparing programmed textbooks for the introductory section of the course. By September they had prepared 710 frames covering the first fifteen hours of conventional instruction (the equivalent of the first five weeks of a three-hour college course). Seventy trainees using only the programmed textbooks were compared with forty-two trainees attending the conventional classroom course. Results: The automated-instruction group spent 27 per cent less time in learning, five times as many of the automated group had scores of 95 or higher on the final objective achievement test, and 87 per cent said they liked the automated course more than other conventional company courses they had taken.

Exhibit 8-4 shows the form that a linear program for developing a more accurate stereotype of the differences between executives and unskilled workers might take (Boice, 1965). Some of the terms and techniques involved in such linear programs are the following:

1. For a trainee to learn well, it is important to tell him whether a response is acceptable immediately after the response is made.
2. Immediate feedback that the response is correct is called a *reinforcing* response.
3. A *formal-prompt* has a form designed to increase the probability of a particular response.
4. *Fading* is a technique which uses formal-prompts by gradually eliminating parts of a definition until it disappears.
5. The per cent of trainees who miss a given step should be less than 10 per cent.
6. A good program should provide for (*a*) immediate reinforcement, (*b*) gradual progression from initial to terminal behavior, and (*c*) control of observing behavior.

EXHIBIT 8-4   *An Illustration of Initial Steps in a Linear Program for Developing Stereotype Accuracy*

---

1. In the following frames one or more words is missing. You will be required to write in the missing word(s) before turning to the next (page, frame) where you find the correct (response).

2. Properly used, this manual will teach you to accurately predict the differences in the interests of executives and unskilled workers. Illustrations or examples will teach you the basic principles involved in the (differences) in interests of the two groups.

3. It will be helpful for you to assume the imaginary role of both the typical executive and the typical unskilled worker. Then, deciding that an executive would be more likely to (prefer) a musical comedy is not at all difficult.

4. As you imagine the typical individual in both groups, note that going to a musical comedy would be more agreeable to (executives) than to (unskilled workers).

5. In the same way, note that unskilled workers would be more likely to (prefer) the sport of hunting.

6. Hunting is a less intellectual and more rugged type of interest than seeing a musical comedy. These differences are typical of the differences between (unskilled workers) and executives.

7. For similar reasons, the usually better educated (executive) would prefer a sport like golf more than would the (unskilled worker).

8. Imagine which would (prefer) to be a corporation lawyer as opposed to being a criminal lawyer. The executive type would probably (prefer) to be a corporation lawyer.

9. The unskilled worker type would prefer the more adventuresome job: being a (criminal) lawyer.

10. In your temporary role as an executive you should (prefer) the interest of "scientific research worker." In your other role as an (unskilled worker) you would be (less) likely to prefer such an interest.

Linear programs work. Why they work and whether a better approach to programming is possible is a subject of debate among experts. The father of teaching machines, Pressey (1963), has this to say:

> Even for the first go-through, they are unsatisfactory, because most important matter to be learned has structure, which the programming destroys except the serial order, and most important learning is integrative and judgmental, so requires a looking about in what is being studied; for all such purposes a teaching machine seems about as hampering as a scanning device which required that one look at a picture only 1 square inch at a time, in a set order . . . . The whole trend of American research and theory as regards learning has been based on a false prem-

ise—that the important features of human learning are to be found in animals. Instead, the all-important fact is that human has transcended animal learning . . . current animal derived procedures in auto-instruction destroy meaningful structure to present fragments serially in programs, and replace processes of cognitive clarification with largely rote reinforcings of bit learnings.

No type of human learning is more "important," more "integrative," or more "judgmental" than learning about people. We react to a person first as a simple whole and only gradually learn to differentiate details within that whole. Linear programming starts with the details and works toward the whole. It would be better to start with the whole and work toward the details. Just how this can be done is not yet certain. Lawson (1966) has developed a theory of human learning that fits the wholistic view as well as some programs for learning in the natural science based on the view. The critical implication: Move, not from the easy to the hard, but from the general to the specific. Applied to stereotypes, this implication suggests that training should begin with the most central difference between one group and another and gradually move toward the details.

THE USE OF TYPICAL CASES

Suppose we have knowledge of a group. The problem still remains of applying the knowledge of the group to predicting persons in the group. The use of typical cases is a way of simultaneously learning a stereotype and applying the knowledge to persons. Doctors, psychiatrists, social workers, and clinical psychologists have long made use of typical cases. They have realized that their value went beyond merely providing an illustration of a principle. They have recognized the worth of the pooling principle (Wakeley, 1961); "Use the information which you have about people whom you know well when you are making judgments about people whom you know less well." Consequently, they have stressed knowing the typical cases *well* and have emphasized the importance of mastering long and complicated case reports and of seeing, talking, and living with typical cases. The more intense the deliberate exposure to a typical case, the more likely it is to balance chance experiences with atypical ones. It is hard, for example, for the son of a rejecting father to understand the thoughts and behavior of an acceptant one.

A critical problem in the use of cases is knowing how typical a person is and in what ways he is typical. Is Morgan (Exhibit 8-5) a typical man? In some respects he is but in some he is not. In the first group of interests, his likes and dislikes correspond to those of the average man; in the second group, his likes and dislikes do not correspond. Per-

Exhibit 8-5   *The Case of Morgan Johnson*

Morgan is a twenty-two-year-old unmarried college senior who is planning to study psychology in graduate school. His parents died when he was four, and he and his younger brother were raised by permissive grandparents in Brooklyn. Of his childhood, Morgan said: "As I grew up, I always had the feeling that I was inferior to everybody else because I had no parents. In grade school, I was very loud and boisterous and made persistent attempts to dominate my peers and to excel in everything I did." Today he places emphasis on being a "well-rounded scholar." About his values, he now says: "I do not believe there are any determining forces in the universe that make us what we are; everybody rules his own destiny. I can think of nothing more important than being a good friend or having good friends, but I don't think it is possible to have more than a few really close ones. I place little value on material things: cars, clothes, etc."

Morgan filled out the Strong Vocational Interest Blank that requires the respondent to answer "Like," "Indifferent," or "Dislike" to a long list of interests. Below are the responses that Morgan made to some of these interests. Opposite his answer is the per cent of American men who made the same response.

INTEREST	MORGAN'S ANSWER	PER CENT OF MEN GIVING SAME ANSWER
	STEREOTYPE RESPONSES	
1. Driving an automobile	Like	77
2. Meeting and directing people	Like	58
3. Progressive people	Like	85
4. Independents in politics	Like	52
5. People who have done you favors	Like	83
6. Quick-tempered people	Dislike	67
7. "Roughhouse" initiations	Dislike	68
8. Music teaching	Dislike	65
9. People who talk very loudly	Dislike	80
10. Acting as cheerleader	Dislike	68
	INDIVIDUAL RESPONSES	
11. Fortunetellers	Like	5
12. People who always agree with you	Like	5
13. Floorwalker	Like	2
14. Politician	Like	18
15. Labor arbitrator	Like	19
16. Economics	Dislike	7
17. Travel movies	Dislike	3
18. Thrifty people	Dislike	4
19. Regular hours for work	Dislike	17
20. Taking long walks	Dislike	8

haps what is needed for the most effective training is a series of cases which move from the typical to the atypical. In any use of this form of the typical case method, however, the trainee would learn an accurate stereotype of a group while focusing on a person in it.

Stereotypes dominate our judgments. Contrary to widespread opinion, the dominance is usually helpful, for our stereotypes often lead us to surprisingly accurate judgments of a person. We have suggested ways in which our use of stereotypes might be expanded and improved and the crucial part that the social sciences can play in the process. No person, however, is a completely typical member of any group or combination of groups. Even two chicken eggs are not the same. It is to the judgment of individual qualities, therefore, that we turn in the following chapter.

Chapter Nine

THE INDIVIDUAL

As WE HAVE NOW seen, our sensitivity to a person is determined by the accuracy of our level and spread, of our assumptions of similarity, of our observations, and of the knowledge we have about the groups to which the person belongs. What else is there? The question is pervasive and controversial. We return to it in order to understand the importance of individual accuracy and to ways of improving it through training.

The Battle for Uniqueness

Allport has been a defender of uniqueness. In 1937, he demanded that psychology expand its boundaries, revise its methods, and extend its concepts in order to better understand the single concrete mental life:

> This demand is thoroughly radical. It is directed against the practice in general psychology of drawing the blood and peeling the flesh from human personality. . . . By stripping the person of all his troublesome particularities, general psychology has destroyed his essential nature. The newer point of view reverses the perspective . . . the integral, three-dimensional, and unique individual emerges as the salient feature.

In 1962:

> One marvels, for example, at the correctness with which insurance companies predict the number of deaths that will occur by highway accidents, from cancer or from suicide. The chances of a hypothetical average man for survival or death are all the insurance business wants to know. Whether Bill himself will be one of the fatal cases it cannot tell—and that is what Bill wants to know. . . . The situation is exactly the same in psychology.

The defenders of uniqueness see as a model of their "enemy" a legendary vocational psychologist. This psychologist told a young man seeking guidance that it would be necessary to take a fourteen-hour battery of tests. The young man hesitated because fourteen hours seemed like a lot of time. "Oh well," said the great psychologist "don't worry about that. If you're too busy, you can arrange to have my assistant take these tests for you. I don't care who takes them, just so long as they come out in quantitative form." The enemy, however, likes the following kind of true story (Meehl, 1957) :

> Back in the days when we were teaching assistants, my colleague Mc-Corquodale was grading a young lady's elementary laboratory report on an experiment which involved a correlation problem. At the end of an otherwise flawless report, this particular bobbysoxer had written "The correlation was seventy-five, with a standard error of ten, which is significant. However, I do not think these variables are related." McCorquodale wrote a large red "FAIL" and added a note: "Dear Miss Fisbee: The correlation coefficient was devised expressly to relieve you of all responsibility for deciding whether these two variables are related."

We cannot, however, make inferences about unique people, a philosopher says (Reade, 1938, pp. 19–20) :

> It is obvious, surely, that when "individual" signifies uniqueness neither from it nor to it can there be any inference whatever. . . . If we propose to make an inference from one man, one triangle, or one anything else to others it can only be in virtue of what is common to two or more. The moment we touch the unique all inference (and indeed all science) comes to an end.
>   What, then, is the "particular" for the purposes of inference? Paradoxical as it may sound, it seems that it cannot be anything but the universal. Dissect or analyze the individual, dissolve Plato into "man," "Athenian," "philosopher," and he can become apparently the goal or source of many inferences. But leave him as Plato, the unique and unapproachable, and he will mock at deduction, induction, and all similar pretences. Before the individual can be brought within range of inference it has to be transformed into a specimen, an example, an instance . . .

The battle, is not over whether one should or should not make inferences. Both sides do. The difference concerns the direct method of understanding a person. Sarbin, Taft, and Bailey (1960) have listed the following major differences between the defenders of uniqueness and their opponents:

1. The defenders of uniqueness aim at an artistic "understanding" of a person rather than the construction of statistical-general laws.

2. They are interested in the "whole" personality rather than part of it.
3. They focus on the person as an individual rather than as a member of the class.
4. They favor intuition rather than logical analysis as a method.
5. They stress combining impressions into patterns rather than adding them.

Which approach is more valid? The upholders of uniqueness lean heavily upon consensual and congruent validation. An example of consensual validation: A perceiver reaches the conclusion that "Jones is a highly creative person." If other perceivers reach the same conclusion, then the conclusion of the first is consensually validated. In congruent validation, a perceiver accepts an inference as correct if it is congruent with his theories about human nature. An extreme example: A paranoiac has the implicit theory that the world is filled with people hostile to him. His bus is late. He infers that the bus driver is hostile to him. His inference has congruent validity, for it is consistent with his theory. Sabin et al. (1960) conclude: "Consensual validation is only a makeshift; congruent validation harbors an intrinsic logical fallacy; prediction as a test of knowledge . . . is by far to be preferred to the other methods of validation."

The scientist is a human being. As a scientist, he is interested in making correct predictions about people. As a human being, he is concerned with how he feels about a person, how the person feels about himself, and how he gets along with the person. William James said: "Probably a crab would be filled with a sense of personal outrage if it could hear us class it without ado or apology as a crustacean, and thus dispose of it. I am no such thing! I'm MYSELF, MYSELF alone." We like to feel that we are unique and feel better and generally do better when we think we are and other people act as is if we are. Perhaps it is an awareness of some such feelings that generate the steam in the uniqueness boiler. The scientists minimize such feelings and opt for predictive accuracy; the upholders of uniqueness minimize predictive accuracy and opt for human feelings. Our feelings and our inferences about a person overlap; they are not, however, the same thing. Many people, including clinicians, are not so much concerned with making correct inferences about people as with helping them. Our concern, however, is with predictive accuracy.

The Measurement of Individual Accuracy

Individual accuracy is what is left when the influences of level, spread, and stereotype have been removed. What is left? Theoretically,

Exhibit 9-1 *The Case of Earl and Frank*

Earl and Frank, identical twins, were born in a Midwestern city of uneducated and unmarried parents. When the boys were six months old, they were turned over to their mother's sister. She kept Frank but placed Earl with a family who had advertised their wish to board a baby. This family soon assumed full responsibility for Earl and took him to a city in the Northwest without consulting the aunt of the boys. Earl's foster father was a college graduate and a successful salesman; Frank's, a streetcar conductor. Earl graduated from college; Frank attended high school for only six months, though later he attended night school. Earl was raised in comfort; Frank was brought up with little economic security by his fond aunt. Both twins had a pleasant home life with only moderate discipline. After they were separated, the boys did not see each other until they were fifteen years old and did not know they were twins until they were twenty-three.

They were both interviewed and tested by psychologists when they were thirty-seven years old. At the time of the study the twins were living in the same surburban community. The psychologists made personality ratings of the twins based on their interviews with them. Ratings were also obtained from their wives. In addition, both Earl and Frank took an individual intelligence test, the Rorschach Ink Blot Test, and the Strong Vocational Interest Blank (Burks and Roe, 1949).

The twins were remarkably similar in many respects: in height, hair, fingerprints, good health, poor spelling, ratings on many personality traits, vocational-interest scores, etc. In some respects, however, they were different. For the following statements, indicate the name of the twin to whom you think the statement applies, marking "E" for Earl and "F" for Frank. (The correct answers are in italics.)

E	F	1. Was more energetic.
E	*F*	2. Had an IQ of 83 while his brother had an IQ of 96.
E	*F*	3. Was warmer in his personal relations.
E	F	4. Spoke of his brother with condescension.
E	*F*	5. Was less pompous.
E	*F*	6. Had a higher score on the minister vocational-interest scale.
E	*F*	7. Was more interested in athletics.
E	F	8. Was more "cagey," less willing to give himself away.
E	F	9. Was bothered by the gap between his aspirations and his ability to achieve them.
E	F	10. Was less stable emotionally.
E	F	11. Was more self-conscious.
E	F	12. Said what he wanted most in life was a good business with men working for him.
E	*F*	13. Said that what he wished most was the happiness of his family.
E	*F*	14. Was more cooperative with the psychologist.
E	F	15. Was more eager to impress people.

nothing: "The moment we touch the unique all inference (and indeed all science) comes to an end." Practically, the more the influences of level, spread, and stereotypes are reduced, the closer we approach the unique.

The prediction of the differences between identical twins eliminates level and spread and greatly reduces stereotypic cues for inferences. Consider, for example, the case of Earl and Frank (Smith, 1961) shown in Exhibit 9-1. They are identical twins; the perceiver cannot use his stereotypes about the differences between the sexes, age groups, appearance, and so on as a basis for making inferences about the differences between them. As the prediction requires only that the perceiver differentiate between the two, the influence of level and spread are eliminated. By individual accuracy, then, we mean the ability to differentiate between individuals when group membership cues are reduced to a minimum. Stereotype accuracy requires differentation between the average members of different groups. By contrast, individual accuracy requires differentiation between individuals in the same groups.

THE GROSSMAN TEST OF INDIVIDUAL ACCURACY

In the development of his test of individual accuracy Grossman (1963) used three men and three women of varying ages and backgrounds. They were presented to the perceivers by means of five-minute filmed interviews. Exhibit 9-2 gives a sample of statements from the male test. As the perceiver is required to match one of the men to each of the statements, the influences of level and spread are eliminated. As the subjects are all men, the perceiver cannot use his stereotypes about the differences between men and women as a guide.

Grossman also eliminated other less tangible influences of stereotypes. The first form of the test included 240 statements; the final form, 120. The initial forms were taken by over a hundred students who also took the Johnson test of stereotype accuracy (Chapter 8). Grossman selected for his final form statements that discriminated between those with low and high scores on his test but did not discriminate between those with low and high scores in stereotype accuracy. The procedure was successful. A new group of students took the revised individual accuracy test and the stereotype test. Scores were unrelated ($r = .12$).

Grossman also attempted to make the test as general as possible. Exhibit 9-3 shows the final distribution of items in his test. Note that the test includes subtests for men and for women and subtests for judging what the individuals think of themselves and for judging what their friends think of them. In addition, the second-person subtests required the respondent to predict how the individuals rated their religious beliefs,

EXHIBIT 9-2 *Test of Individual Accuracy (Men)*
(Grossman, 1963)

Directions: This is a test of your ability to judge men. you are going to see five-minute filmed interviews with three men: Mr. G., Mr. W., and Mr. Z. All the men in the film filled out a series of attitude and personality scales and close associates rated them on a series of traits and gave thumbnail sketches of them. The statements below are based on the answers that the men and their friends gave. If you think the answer to a particular question is Mr. G, circle "G"; Mr. W., circle "W"; Mr. Z., circle "Z." Assume that the correct answers are the answers given by the men and their associates. Assume, also, that the correct answers are about equally distributed among the three men.

SECOND-PERSON PREDICTIONS

Religious Beliefs

Mr. G., Mr. W., and Mr. Z. filled out a rating scale concerned with their religious beliefs. Which one answered in the following manner?

G W Z   1. Agreed that "I'm unable to accept the idea of life after death, at least not until we have some definite evidence there is such a thing."

G W Z   2. Agreed that "God will punish those who disobey his commandments and reward those who obey Him (either in this life or a future life)."

Adjective Check List

The three men were each given pairs of adjectives and were asked to choose the one which they thought was a better description of themselves. In each of the pairs below only one of the men checked the adjective underlined. Circle "G" if you think it was Mr. G.; "W" if you think it was Mr. W.; "Z" if you think it was Mr. Z.

G W Z   3. *Arrogant*—apathetic
G W Z   4. *Changeable*—tense

Personality Inventory Items

Which one of the three men answered false to the following statements?

G W Z   5. I like to be the center of attention.
G W Z   6. It is easy for me to talk to strangers.

Which of the three answered true to the following statements?

G W Z   7. I easily become impatient with people.
G W Z   8. My hardest battles are with myself.

Exhibit 9-2 *Test of Individual Accuracy (Men) (Continued)*

THIRD-PERSON PREDICTIONS

Thumbnail Sketches by Associates

Close associates of the three men wrote thumbnail descriptions of them. Which one was described as follows?

G W Z   9. "Enjoys almost all good art and music."
G W Z   10. "Enjoys himself at parties, but is not much noticed."

Ratings by Associates

The three men were also rated by their associates on a series of personality traits. Which one was rated as follows?

G W Z   11. Least confident
G W Z   12. Most careful

---

how they filled out a personality inventory, and which of pairs of adjectives they chose to describe themselves. The third-person subtests require the respondent to predict both how the friends of the individuals rated them on a series of traits as well as how their friends informally described them. Scores on the subtests were related: Good judges of men were good judges of women; good judges of what people thought of themselves were good judges of what their friends thought of them.

What kind of people obtained high individual accuracy scores? Grossman picked 25 high scorers and 25 low scorers and contrasted their responses on more than six hundred personality inventory statements. He then picked the statements that most sharply differentiated the low and

Exhibit 9-3 *The Distribution of Questions on Grossman's Test of Interpersonal Sensitivity*

| | KIND OF PREDICTIONS | | |
SUBJECTS	SECOND PERSON	THIRD PERSON	TOTAL
Men (3)	30	30	60
Women (3)	30	30	60
Total	60	60	120

high scorers. Those of high individual accuracy more often answered "true" to the following statements.

1. I occasionally act contrary to custom.
2. The notion of divine inspiration may be mistaken.
3. I would rather read an article about a famous musician than about a famous financier.
4. I would rather grow inwardly than be a success in practical affairs.
5. I like continually changing activities.
6. I believe that the individualist is the man who is most likely to discover the best road to a new future.
7. I generally talk very quietly.
8. I like to associate with emotional people.
9. I usually enjoy spending an evening alone.
10. I have occasionally felt contempt for the opinion of others.

In general, the high scorers were more tough-minded, more empirical, more skeptical, readier for change, more individualistic, and more nonconforming. Johnson (1963) found similar qualities related to high stereotype-accuracy scores. However, those of high stereotype accuracy were more considerate of others and more concerned about problems of effective leadership and organization; those of high individual accuracy were not. In fact, the statement that most sharply differentiated those of low and high individual accuracy was "I enjoy being a leader of people." The high scorers answered "false." It seems that those of high individual accuracy are more interested in individuals than in groups. They also are more critical and discriminating about people.

Social Roles Versus Psychological Traits

I observed that a man is redheaded and predict that he is quick-tempered. From what I know of him, I have predicted something that I do not know. In the process, I have used a theory about people. That is, I have assumed a relationship between red hair and temper. Our theories may be implicit or explicit. Often, as in the following case, we may have a dominating implicit theory that conflicts with an explicit theory (McGregor, 1960, p. 7):

A manager states that he delegates to his subordinates. When asked, he expresses assumptions such as, "People need to learn to take responsibility," or "Those closer to the situation can make the best decisions." However, he has arranged to obtain a constant flow of detailed information to police their behavior and to "second-guess" their decisions. He says, "I am held responsible, so I need to know what is going on." He sees no inconsistency in his behavior, nor does he recognize some other assumptions which are implicit: "People can't be trusted," or "They can't really make a good decision as I can."

If we make a prediction about a person, it can only be by virtue of what he has in common with at least one other man. What can one man have in common with a second man that differentiates them from other men? They may share a common role. Both men may be psychologists, executives, doctors, policemen, carpenters, coal miners, Australians, college students, fraternity brothers, etc. They also may share a common psychological trait: they both may be bold, extroverted, tough-minded, problem-centered, irritable, etc. That is, we may make predictions about a person from knowing the social role he is playing or from knowing a psychological trait that he has.

Our stereotype accuracy primarily depends upon knowing the social roles that a person is playing and upon knowledge of these roles; individual accuracy depends upon knowing the traits that a person has and upon our knowledge of these traits.

Formal personality theories vary in the stress that they place upon social roles and psychological traits. The theories of Fromm, Horney, Lewin, Murphy, and Sullivan place a heavy weight upon the groups to which people belong and the social roles they play in them. On the other hand, the theories of Allport, Freud, Jung, and Sheldon pay more attention to psychological traits.

Methods of studying personality also vary in their stress upon roles and traits. Cross-cultural methods are concerned with social roles while psychological test methods are concerned with traits. Psychological tests, in turn, vary in the stress they place upon the relationship of traits within the individual and upon trait differences between individuals. The Rorschach and the Thematic Apperception Tests are concerned with the patterning of traits within the individual; personality inventories, with individual differences in traits. Our present concern is with individual differences.

The Improvement of Individual Accuracy

Realistic practice and feedback can be confidently expected to result in improvement in level, spread, empathic, observational, and stereotype accuracy. Not so with individual accuracy. Kepes (1965) gave six hours of training to 57 college students in making differential predictions about people. The training sessions involved discriminating between three individuals who were sometimes presented in written cases, sometimes in taped interviews, and sometimes in live interviews before the training group. Detailed feedback and discussion followed each effort at prediction. To evaluate the success of the training, each trainee was matched with a student who had the same initial score on the film test of individual accuracy (Grossman, 1963). Result: Significant but small improvement. Practice and feedback are not enough. Other principles must be incorporated into successful individual-accuracy training. Here are some that seem relevant.

ROLES BEFORE TRAITS

In the last chapter as well as in earlier ones we have presented evidence contrasting the success of stereotypes with the success of individual impressions as bases for predicting behavior. The evidence is overwhelming in favor of the stereotypes. We are much better at predicting the behavior of a person from a knowledge of the social roles that he is playing than from our impressions of his psychological traits. The differences between the behavior of a Negro cotton picker in Alabama and the president of a Minnesota mining firm are much more accurately predicted from the differences in their roles than from differences in their traits.

It takes a difference in stereotypes as well as in anything else to make a difference in predictions. Normally, for example, the height of players on two basketball teams makes a difference in which team wins. However, if the players on the two teams are the same height, difference in height can make no difference in the outcome predicted for the game. Again, differences in the intelligence of students in a class may account for much of the difference in grades. However, if all students have the same IQ, differences in intelligence can make no difference in grades. Now differences in the groups to which persons belong make accurately predictable differences in their behavior. However, if two persons belong to the same groups and are playing the same roles, group differences can make no difference in their behavior. In general, the greater the differences in the roles that two persons are playing, the more accurately we can predict differences between them on the basis of our stereotypes; the smaller the differences in social roles, the more important traits become as a determinant of differences. The principle may be stated as follows: Differentiate between people first on the basis of their roles; differentiate within roles on the basis of traits.

An exact and complex comparison of the accuracy of predictions based on stereotypes versus the accuracy of predictions based on personal judgments supports the principle. Cline and Richards (1962) first had six people rate themselves on a series of scales concerned with their religious attitudes. The first statement in the inventory illustrates its general form:

1. God will punish those who disobey his commandments and reward those who obey him.

   a. Strongly agree
   b. Agree
   c. Neither agree nor disagree
   d. Disagree
   e. Strongly disagree

The authors had judges who saw the persons on films predict how each of them had filled out the inventory. They compared the success of these individual predictions with predictions based on stereotypes. The comparisons were based on three different measures of sensitivity: a measure of stereotype accuracy, a measure of individual accuracy, and a measure of total accuracy. The method of deriving predictions from stereotypes was as follows: The first step was to give the same inventory taken by the six individuals to a large number of people. The next step was to divide this group into lower and upper halves on the basis of the total scores. Then the average answer on each of the statements was computed separately for the lower and upper halves. Finally, it was "given" to the method whether each of the six people being predicted were in the lower or the upper half. If a person was in the lower half, it was predicted that he would respond to each of the 12 items in the same way that the average person in the lower half had responded. If he was in the upper half, then it was predicted that he would respond in the same way as the average person in the upper half. These stereotype predictions were compared with the actual answers that the six people had made. Results: The predictions made by stereotypes resulted in more accurate stereotype and total scores. The judges, though, had superior individual accuracy scores, i.e., they were better at predicting differences between the individuals in the films. Conclusion: Contrary to common opinion among clinicians, the activity at which they are most likely to exceed the actuarial is not in making predictions about a unique individual but in predicting differences among persons who are grouped in the same class. For example, assume that we have talked to a man and a woman and are then asked to predict which would be more enthusiastic about each of a series of activities. If we know that the average man is more enthusiastic about an activity, we would predict that this particular man would be more enthusiastic. If we know that men and women are equally interested, then and only then would it be best to base our predictions on our interview impressions.

FACTS BEFORE GUESSES

As the social roles of persons become more alike, we more frequently assume a relationship between a trait and the behavior we are predicting.

The assumed relationship may have empirical support or it may not. The advice to use supported before unsupported relationships reflects one of two major conclusions of the study of clinical inference and cognitive theory by Sarbin et al. (1960): "Wherever experience tables are available for the prediction of conduct, inference from such tables should be used rather than inference from untested hypotheses."

Hypotheses can have a cancerlike effect on predictions. Five clinicians were given 462 responses made by 30 patients, 6 in each of five diagnostic categories: schizophrenia, neurosis, organic brain damage, retarded, and normal. For each response the clinicians were asked to decide in which category the patient belonged. Hunt, Schwartz, and Walker (1964) had previously noted that clinicians operated on the hypothesis that confusion in thinking and schizophrenia were related. The more severe the confusion indicated by a response, the more likely the clinician was to believe that it was made by a schizophrenic. To test the practical effects of the hypothesis, the authors first rated all the responses from low to high confusion. The clinicians diagnosed 31 per cent of the low confusion responses as schizophrenic although only 20 per cent actually were (6 out of 30). They diagnosed 81 per cent of the high confusion responses as schizophrenic. They were wrong on every one. All of the high confusion responses were made by patients who were mentally retarded or had organic brain damage. If the clinicians had had experience tables showing the frequency with which different types of patients had confused reactions, their diagnoses would have been much more accurate.

Predictions based on facts are not perfect, but they are better than those based on hypotheses. In 27 studies where predictions based on an empirical formula were compared with predictions based on the institutions and hypotheses of experts, the formula never failed (Meehl, 1959). Some of the formulas were crude. When they become more sophisticated, as they are continually doing, their superiority will become even greater. The conclusion: Cooperate with the formula by starting where it stops. Suppose a formula for predicting the success of college applicants selects the 10 in a 100 most likely to succeed but only 5 can be admitted. The hypothesis maker can pick the 5 from that 10. Suppose a formula picks the 10 in a 100 patients who are most likely to benefit from psychotherapy but only 5 can be treated. The hypothesis maker can pick the 5, etc.

EXPLICIT BEFORE IMPLICIT HYPOTHESES

When shall we use our heads instead of the formula (Meehl, 1957)? We should use our heads when there is a special case that is an obvious exception to the formula. For example, "If a sociologist were predicting whether Professor X would go to the movies on a certain night, he might have an equation involving age, academic specialty, and introversion score. The equation might yield a probability of .90 that Professor X goes to the movie that night. But if the family doctor announced that Professor X had just broken his leg . . ." It is the nature of special cases, however, that they are rare.

We can confidently use our heads when we know a great deal about the people we are differentiating. Students of the author were asked to predict how he had answered "like," "indifferent," or "dislike" to 30 items on the Strong Vocational Interest Blank. The average student made accurate predictions on less than 50 per cent of the statements; his wife missed only 1 of the 30. More generally, Newcomb (1963) had men in a cooperative house rank what they thought were the major interests of the other men in the house. After two weeks, 25 per cent of the predictions were highly accurate; after four weeks, 40 per cent. That accuracy normally compares with length of acquaintance is obvious, but it still needs to be stressed. Practically all the conclusions reported in this book are based on brief contacts between perceiver and the person he is perceiving, many for less than five minutes and few for more than an hour. The absence of studies among perceivers who have had long relationships with the person they are perceiving is one of the most significant gaps in our knowledge of sensitivity.

We have to use our heads when we have no formula or have no time to use a formula. Clinicians have a storehouse of tests that they may use to develop formulas; they still only rarely have experience tables upon which to base their predictions. The man in the street, who is our primary focus of attention, almost never does. He is therefore forced to use his theories about people in making predictions from what he has observed to what he has not. It is for this situation that Sarbin et al. (1960) have made the second of their two major recommendations: "Where formal or informal experience tables are absent, the clinician should recognize *explicitly* that his decisions, which may be far-reaching, are made on the basis of unconfirmed hypotheses."

The common sorry fate of the user of implicit and unconfirmed hypotheses is indicated by one result of a classic study. In 1946, hundreds of students already admitted to psychology graduate schools throughout the country came to Ann Arbor for a week of evaluation of their probable success by dozens of experienced psychologists (Kelly and Fiske, 1951). In one part of the experiment, the psychologists predicted the academic success of the students by answering this question: "How well will this student: effectively master course work content; successfully complete courses in general psychology, clinical psychology, statistics, and related fields; satisfy language requirements for the doctorate; pass general examinations?"

The ratings were made on an eight-point scale. Sometimes they were based on credentials alone (transcripts of college grades, references, etc.), sometimes on test scores, sometimes on interviews, and sometimes on a combination of these. The students then returned to their graduate schools. After three years, their professors in graduate school ranked the students on their academic performance from the best to the worst. These rankings were used to test the validity of the ratings made years before. The ratings made on the basis of credentials alone correlated .26 with actual performance in graduate school; the ratings made on the basis of credentials plus scores on objective tests correlated .36; and the ratings made on the basis of credentials plus a two-hour individual interview with the student correlated .32. The two-hour interview slightly decreased the validity of the predictions. The interviews probably stimulated the clinicians to formulate many hypotheses about the interviewees; they did not stimulate predictive accuracy.

In a more recent study (Golden, 1964) experienced clinicians predicted the responses of five patients from a knowledge of their scores on the Rorschach and Thematic Apperception Tests. Predictions were made sometimes on the basis of one test and sometimes on the basis of various combinations. Result: Accuracy did not increase as the amount of information given to the perceiver increased. Conclusion: "It is conceivable . . . increased amounts of data resulted in greater reliability up to a certain point, perhaps diminishing as more and more information was needed, and finally stabilizing at a uniformly low level. What is needed in future research . . . an examination of the inferential process itself, and, in particular, the cognitive activity of the clinician." Let us make hypotheses explicit and study their effectiveness.

EMPIRICAL BEFORE NONEMPIRICAL THEORIES

Hypotheses are derived from theories, and theories are also best made explicit. What is the best theory? In general, "a theory serves the dual functions of unifying known empirical findings, and suggesting new empirical relations to be explored." Theories are used by research workers to guide their research activities, by psychotherapists as an aid in helping their clients, or by perceivers as a way of improving the accuracy of their differentiations between individuals. The purpose determines the theory.

The world is a dazzling array of things to see, describe, explain, and predict. To prevent himself from being blinded or confused by complexities, the research worker must simplify his task. Mechanical devices help: The telescope limits the astronomer's attention to one part of the heavens; the microscope fastens the biologist's attention upon one part of his environment. A theory provides an even more powerful way of simplifying things, for it not only tells the researcher what to look for but also what not to look for or worry about. As an aid in the scientist's quest for knowledge, it is less important that a theory be true than that it generate hypotheses that can be proved false.

Consider Sheldon's theory of the relationship between body types and personality traits. It is a comparatively simple theory from which it is possible to derive many concrete hypotheses that can be readily tested. The theory, for example, states that thin people smoke less than fat or muscular people. Plath (1959) compared the smoking habits of thin, fat, and muscular people. Results: Thin people smoked more than fat or muscular people. The hypothesis was false, but it was derived from a useful theory. It lead to the testing of an hypothesis and to an expansion of knowledge.

The primary aim of the psychotherapist is not to expand general knowledge but to promote constructive changes in his clients. Most American psychotherapists have chosen psychoanalytic theory as the most suitable for their purpose, for it focuses upon what should be changed and what can be changed. The constitutional psychology of Sheldon is entirely unsuited for this purpose, for it focuses upon what cannot be changed. On the other hand, psychoanalytic theory is almost equally unsuitable for the research worker, for it is hard to derive concrete hypotheses from this theory. It is even harder to devise ways in which they can be confidently falsified. For example, an hypothesis derived from psychoanalytic theory is that paranoia results from inadequate repression of homosexual impulses. In spite of considerable research effort, no one has satisfactorily proved or disproved this hypothesis.

What kind of theory will best lead the perceiver to improvements in his individual accuracy? There seem to be at least four requirements: (1) The theory should stress individual differences; (2) the theory should stress observations the perceiver can make; (3) the observed differences should suggest hypotheses about related differences; and (4) the hypotheses should be verified. Sheldon's theory would be a poor choice. It does stress individual differences; it does suggest observations that the perceiver can easily make (difference in the physique of individuals); and it does lead to many concrete hypotheses. Unfortunately, all the tested hypotheses have either been proved false or been so overstated as to result in false predictions. The theory leads to more confident and explicit predictions but also to more mistaken ones.

Freud's theory seems to be an equally poor choice. In the first place, it stresses, not individual differences, but the dynamic organization of traits within the individual. In the second place, it does not lead to observable differences (How can one observe whether a person has forgotten or has repressed a bit of information? How can one observe that a person is a latent homosexual?). In the third place, while it suggests many hypotheses, few are verifiable. Finally, the correctness of the hypotheses is uncertain. The inadequacy for prediction purposes is supported by the chronic failure of clinically trained psychologists to make more accurate predictions than other groups.

Where, then, should we find a better choice? The theory, first of all, should have a trait approach which looks at a person as an individual, definable in terms of a qualitative or quantitative difference from others. The theory should also guide observation. A giant step in this direction is to narrow the range of traits with which the perceiver must concern himself. There are, for example, almost twenty thousand possible trait names in the dictionary. Cattell (1956) has narrowed the list to sixteen: will control, emotional stability, positive character, self-sufficiency, radicalism, sophistication, dominance, emotional sensitivity, etc. The traits, if they are to lead to accurate predictions, should have an empirical base. Cattell's traits do, for they grow from long study of the ways that persons describe themselves on inventories.

A Training Proposal

Thus far, no kind of training seems to make any appreciable improvement in individual accuracy. We have speculated about the principles that an effective program would stress: roles before traits, facts before guesses, explicit before implicit hypotheses, and an empirical trait theory before a speculative, dynamic one. It remains to suggest how such principles might be translated into effective training.

The trait list should be further simplified. While 16 traits are measurable, it is unlikely that they are observable. Linden (1965) has reduced the list to 5. He factor-analyzed the 25 traits isolated by Hershey (1958) from a study of traits measured by other personality inventories (Smith, 1961, p. 64). The five factors appearing from this analysis and the traits most highly saturated with the factor were:

1. IMPULSIVE	versus	CONTROLLED
Unambitious		Ambitious
Unorganized		Organized
2. RATIONALISTIC	versus	EMPIRICAL
Resistant to change		Readiness for change
Religious		Sceptical
Conforming		Nonconforming
Nonscientific		Scientific
3. INTROVERTED	versus	EXTROVERTED
Introverted thinking		Extroverted thinking
High artistic values		Low artistic values
Low economic values		High economic values
4. CAUTIOUS	versus	BOLD
Submissive		Dominant
Unenergetic		Energetic
Low self-confidence		High self-confidence
Pessimistic		Optimistic

EMOTIONAL	versus	CALM
Critical		Amiable
High sensory awareness		Low sensory awareness

Based upon this analysis, Linden developed the Protebob Personality Inventory which consists of 200 items measuring the five traits. The trait measures are highly reliable, none of the reliabilities being less than .80. The traits are also quite independent, none of the intercorrelations being greater than .30. Sample statements from each of the scales are given in Exhibit 9-4.

EXHIBIT 9-4   *Sample Statements from the Protebob Personality Inventory* (Linden, 1965)

IMPULSIVE VERSUS CONTROLLED

1. I find it rather hard to keep to a rigid routine.
2. I generally go from one thing to another in my daily life without a great deal of planning.
3. I frequently obey whatever impulse is strongest.
4. I believe in getting as much fun as I can out of life.
5. I feel that friendship is more important in life than anything else.
6. I set very difficult goals for myself.
7. I enjoy work more than play.
8. I am guided in all my conduct by firm principles.
9. I think more for the future than for the present.
10. I really don't like to drink alcoholic beverages.

RATIONALISTIC VERSUS EMPIRICAL

11. I am more interested in general ideas than in specific facts.
12. I trust in God to support the right and condemn the wrong.
13. I carry a very strict conscience about with me wherever I go.
14. In matters of conduct I conform very closely to custom.
15. I take pains not to incure the disapproval of others.
16. I am more interested in what I see and hear than in abstract principles.
17. I have occasionally doubted the reality of God.
18. In the long run, science provides the best hope for solving the world's problems.
19. I often act contrary to custom.
20. Compared to your own self-respect, the respect of others means little.

INTROVERTED VERSUS EXTROVERTED

21. Daydreams are an important part of my life.
22. My head is always full of imaginative ideas.

EXHIBIT 9-4 *Sample Statements from the Protebob Personality Inventory (Continued)*

23. I prefer friends who have well-developed artistic tastes.
24. I like abstract paintings.
25. I would prefer to read an article about a famous musician than a financier.
26. I can deal much better with actual situations than with ideas.
27. I tend to accept the world as it is and not worry about how it might be.
28. I would rather be a salesman than an artist.
29. I am an extremely practical person.
30. I think there are few more important things in life than money.

CAUTIOUS VERSUS BOLD

31. I generally keep in the background at social functions.
32. I am inclined to limit my friends to a few people.
33. I am frequently discouraged by my own inadequacies.
34. I am cautious about undertaking anything that might lead to humiliating experiences.
35. I prefer quiet games to extremely active ones.
36. I enjoy speaking in public.
37. I am a very adventurous person.
38. I have frequently assumed the leadership of groups.
39. I am very optimistic.
40. I spend myself freely as I have plenty of energy.

EMOTIONAL VERSUS CALM

41. I have sometimes corrected others, not because they were wrong, but only because they irritated me.
42. I am rather spontaneous in speech and action.
43. I am easily moved to laughter or tears.
44. I have very strong likes and dislikes.
45. I have sometimes gotten so angry that I felt like throwing and breaking things.
46. I find that my life moves along at an even tenor without many ups and downs.
47. I can stand pain better than the average person.
48. I am practically always tolerant even in dealing with people that I don't like.
49. I am a rather objective and matter-of-fact person.
50. I suppress my emotions more often than I express them.

The first phase of training, it is proposed, would be to instruct trainees in the nature and relationships of the traits. Trainees have widely varying and mistaken ideas about their relationships (See Exhibit 3-1). For example, most trainees who have the traits explained to them have the implicit theory that boldness and extroversion are highly correlated. In fact, they are unrelated. Some think of the traits as generally very highly related while others think of them as relatively independent.

The second phase of training would be to instruct the trainees in relevant stereotypes. On many of the traits there are significant differences related to age, sex, social class, educational status, and occupational interests. These differences provide clues for establishing trait differences between persons. Along with such training would go training in observing verbal and expressive cues related to differences in traits. What behavior in an interview situation, for example would be related to the cautiousness or boldness of the interviewees?

The final phase of training would involve practice in making differential predictions about individuals from differences in their place on trait dimensions. Informal and formal "experience tables" would make this phase of training more efficient. Even without such tables, however, it seems likely that frequent feedback to the trainees would improve accuracy at this stage.

The five traits have been used here to make the outlined training proposal somewhat more concrete. Other trait systems might do better. The essentials of the training proposal are (1) substitute an explicit and empirical trait theory for whatever implicit theory the trainee is using; (2) develop the trainee's skill in placing individuals along these trait dimensions with the aid of stereotypic and observational cues; (3) give him practice and feedback in making inferences about individuals from their positions on these dimensions. How well would the system work? An experimental evaluation can provide the only good answer. It would do at least as well as any other system—which apparently is not saying very much.

Part Five

IMPLICATIONS AND APPLICATIONS

Chapter Ten

QUESTIONS AND ANSWERS

THE PRECEDING chapters differentiated sensitivity into six components and sketched their nature and origins. It remains to reintegrate these components and to examine their significance for education. The reintegration we shall try in this chapter; the examination, in the next. Here our concern is with summary answers to some general questions about sensitivity.

What Is Sensitivity?

Sensitivity is the ability to predict what a person will feel, say, and do about you, himself, and others. There are processes that lead to this ability and there are consequences of having it. We however have focused upon the result, not upon the causes of the result or its consequences. We have shown how this result can be measured: We can present persons to be judged, specify what judgments are to be made, and determine their accuracy with objective precision.

Sensitivity is not a single unified trait. Like intelligence, it is factorially complex, made up of relatively independent components. Some of these components lie entirely within the perceiver; some, in the interaction between the perceiver and the person; and some, in the person being perceived. The failure to appreciate the component nature of sensitivity has been the major cause of measurement failures; it has been a major aim of the present work to indicate what these components are and how they can be measured. Experience indicates that the components of level, spread, empathic, observational, stereotype, and individual accuracy can be measured with the same precision as other abilities when the same psychometric techniques are employed.

Who Is Sensitive?

Kelly and Fiske (1951, p. 202) concluded their extensive study of procedures for the selection of clinical psychologists with the statement:

> It is our belief that there are a few relatively gifted individuals whose intuitive insights may provide a basis not only for superior prediction in individual cases, but the development of new and powerful techniques for the evaluation of personality and the prediction of individual behavior. . . . If this should be the case, it is essential that efforts be made to identify the methods employed by such persons so that these methods may be communicated to others in training.

The more we know about sensitive people, the better sensitivity training can be done. Identifying the traits of sensitive people is harder, however, than measuring sensitivity. The first step requires the identification of sensitive people. To take the step without stumbling requires an adequate measure of sensitivity. Once the step is taken, it is necessary to have adequate measures of personality to which the measure of sensitivity can be related. The minimum requirement for the measure of traits is that they be independent of the measure of sensitivity. Most studies of the question do not meet this minimum requirement. Their results, consequently, are conflicting.

A useful study of the traits of sensitive people requires (1) an adequate number of judges; (2) an objective measure of sensitivity; and (3) an objective measure of personality traits. Three studies that meet these minimal requirements are shown in Exhibit 10-1. The studies used different measures of sensitivity and of personality so that the results are not all comparable. The results that are positive, comparable, and consistent are shown. The pattern is clear: the sensitive are more intelli-

EXHIBIT 10-1   *Traits of Sensitive People*

CLINE (1955)	CHANCE AND MEADERS (1960)	GROSSMAN (1963)
High social responsibility	High affiliation and independence, low hostility	Considerate and constructive leadership attitudes
Antifascistic, tolerant, and liberal		Readiness for change and humanitarian religious views
High intelligence test scores and intellectual efficiency		High verbal intelligence and college grades

gent, more tolerant, and, above all, more independent but responsible and considerate in their relations to others. Less consistent results indicate that the sensitive are more imaginative, more dominating, and less gregarious.

Why these particular traits? Most of what we know about people we have learned informally. The sensitive people are simply those who have learned the most. In learning anything, we need to be motivated to learn it, to be aware of what there is to learn, to take an active attitude in learning it, and to know whether we have learned it. The process applied to learning about people can be diagramed in the following way.

Motivation to	Openness to	Participation	
understand	→ experiences	→ in a	→ Feedback
people	about them	learning process	

The most sensitive person is the most highly motivated, most open to new experiences, most ready to participate in learning about them, and most able to assess the adequacy of what he has learned.

Motivation is the first essential: men learn what they want to learn. What a person says about his motivation, however, is no safe guide to what it is. In one evaluation of sensitivity training, those who expressed the greatest eagerness to learn about people learned the least (Miles, 1960). What is the successful motivational pattern? The top line of Exhibit 10-1 suggests the answer. The sensitive are people who find their greatest satisfactions in human relations, who are considerate and responsible in dealing with others, who want to give to others rather than to get something from them, but who are not dependent upon them. The findings of Bronfenbrenner et al. (1958) support the pattern. Of 24 traits of students attending a dinner-discussion meeting, those which most sharply separated the sensitive from the insensitive involved the ability to relate to others in a considerate, reasonable, and flexible way.

While Cline found that the sensitive are immune to symptoms of serious disorders (hypochondriasis, schizophrenia, etc.), they are not remarkable for their stability. In fact, the sensitive may be more anxious than the insensitive. Trumbo (1955) matched 25 anxious students with 25 unanxious ones on the basis of sex and intelligence. The anxious had higher predictive accuracy. The experiment was repeated with the same result. It was first thought that the anxious might have done better because they took more time in completing the test. A check, however, showed that the anxious took less time. It may be as Wedeck (1947) found among fourteen-year-old London school girls that the accurate are more physiologically sensitive: "They are like instruments in a perpetual state of vibration . . . extreme susceptibility of their nervous systems . . ."

William James appears to have been a person of this type (Perry, 1935, p. 682) :

> In speaking, first, of James's sensibility, I do not mean his susceptibility to feeling or emotion, but the acuity of his senses—the voluminousness and richness of the experience which he received through them, and the prominence of that experience and of its underlying motive in his life as a whole. . . . He wanted to see people who he knew . . . he was quick also to discriminate nuances of sound, especially in the quality of a human voice. His psychological writings testify to his discrimination of organic sensations.

It may be, however, that the sensitive are no more anxious than the insensitive, but merely freer in admitting their anxieties.

To learn about people, a person must be open to new experiences. He must be sympathetic to new ideas about people and capable of looking at old facts about them in new ways. The more curious, plastic, and nondefensive he is, the more likely he is to learn. The traits indicated in the second line of Exhibit 10-1 support the interpretation. The sensitive are more empirical, skeptical, tolerant, liberal, and readier for change than the insensitive.

An active attitude is also important for effective learning. The learner must not only be eager and ready to learn but also to seek information, make inferences, and test them out in practice. An active attitude has more to do with listening than with talking. For example, class sessions at the University of Chicago were recorded. The tapes were later played back to each student in the class, and he was asked to report what he had been thinking about at the time. The reports of the students were rated for their relevance to the topic being discussed. The amount of time that the same students spent in active class participation was also rated. Their achievement in the course was also measured by objective examination. Talking time had no relation to achievement; the relevance of thinking did (Bloom, 1953).

Learning about people requires boldness—a willingness to approach people, ask questions, and express feelings. Both Cline (1955) and Kelly and Fiske (1951) found that the most sensitive had high scores on the MMPI Capacity for Status Scale ("ambitious, active, forceful, insightful, resourceful, ascendant, and self-seeking"). Chance and Meaders (1960) also found the sensitive to be more independent and dominating. Boldness is particularly relevant in training, for the trainee who is a bystander will not learn. Cline and Richards (1959) found that their most sensitive participants were described by their fellow trainees as egotistical and conceited; they also described themselves as egotistical and conceited. The authors concluded that the sensitive person is

... a person who possesses a considerable amount of ego strength, self assuredness, and even conceit (probably to the point of occasionally irritating others). He is somewhat independent (emotionally) of other people and is not particularly concerned about how they regard him. He has tendencies toward leadership and dominance and has little psychic difficulty in initiating action or making decisions about things in his environment.

The greater boldness of fast learners was established more precisely by Hershey (1960). He divided fifty students into 10 five-man discussion groups according to their social boldness scores, the first group having the highest boldness scores; the second, the next highest, etc. Trumbo's written test of the ability to predict behavior was given before and after the 10 training sessions. Result: The bold groups improved more than the cautious groups. Observations indicated that the bold groups expressed their opinions more freely, seemed more willing to listen to others, and more willing to change their own opinions. What is true for trainees learning to be sensitive seems also true for housewives learning about foods. The bold more often consult their husbands, friends, and newspaper ads about purchases than the cautious do (Trier, Smith, and Shaffer, 1960).

The more a trainee is told how he is doing, the faster he learns. Everyday life provides little systematic feedback about the accuracy of our judgments of others. The sensitive are intelligent enough to make good use of the little they do get. The ability to consider and to make sense out of factual fragments about people seems to be a core aspect of relational thinking and is closely correlated with both chronological and mental age (Gollin, 1958). Intelligence is the most certain correlate of sensitivity. Of 20 studies relating intelligence to sensitivity published between 1915 and 1963, all were positive, the median being .30. Four different measures of intelligence are represented in Exhibit 10-1: scores on the Henmon-Nelson general intelligence test, scores on the scholastic aptitude test, grades in college, and scores on the MMPI scale measuring intellectual efficiency.

In sum, the most sensitive person is the one best equipped to learn about people. He is curious about and deeply involved with others but is neither gregarious or undiscriminating. He is open to people and nondefensive in his relations with them. He is frank about himself and bold, but not hostile, in his dealings with others. He is an intelligent user of complex concepts.

If this is really the basic pattern, then we seem to be making incomplete use of it in the selection of candidates for "sensitive" jobs: clinical psychologists, counselors, social workers, etc. The requirements of professional training as well as the availability of intelligence tests ensure that the intelligence criterion is being used and probably overused. Since openness to experience and readiness for change are related to intelligence and educational level, it is likely that adequate attention is being given to this variable. On the other hand, the need for nonaggressive boldness and independence is probably being underemphasized. A considerate and deep involvement with people—the trait most clearly and intimately related to sensitivity—is the one that seems most neglected. While its importance is given some recognition, it is easily confused with gregariousness and general amiability. Few concrete steps to remedy this weakness seem to have been taken. Scores on the clinical psychology scale of the Strong Vocational Interest Blank tap this trait. The test is easy to administer and is one of the few to be related to success as a clinical psychologist (Kelly and Fiske, 1951). It is rarely used by psychology departments in the selection of their graduate students.

What Are the Causes of Insensitivity?

Some people are more sensitive than others. All, however, make errors in their judgments. As we examined the components in the preceding chapters, we pointed out the most common and serious of these errors. A summary view follows.

THE RIGIDITY OF LEVELS

Even after the briefest exposure, we can gain a clear picture of what a person is like. Our pictures, however, vary widely from the darkest gray to the rosiest pink. Some people think that most people are "no damn good" while others think the best of everyone. The general level at which a perceiver operates reflects the stable and central personality quality. It also has a pervasive influence on all his judgments of himself and others.

Regardless of his level, a perceiver tends to think that it is he who is in closest touch with reality, that the general level of his judgments is the most accurate one. Levels are highly resistant to change, as every instructor knows who has tried to persuade his colleagues to accept a common distribution of student grades. One reason for the resistance is that every level is sometimes and from some point of view correct. The low leveler who thinks little of himself is likely to be closer to what others think of him, for we tend to exaggerate our worth in the eyes of others. The high leveler, on the other hand, who thinks well of himself and others is likely to be in accord with what others think of themselves. In objective situations, sometimes the pessimist and sometimes the optimist is more likely to be right. The situation may be so difficult that the person who says, "He won't do it," is almost certain to be right; it may be so easy that the person who says, "He will do it," is more likely to be right.

The problem is not so much the level that a perceiver has as the inflexibility of his level. More or less regardless of his own qualities, of whom he is rating, or of what he is rating, perceivers tend to stick to a constant level. The most sensitive are those who have learned to adapt their level realistically to changing persons and situations.

THE PREVALENCE OF SIMPLE THINKING

We perceive a person as a unified and simple whole. So strong is this tendency that it is hard to avoid describing everyone as good or bad, right or wrong, strong or weak. Gollin (1954) showed students films of a girl in a "moral" and in an "immoral" scene. When asked to describe the girl afterward, half of the students described her as simply moral or immoral. More than a quarter described both moral and immoral facts but did not try to account for the inconsistencies. The smallest group tried to account for the conflicting facts.

One common way of achieving a simple picture of a person is to fail to observe or to forget facts that do not fit. Even when we retain the facts, however, we can put them in the corner of the picture. The commanding officers below who assessed their subordinates were able to achieve this end (Whisler and Harper, 1962, p. 220):

> A quiet, reticent, neat appearing officer—industrious, tenacious, diffident, careful and neat. I do not wish to have this officer as a member of my command at any time.

> Is keenly analytical, and his highly developed mentality could best be used in the research and development field. He lacks common sense.

> Never makes the same mistake twice but it seems to be that he has made them all once.

A common way of maintaining a simple picture is to accumulate an excessive number of facts, some of which are ambiguous or conflicting. It is then possible to consciously pick facts that fit the picture we had before the facts were accumulated.

THE DANGERS OF PSYCHOLOGICAL-MINDEDNESS

It is commonly assumed that the development of a psychological orientation toward people by the mastery of the vocabulary, facts, and theories of psychology is a valuable way of increasing sensitivity. The studies summarized in Chapter 1 do not support this view. Those with training in psychology never fare better and sometimes fare worse than those without training. The most pointed study of the question (Chance and Meaders, 1960) showed that those who were most psychologically minded were least accurate in their judgments.

The dangers of psychology lie more in the point of view of the knower than in what he knows. Preoccupation with the psychological underground leads one to overlook significant facts that lie on the surface. This preoccupation may also lead to the view that we are all moved by primitive and blind impulses when, in fact, we are largely reasonable players of social roles. It is also hard to see in the underground and thus easy to mistake our own projected feelings for the reality. Perhaps most relevant of all, the most enthusiastic proponents of psychological-mindedness are not those with deep involvement with others but those with a desire to protect and enhance their own self-esteem. Mastery of the "psychological point of view" may be comforting, but it may also be deceptive.

THE ERROR OF LEAST EFFORT

It is possible to surface after a dip in the literature of sensitivity with the idea that we are generally preoccupied with assessing the fundamental nature of the people we meet. We are usually interacting with others in well-defined situations where we are playing rather specific roles. We are seeking, therefore, information that is relevant to the role we are playing. The question most likely to be before us is not: What is he like? It is: What do we do next? Jones and Thibaut (1958) state the implication in this way: "The perceiver in any social situation will act in such a way as to reduce the need for information to sustain the interaction process." We seek to know the least amount about another person that is consistent with playing our part effectively.

The greatest gap between possible and actual accuracy lies in the area of observation, for we are capable of observing much more about people than we usually do. Thus, we can predict with a high degree of confidence that scores on any test of observational accuracy will improve on the second trial. Improvement is a matter of knowing what is wanted and wanting to do it. It is easy to improve observation by improving accuracy of observations made. There is so much room for it.

"Observation" as used by psychologists generally does not mean observation. Rather, it means reporting inferences on the basis of observations that are not reported. In the typical interview study, for example, the focus is upon the interviewer's judgments of the intelligence, industriousness, cooperativeness, etc., not upon the appearance, actions, and statements of the interviewee.

FAULTY STEREOTYPES

A stereotype is our picture of the social role the members of a particular group play; stereotype accuracy is the adequacy of our knowledge of these roles; and stereotyping is the process of applying our knowledge of these roles in making predictions about how individuals will behave. Stereotyping has been condemned as having a distorting and paralyzing effect upon our judgments of others because it can lead to wrong predictions. Again and again, however, we have seen that stereotyping a person leads to more accurate predictions than considering him as a "unique individual."

Stereotyping is inevitable; it is also helpful. Still, stereotypes can often be mistaken and misused. Stereotype accuracy depends, in part, upon the number of persons in the group we have known. Not infrequently, the number is one. We meet an Australian, form an impression of his personality, and use that impression in making predictions about all Australians. Even more serious, the number may be none. Children and adults learn stereotypes from those about them without any firsthand experience with the groups: Koreans, Negroes, Jews, Texans, Catholics, etc. The condemnation of stereotypes seems itself to result from a mistaken stereotype. The ignorant, the unintelligent, the authoritarian, and the ethnocentric overuse and misuse stereotypes. Such people prefer simplified and overgeneralized concepts and use them in a blind fashion (Rokeach, 1960). It has been implicitly assumed that because this group misused stereotypes, all groups do. The assumption is not correct. However, even those who are not chronic misusers of stereotypes and who have had time to observe many members of a group still make mistakes. One of the most certain ways of reducing these mistakes is through training in stereotype accuracy.

THE CANCEROUS HYPOTHESIS

One sort of error is so typical of judgments of personality, so persistent, and seemingly so unavoidable, that it should be constantly borne in mind. It is the result of a hypothesis that, like cancer, grows in a wild uncontrollable way. It is a product of oversimplification, overgeneralization, and overspeculation. It may grow from an assumed relation between a physical quality and psychological ones. Thornton (1943) took two photographs each of four men and four women. In one photograph they wore glasses; in the other they did not. He projected these on a screen and asked groups of judges to rate the person on a series of personality traits. Result: When the persons were wearing glasses, they were judged as more intelligent, more dependable, more industrious, more honest, etc. In similar experiments, persons who were smiling were judged as more honest, more kind, more humorous, etc. Girls wearing lipstick during interviews were judged as more frivolous, more anxious, more interested in men, etc. (McKeachie, 1952).

The hypothesis may relate a particular psychological trait to a general psychological state. Schizophrenics, for example, are confused in their thinking. Therefore, the hypothesis goes, the more confused a person is, the more likely he is to be schizophrenic. Clinicians classified mental patients into various categories of mental illness. They varied in their symptoms of confusion. The more confused the thinking, the more frequently the patients were classified as schizophrenic. Almost all the patients that showed high confusion were classified in this manner; none of the classifications were correct (Hunt et al., 1964).

Implicit and cancerous hypotheses may play a dominant part in important decisions. A great university in Texas needed a new head for their economics department and the autocratic president announced his choice. All the members of the department signed a petition protesting the appointment by saying that the candidate was "unimpressive." His dwarflike physique played a large part in the discussions of his unimpressiveness. Nonetheless, he was appointed, was successful, and became dean. The country was combed for his replacement and there was general agreement on the best man for the job, though it was incidentally remarked by those who recommended him that "he tends to talk a great deal when he is nervous." He came, was interviewed, and was rejected because he seemed "arrogant, egotistical, and opinionated."

How Can Selection Be Improved?

The man buying a pair of shoes is not interested in understanding the fundamental nature of the salesman and there is no special reason why he should be. Most social interactions are of this type. There are, however, interactions where the aim is to achieve the highest possible predictive accuracy. Notable among these are selection situations: the employment director picking candidates for jobs, the executive picking subordinates to promote, the admissions officer selecting candidates for the freshmen class, the clinician selecting clients for therapy, etc. Personal impressions via interviews, though costly, are a nearly universal part of the process. Studies regularly show, however, that such impressions contribute little to predictive accuracy. They would contribute if the following principles were more often applied.

Instead of rating each applicant on a scale from poor to outstanding, rank all applicants from the best to the worst. Regardless of whom they are rating, some raters habitually rate low and some high; some habitually use the middle ratings and some use the extremes. Rankings eliminate the large and largely irrelevant errors in prediction due to individual differences in level and spread. These sources of error are well understood as are the techniques of eliminating them: rankings, forced-choice distributions, paired-comparisons, etc. Unfortunately, the techniques are too infrequently employed. Even in research studies of sensitivity nearly half employed ratings. Rankings should be substituted for ratings whenever it is possible to do so. The only exception occurs when the focus is upon finding out something about the rater rather than the ratee.

The general question should not be: How good is this man? It should be: Who is the best of the men available? Considerable time is often spent in long interviews or in the accumulation of voluminous records in order to increase the amount of information and thereby, it is assumed, the accuracy of the judge's predictions. Much of the time is wasted, for judges soon reach a saturation point in the amount of information they can absorb and use effectively. Meehl (1959), for example, measured the accuracy with which therapists could predict the Q-sort responses of clients after the first, second, fourth, eighth, sixteenth, and twenty-fourth sessions. Peak accuracy was obtained between the second and fourth interview.

We form impressions of people quickly. If these early impressions are formed on the basis of vivid but inconsequential facts, the final impressions are likely to be in error, for later information is made to fit the early impression. How a person looks and acts when we meet him is a prime source of vivid first impressions of dubious validity: lipstick, glasses, dirty fingernails, loud voice, etc. Consequently the recommendation: "Read before you listen; listen before you look." The first part of the recommendation can be put into effect by arranging that judges systematically study the record of a person and make preliminary judgments before seeing him; the second, by having the judges listen to taped interviews before seeing him. The written record, of course, should stress central and significant facts. In any case, however, impressions based on such records are likely to be less vivid and therefore more subject to change than those based on a brief meeting with a person.

Everything that can be done should be done to delay the formation of impressions (Hyink, 1965). We judge too rapidly and forget too slowly. Furthermore, we start at what we consider the heart of the person. Instead, we should begin at the fingertips, making peripheral and less important judgments before the more important ones. The ordering of judgments that the perceiver is asked to make may help in this process. The ranking of traits within the person rather than rating his overall worth also delays impression formation. It might also be useful to train judges to write their impressions and to search solely for facts that are inconsistent with those impressions.

First impressions should be based on the most significant facts about the person. In the selection of people, these are the facts that are known to be related to the kind of success that is being predicted. We have returned once more to the problem of clinical versus actuarial prediction. We repeat, once more, the solution: Use experience tables before personal impressions whenever they are available; use personal impressions to discriminate between persons placed in the same category by the experience tables; and vary from the experience tables with increasing caution as the variation increases.

How Can Training Improve Sensitivity?

Effective training should focus upon the unified person, make it easy for the trainee to change his theories about people, and provide realistic feedback. Like all principles, these are easier to state than to successfully apply.

THE GOALS OF TRAINING

The more meaningful the aims of a program are to the trainees, the more effective the program is likely to be. What is most meaningful to trainees is training that aims to help them solve their problems. For most people most of the time their sensitivity is no problem to them. They are generally satisfied and often complacent about their ability to understand others. Consequently, training programs tend to focus upon situations where sensitivity is a problem to the trainees: executives who do not understand their subordinates, teachers who do not understand their students, parents who do not understand their children, counselors who do not understand their clients, married people who do not understand their partners, members of the Peace Corps who do not understand the people with whom they will be working, etc.

The more realistic the aims, the more effective the training. The aims of a program may be meaningful without being realistic, i.e., they may concern a problem that is serious to the trainees without making any contribution to its solution. The component approach contributes to the realism of aims by breaking down the global problem into more specific ones. One of the major problems of our time, for example, is the improvement of understanding between Negroes and whites. The components of sensitivity enable us to analyze the problem. Whites may rate Negroes at a lower level than Negroes rate themselves and lower than Negroes, in fact, are. Whites may use too wide a spread, i.e., may assume that all Negroes have very low ambition and very high athletic ability, etc. Whites may have low empathic accuracy, i.e., assume less similarity between their own feelings and the feelings of Negroes than actually exists. Whites may lack stereotype accuracy, i.e., may be as ignorant of the customs, culture, and attitudes of Negroes as they are of Russians. They may lack individual accuracy, i.e., they may be unable to differentiate between the feelings and behavior of different Negroes. Negroes may make the same kinds of errors in judging whites.

THE MEASUREMENT OF SENSITIVITY

The more reliable and valid the measures of goal achievement, the better the training is likely to be. The use of such measures during training gives the trainees the knowledge of results that is necessary for effective feedback. Their use after training shows how successful the training has been and how it might be made more successful. The effort to develop and improve measures provides a beneficial circle, for the process is likely to result in revising the goals to make them more meaningful and realistic.

Many of the measures we have discussed provide a framework for measuring Negro understanding of whites. The development of comparable measures of white understanding of Negroes is straightforward but not easy. It would require case studies, photographs, tape-recorded interviews, sound films, opportunities for controlled interactions between Negroes and whites, etc. It would require criterion data gathered from the Negroes to be used in determining the accuracy of predictions. Most difficult of all, it would require incorporating into the measuring instruments the kinds of feelings and behavior that are most often misjudged and are most significant for the general improvement of understanding.

THE SEQUENCE OF TRAINING

What is the best sequence for training? Would it be better to train Negroes and whites to adopt more accurate levels in judging each other or would it be best to improve first their individual and then their level accuracy? Should training in empathic accuracy come before or after training in observational accuracy? Should training in stereotype accuracy come before or after individual accuracy? While there are no confident general answers to such questions, the training time available often provides the practical answers.

Sensitivity training generally tries to do too much in too little time. An hour lecture with the aim of increasing the general sensitivity of whites to Negroes is foredoomed to failure. However, the same hour spent with the more limited goal of improving level accuracy might have a better chance of success. Suppose that a group of whites were given a series of written cases designed to measure only their second-person level accuracy in judging Negroes. The whites, after reading a thumbnail sketch of a Negro, would rate him on traits as they thought the Negro had rated himself. The level errors of the whites would then be calculated and reported back to them. Even in an hour, the process with feedback would be repeated several times. Under these circumstances, there is a realistic chance that the whites would improve their ability to understand the general level at which Negroes rated themselves.

THE REDUCTION OF DEFENSIVENESS

In an Eastern city, instances of racial conflict had occurred. Aroused citizens forced the local police to introduce an eight-hour course dealing with the backgrounds of group antagonism and the policeman's role in preventing and handling outbreaks. The police officers who attended the compulsory course were resentful. A sense of injustice together with their own prejudices created a condition of tension that made instruction almost impossible. Every step in the course of instructions provoked expressions of hostility from the class. Often the class would complain: "Why does everyone pick on the police?" "We've never had any trouble. Why do we need this course?" "The Negro leaders ought to control their people and not set them against the police."

The instructor offered no counterarguments and listened sympathetically to the outbursts. Gradually a change seemed to occur. For one thing, the class became bored with its own complaining. The attitude at the end was: "We've had our say; now we'll listen to what you have to say on the subject." Furthermore, there were so many obvious angry overstatements that a certain sheepishness crept in. Thus, the man who earlier had said, "We've never had any trouble; there is no problem here" eventually told of several incidents of conflict that he had encountered and did not know how to handle. Observers in the course noted that during the last two meetings the lessons commenced to register and sensitivity to increase (Allport, 1945).

The above was only incidentally concerned with the development of sensitivity. Suppose, however, such development had been the primary aim. How could defensiveness have been more speedily reduced? Limiting the goal to the development of sensitivity rather than to the more global purpose of increasing effectiveness in dealing with racial conflicts would probably have helped. Limiting the goal of any particular hour to one aspect of sensitivity may have further reduced it. Within any particular hour tension might have been reduced by starting with written cases and then going on to films. Finally, use of objective criteria which provide a measure of the correctness of judgments would also assist in reducing defensiveness. Psychiatrists and psychologists are well acquainted with the tendency of clients to resist correction of their insensitivities. They vary in their opinions of how to handle the resistance. Those of a psychoanalytic persuasion are more likely than those of a Rogerian or existentialist persuasion to stress the necessity of such correction in spite of the resistance. Sensitivity Training also recognizes the omnipresence of resistance and varies in methods of handling it.

It is likely that much of the resistance can be eliminated by the proper sequencing and structuring of training. The more global the threat the trainee perceives, the greater his resistance is likely to be. It is quite possible, however, for training to begin with situations that involve little or no threat—the judging by the trainees of neutral qualities of persons presented in written cases, for example. As the trainee develops sensitivity in dealing with such unthreatening situations, his capacity for dealing with greater threats should increase.

THE METHOD IN RELATION TO THE GOAL

Many methods are used in sensitivity training: lectures, group discussions, case studies, role playing, T groups, etc. As a principle, no one would question that the best training method in any area is the one that best achieves its goal. In practice, the principle is rarely applied. The method is the thing. One good reason for this thinking is that the aims of a program are often so vague and general that any method might with equal force be defended as a good way of achieving it. The proponents of a new method are also often so enthusiastic and zealous that they wish to blanket the educational system with it. The adherents to an old method, on the other hand, are often so preoccupied with their status in the system and its impact upon the public, accrediting bodies, and other educational organizations that they have little time and no desire to determine its impact on learners. Consideration of a possible program to develop Negro-white sensitivity illustrates a more constructive way of looking at the relationship between goals and methods.

The goals of a training program to increase Negro-white sensitivity, like the goals of all sensitivity training programs, are numerous: to increase level and spread accuracy, to improve the accuracy of empathy, and to improve stereotype and individual accuracy. Written cases are most convenient and may be the best method of increasing level and spread accuracy. Role playing may be the most effective way of increasing empathic accuracy. On the other hand, reading, lectures, and group discussions may be the best way of increasing knowledge of Negro culture (stereotype accuracy). Films may be best for improving observation and the ability to make differentiations between people. There is doubt about the best way of achieving any of these goals; there is no doubt that no one method will be best for all.

It might seem at first glance that training methods that stressed interaction between Negroes and whites would be the most effective method. Yet it is the most time-consuming, the hardest in which to achieve adequate feedback, and the method most likely to arouse disruptive defensiveness. It should, therefore, be limited to those aspects of training where it is necessary. It is most necessary in assuring that what is learned in the classroom is applied to everyday life. As a method, therefore, it seems best confined to the final phases of training. Here one can provide the opportunity to apply what has been learned to life situations which are still under some control.

THE EVALUATION OF TRAINING

The importance of evaluating training has been so incessantly urged upon the reader that, by this time, he may have reached the conclusion that the stress is a somewhat eccentric preoccupation of the author. To combat this impression and to place the problem in the broadest context, we quote from the conclusion of a comprehensive survey of the American educational system by more than twenty-five authors (Miles, 1964, pp. 657–661):

> Educational innovations are almost never evaluated on a systematic basis. Perhaps every educational researcher ought to spend part of his apprenticeship painstakingly illuminating this text on parchment: "The creators of experimental programs . . . have little question about the efficacy of the changes they have introduced. They know that the courses they have developed are the best possible under existing conditions; and in the light of this assumed fact, systematic evaluation seems superfluous." To illustrate: it has been pointed out that less than half of 1 percent of nationally financed experimental programs in a large state were systematically evaluated; that it was never really decided whether a multimillion-dollar program of teacher education was worth the money and effort; and that reading instruction has not really been influenced by research findings for the past thirty years.
>
> In the absence of evaluatory evidence, substitute bases for judgment are used, such as educational ideology, sentiment, or persuasive claims by advocates or salesmen. Most educational decisions appear to be made in an intuitive, prudential manner. Sometimes the merits of an innovation are said to be "self-evident"; for example, the various positions on methods of teaching reading seem to have antedated the advent of research to test them. More frequently, the opinions of users and clients are invoked. Informal student reactions and teacher responses are assessed; perceived student boredom is taken as an indicator of lack of learning, and the extra enthusiasm of teachers and students usually found in a new program (with its additional encouragement, recognition, and shared wishes for goal accomplishment) is mistaken for the success of the innova-

tion. *Yet no hard data have been collected,* and decisions to terminate or continue the innovation are founded on sand.

For these reasons, among others, many apparently promising innovations have been abandoned before they have had a chance to "put down their roots"; and apparently poor (or at least implausible) educational practices have persisted for decades. Faddism, cycles of educational practice, and capricious shifts based on single research studies of doubtful validity are further consequences.

Several reasons for the infrequency of evaluation have been suggested. The primary one is that there are few clear criteria of educational effectiveness. Since *really* confronting this possibility would be too alarming, it is usually suggested that educational objectives are "difficult to evaluate" . . . . Adequate evaluation of an innovation is expensive in the time and money; for example, serious evaluation and revision of a new physics curriculum cost three times that required for the original production. It also requires the use of controlled situations and measurable procedures, maintained for a significant period of time, and careful measurement of effects; these conditions are not usually met in educational practice . . . . education—both its practice and its study—constitutes a kind of anachronistic folk subculture, a pocket of *Gemeinschaftlich* life in the midst of an otherwise rationalized world.

Everything said about education in general goes with at least as much force for sensitivity training.

Chapter Eleven

SENSITIVITY FOR EDUCATION

WE HAVE NOW SAID a good deal about sensitivity and how it might be developed. Thus far, however, we have said little about *why* it should be developed and where it should be developed. It remains, therefore, to examine the place of sensitivity as a goal in the educational system.

The Value of Sensitivity

Increased understanding of others is generally not desired for itself; it is desired for the value of its assumed consequences. Some see it as a way of avoiding threatening interpersonal situations; others, as a way of satisfying personal power needs (Coyle, 1955):

> "Mr. Coyle, I don't want to criticize you as a psychology teacher but you haven't taught this class one thing about how to fool an employer about our qualifications for the job—or how to pad our job resumes—or, for that matter, how to cut angles in general."
>
> Unfortunately, this college student spoke for possibly the majority of the class which I daresay was a relatively representative sample drawn from the New York City population. In one of several efforts to develop value consciousness, if not values themselves, *What Makes Sammy Run* was assigned as supplemental required reading. Subsequent class discussion of this book and polling revealed that a substantial majority considered Sammy "a pretty good guy," "smart," "nobody's fool," "definitely not a sucker." Several volunteered that they had learned a lot from Sammy that "would come in handy." The three or four students who spoke out against Sammy's values or "unifying philosophy of life" were slychologized by their classmates as being "jealous" or as lacking "the courage Sammy had."

Still others see understanding as a tool for teaching and helping others.

Some of the hopes for and fears about sensitivity are dispelled by the difficulties involved in actually increasing sensitivity. Some are dispelled by an examination of the qualities of those who are sensitive and those who are not. However much they may desire understanding in order to manipulate others, authoritarians and power seekers are insensitive. It may even be that increasing their sensitivity would decrease their authoritarianism and power orientation.

What are the *actual* consequences of sensitivity? To answer the question with any confidence we need many studies where measures of sensitivity have been related to measures of assumed consequences. Only three come to mind. In one, army leaders who were accurate in observing and remembering details about the lives of their subordinates were more competent leaders on the battlefield (Showel, 1960).

In the second study, 15 married couples predicted their respective spouses' responses to 55 items on a personality inventory (Dymond, 1954). Their scores were then related to the happiness of the marriage as rated by the marriage partners and by an outside judge. The happily married were more accurate in their predictions than the unhappily married: "Married love is not blind, and ignorance is not connubial bliss. The better each partner understands the other's perceptions of himself and his world, the more satisfactory the relationship."

The third study concerned 100 teachers and their 2,800 pupils in grades 4 to 6 (Gage, 1958). The hypothesis examined in the study: The better a teacher understands her pupils, the more effective she will be. Three measures of understanding were used: (1) the ability of the teachers to predict which of a pair of test questions (there were 60 pairs) would be missed by the largest number of fifth-grade pupils; (2) their ability to predict which pupils would be chosen by each pupil in responding to a sociometric question; and (3) their ability to rank personal problems in the way that different pupils in their classes had ranked them. The effectiveness of a teacher was determined by the answers given by her pupils to three questions: (1) "Does your teacher make sure not to hurt your feelings or make you feel afraid?"; (2) "Does your teacher know which pupils you like best in this class?"; and (3) "Does your teacher explain school work so you can understand it?" Result: *None* of the measures of sensitivity were related to any of the measures of effectiveness. Interpretation:

It may still be true that understanding is necessary for effectiveness; our results may indicate merely that individual differences among teachers in such understanding are not great enough to make any discernible difference in their effectiveness. For example, visual acuity is necessary to teacher effectiveness, but individual differences in such acuity are negligible as sources of variance in teacher effectiveness. Most teachers have enough visual acuity to do their job. In the same way, perhaps, teachers may understand their pupils well enough for the ordinary requirements of classroom activity.

We need more and better studies of the relationships between sensitivity and interpersonal competence. From these too few studies we can only conclude that the relationship between sensitivity and competence depends upon who is understanding what and how success is being measured. Thus, the success of military leaders in action depends upon their knowledge of their subordinates; the happiness of couples depends upon their mutual understanding of each other; but differences in the ways that pupils perceive their teachers is not related to differences in their teachers' understanding of them. Like reading, writing, and arithmetic, sensitivity is irrelevant to some problems, relevant to others. It is highly relevant, most would agree, to the psychotherapist dealing with his clients.

Clinical Training

The importance of sensitivity for the psychotherapist is universally acknowledged, though never more eloquently than by Carl Rogers (1961):

> To understand is enriching in a double way. I find when I am working with clients in distress, that to understand the bizarre world for a psychotic individual, or to understand and sense the attitudes of a person who feels that life is too tragic to bear, or to understand a man who feels that he is a worthless and inferior individual—each of these understandings somehow enriches me. I learn from these experiences in ways that change me, that make me a different and, I think, a more responsive person. Even more important perhaps is the fact that my understanding of these individuals permits them to change. It permits them to accept their own fears and bizarre thoughts and tragic feelings and discouragements, as well as their moments of courage and kindness and love and sensitivity. And it is their experience as well as mine that when someone fully understands those feelings, this enables them to accept those feelings in themselves. Then they find both the feelings and themselves changing. Whether it is understanding a woman who feels that very literally she has a hook in her head by which others lead her about, or understanding a man who feels that no one is as lonely, no one as separated from others as he, I find these understandings to be of value to me. But also, and even more importantly, to be understood has a very positive value to these individuals.

This discussion has not focused upon the processes by which clinicians achieve understanding but upon ways of testing whether the assumed understanding has been achieved. We have assumed that the most incisive and convincing test of understanding, however achieved and of whatever kind, is the ability to predict what a person feels, thinks, and does. We have also assumed that such tests, however imperfect they are now, can be perfected. We do not question the importance of sensitivity for the good therapist; we do question whether it is achieved as often or as deeply as some think.

The uniform failure of clinicians in many studies under many conditions to predict more accurately than nonclinicians raises doubts about their superior sensitivity. Analysis of accuracy on the various components has provided some explanation for the failures of clinicians. People in general make gross errors in both underestimating and overestimating the frequency of desirable behavior in others; clinicians seem prone to underestimate. People in general use too wide a spread in making predictions; clinicians are particularly subject to this error. Empathy is often the result of projection rather than actual understanding; there is no evidence that clinicians are less likely to make such empathic errors. Observation is neglected by people in general; clinicians also have neglected it, for they have conducted no studies of their accuracy in perceiving what persons actually look like and say. Clinicians may have superior stereotype accuracy as far as maladjusted groups are concerned, but there is no reason to believe that their knowledge of other groups is superior. Individual accuracy advances with the increased use of explicit and empirical personality theories. Clinicians appear to make almost as much use of implicit and speculative theories as nonclinicians.

Clinicians play an unusual role with their clients. They have also developed special techniques for playing their role effectively and have had a great deal of supervised practice in playing it. It may well be, therefore, that the role and techniques of the clinician, rather than his sensitivity, are what benefit disturbed individuals. Our limited concern, however, is not with the effectiveness of the clinician in dealing with the client; it is with his sensitivity.

Assuming that sensitivity is related to the clinician's effectiveness, what can be done to improve it? Exhortations are here especially pointless, for those in charge of clinical training are, on the whole, acutely aware of the problems. It is workable solutions that are needed. The most general and serious weakness in clinical training is not the lack of effort to solve the problems; it is the lack of objective tests of the effectiveness of the attempts.

What about the client? The importance of sensitivity for the therapist is widely recognized; its importance for the client has been given only limited recognition. Yet it is often *the* problem for him. The typical client is an excessively low leveler, an extremely narrow or wide spreader, and notoriously inaccurate in his empathies, in his observations of those with whom he must live and work, in his judgments of the groups of did increase in some such quality as psychological-mindedness or empathic drive but not in their actual sensitivity. As in the education of undergraduates and in the clinical training of graduate students, it seems that Sensitivity Training changes processes assumed to be causes of accuracy but does not change accuracy. Whether the goal is to increase the accuracy of the level of empathy, the relationship between assumed and actual similarity, or the accuracy in identifying specific similarities and differences, knowledge of results is essential. Whether the area of training involves increasing the ability to identify and reconcile conflicting facts, conflicting thoughts, or conflicting feelings, feedback is also necessary. All types of training concerned with empathic accuracy give some feedback of some kind; none seems to give enough of the right kind.

No matter what psychology students are told are the aims of the course they are taking, they are given feedback on their knowledge of the vocabulary, facts, and principles of psychology. It is not surprising that they become more psychologically minded, more concerned with the inner states and feelings of people, and readier to use their newly gained knowledge to describe what they think they see. However, the fact that a student becomes more fluent in his use of terms like "repression," "reaction formation," and "projection" does not mean that he has become better able to understand people. To become more accurate, he needs knowledge of the accuracy of his judgment of real persons.

The training of clinicians is much more consciously directed at the goal of empathic accuracy. Here, for example, are the empathic reactions of a therapist with a student client nearing the completion of his professional training. The student is troubled by physical symptoms of weakness, tremulousness, and extreme fatigue and by anxiety over the responsibilities of his approaching professional assignment (Katz, 1963).

THE BEHAVIOR OF THE CLIENT	THE FEELINGS OF THE THERAPIST
Voice is strained, eyes tearful, body agitated. Reports he cannot do his work—instructors make demands impossible for him to meet. Faces calamity. Fears others will discover how weak he is.	Shortly after the opening comments by the client, begins to feel slight depression and mild anxiety.
Talks of nervous breakdown. Pleads for help. Cannot muster any energy for work.	Experiences client's dread with a sense of reality.
Fears to attend his classes. Driven to take up every research suggestion made by instructor no matter how casually made.	Still immersed in the client's mood, senses some of his own feelings about authority figures, the mood of submission as well as actively seeking the approval of a supervisor.

THE BEHAVIOR OF THE CLIENT	THE FEELINGS OF THE THERAPIST
Begins to sob, repeats fear of a break-down. Presents himself as hopeless but still reaches out for help.	Senses a theme of despair which is mixed with a certain lack of conviction about client's claim of utter helplessness.

Our concern is with the accuracy of the therapist's empathy, i.e., is he feeling a "slight depression and mild anxiety" because he is realistically identifying with the client or because he is projecting some of his own irrelevant feelings into the situation? One way of answering the question is for the therapist to communicate to the client what he assumes the client is feeling. The client can then correct or amplify the therapist's impressions. Another way is to have the expert supervisor listen to the taped interview and to correct what he judges to be empathic errors. While such knowledge of results is more adequate than in a formal course, it may not be adequate enough to increase accuracy. It may have its most significant effect in the tendency to identify with his supervisor rather than his client, i.e., to attend to the inner feelings of the client in the way that he thinks his supervisor is doing.

A similar feedback technique is utilized in Sensitivity Training. A rule sometimes made by the trainees is that before anyone can speak his ideas he must first repeat what was said and felt by the person who had spoken before him. Comments after using the technique are commonly like "For the first time in my life I find that I am really listening to what others say." The pattern has these advantages over the client-to-the-therapist or supervisor-to-trainee type of feedback: (1) the relationships involved are not those of superior-inferior type; (2) the perceiver obtains feedback from the rest of the group as well as from the person perceived; and (3) each trainee has a chance to be the perceiver, the person being perceived, and the observer of perceiver-person interactions.

The feedback in clinical training and Sensitivity Training often stresses what the trainee should feel and do rather than what the person actually felt and did. For example, Porter (1950, pp. 12–13) uses the following kinds of exercises to guide trainees in discussions of the attitudes they should take toward their clients:

> PATIENT: I have the queerest feeling. Whenever anything good happens to me—I just can't believe it. I act as though it never happened. And it worries me. I wanted a date with Myrtle—and I stood around for weeks before I got up enough courage to ask her for a date and she said "yes"—and I couldn't believe it. I couldn't believe it. I couldn't believe it so much that I didn't keep the date!

THERAPIST: (Supportive): Well, I'm not sure that you should be so worried about it. It doesn't mean anything in itself, really. (accepting): It just doesn't seem real when something good happens. (probing): I am wondering whether or not these feelings of unreality are associated with any particular area of your life. Would you like to tell me more about what you mean when you said, "Whenever anything good happens to me"?

(Interpretive): You have probably denied to yourself so strongly that anything good could happen to you that when it does it seems unreal.

(Evaluative): You've got to grow up, fellow, and get a little more realistic idea about women.

Having trainees discuss responses they would make in situations like the above may be helpful in developing therapists. Such discussions, however, do not give the trainee any knowledge of how well he understands this particular person. If the same format were reversed, it would. Suppose, for example, that trainees were first presented with an actual interaction sequence between therapist and client. They could then be given five alternative responses of the client to the last remark of the therapist, one of which the client actually made. If the trainee makes the correct choice in a series of such sequences, he would be given some objective knowledge of his understanding of the person. A casual selection of such sequences and alternatives might result in all the trainees' failing to choose the correct response. However, this problem would be readily solved by trying out the sequences and eliminating or revising those that were inadequate.

A more serious problem is that both trainer and trainee resist the win-lose nature of such situations. Such resistance might be reduced by selecting and testing the interaction samples so that trainees were exposed to them according to their difficulty. Participants are often anxious and defensive in realistic social interactions. To meet this difficulty, training could begin with tape-recorded cases and end with actual interactions where the client is asked to write down the last response. The resistance that is universally found in sensitivity training programs might well be reduced by the use of these procedures. In any case, the method would lead to better controlled and more frequent and exact feedback to the trainees.

ROLE PLAYING

Feedback, alone, may not be enough. A trainee may not improve his understanding of a person even though he is given specific knowledge of his ignorance. Practice in playing the role of the person might be of considerable help in overcoming such statements. In role playing the perceiver pretends he is the person and acts out situations as he thinks the person would behave in them. The role player would, of course, have some additional information about what the person is like from what he says. Bronfenbrenner and Newcomb (1948) have given a helpful analysis of some of the verbal and nonverbal aspects of the person which the role player should be aware of and attempt to incorporate into his portrayal of the person:

> *Verbal content:* slips of the tongue, omissions and blocks, sudden shifts in train of thought, frequent repetitions, etc.
> *Voice characteristics:* speed, rhythm, pitch, intensity, dropping or raising of voice, change in speed, etc.
> *Bodily movements and postural adjustments:* relaxed, jerky, abortive, controlled, immobilized, etc.

The comments of both the trainer and other trainees may be of help in developing the adequacy of the role player's performance.

Role playing has been used for many purposes. The critical differences between role playing for the purpose of developing accuracy and for other purposes are (1) the participants play the roles of actual persons with known responses instead of fictional persons with unknown responses; (2) the stress is upon the exact imitation of another person rather than upon a free interpretation that encourages the role player to project his own personality into the situation; and (3) an exclusive concern with understanding the other person rather than with relating to the person in an effective way. The effectiveness of role playing for increasing empathic accuracy for a particular person could be determined by comparing the accuracy of predictions for the person before and after his role was played. Similarly, the general effectiveness of role playing could be assessed by using as a before-and-after criterion accuracy in predicting the responses of persons whose role was *not* played.

but that they fail to measure or control the results. There are literally hundreds of general questions concerning college teaching that need to be answered, and every teacher finds innumerable questions of his own as he proceeds with his work from day to day. If each college teacher would carry on one sound experiment in one course once every five years there would soon be a large body of accurate knowledge about effective methods and desirable subject matter. . . . There are plenty of problems for all tastes.

With the help of colleagues and students, the recommended pace has been maintained.

In the first study, we were surprised to find that participants in class discussions, even when discussion was strongly encouraged, were nonconformists. They were also better informed than nonparticipants about psychology at the beginning of the course, but did not seem to benefit from their participation (Smith and Dunbar, 1951). In a second study, we were surprised to find that students did not particularly care for or benefit from classes run along democratic lines (Johnson and Smith, 1953). In a third study, we were surprised to find that whether students had favorable or unfavorable attitudes toward their psychology teacher and class activities had no relation to how much they learned during the course. Their attitudes toward the university they were attending and toward the importance of being students, however, did (Armour, 1954). In a fourth study, we were surprised to find that those who were most enthusiastic about their participation in small discussion teams learned the least from them (Smith, 1955).

A recent survey of research on teaching at the college and university level had this to say (McKeachie, 1963, p. 1125):

> The major problem in experimental comparison of teaching methods is the criterion problem . . . even a careful definition of desirable outcomes does not solve the criterion problem. In many cases, laudable attempts to measure attitudinal or affective outcomes have led to the conclusion that neither of two teaching methods was superior in achieving this or that goal, when there is no evidence that *any* teaching could affect achievement of the goal as measured by the tests used. At the very least, the experimenter needs to report some index of reliability; even better would be some evidence that the measure is at least sufficiently sensitive to reveal significant changes which occur between the beginning to the end of the semester. If there is no change on a variable over a semester, it is unlikely that two teaching methods will differ in the amount of change they yield.

The importance of the criterion and the difficulties in absorbing its importance cannot be overemphasized. One instructor of graduate students included the following question on all of his examinations:

The most universal, important, and difficult problem in conducting research in any field of psychology involves the: (1) criterion, (2) criterion, (3) criterion; (4) criterion, (5) criterion.

As our studies progressed, we became increasingly concerned with the criterion problem. On the rare occasions when an evaluation of teaching is attempted, the most common criterion is student satisfaction. Instructors like students to leave their classes with warm feelings about their experience. Student satisfaction, however, is closely related to whether the teacher does what the students expect him to do. Marked deviations from the conventional role are almost inevitably rated lower than more conventional teaching behavior. The relationship between satisfaction and achievement is more puzzling. The more satisfied a student was with our unconventional procedures, the *less* he learned about the vocabulary, facts, and principles of psychology (a correlation of —.29 in the Johnson and Smith study).

A clue to the puzzle was provided by one of the results of the study of democratic leadership. Two of the criteria used in the study were scores on a class evaluation scale and gains from the beginning to the end of the course on a long objective examination. A test of sensitivity to psychological problems was also taken by all students in the democratic and conventional classrooms at the end of the course. Scores on it were used as a third criterion in the evaluation of the success of training. The sensitivity test consisted of the following two problems:

1. The President of the Sophomore Class appoints a committee of seven students to make plans for a class dance. When the committee meets, practically all the talking is done by two people. *List* as many psychological *questions* as you can think of that are suggested by this statement.

2. Two married women of about thirty decide to learn to type, each practicing alone in her spare time. After a month of such practice one types fast and inaccurately, the other slowly and accurately. *List* as many psychological *questions* as you can think of that are suggested by this statement.

In scoring the test, each test paper of a student from a democratic class was paired with the test paper of the student from the lecture class with whom he had been matched at the beginning of the course on the basis of democratic attitudes and achievement. The 31 pairs were randomized and given to an advanced graduate student who had done previous research on complex judgments with the following instructions: "Read these by pairs and check the one of each pair that shows the most psychological curiosity and insight. Don't be influenced by vague generalities. Look for specific plausible hypotheses." Result: 23 out of 31 judgments favored students from the democratic class. Conclusion: "The democratic procedures did increase sensitivity to psychological problems."

Hundreds of thousands of students have now graduated from colleges and universities with majors in psychology. What impact has their training had? It has influenced some to go to graduate school and to become psychologists. All have a better understanding of what psychology is and know more about what psychologists do, and most have a more favorable attitude toward psychology and psychologists. But Carl Rogers (1961) has said: "I realize increasingly that I am only interested in learnings which significantly influence behavior." What significant influence has the teaching of psychology had upon those taught? No one has more than a shred of evidence to support his answer. What learning could have a significant influence? I have become increasingly convinced that the development of sensitivity can be an important, realistic, and measurable goal of instruction in psychology at the undergraduate level. Where sensitivity is viewed as the primary goal, student satisfaction and mastery of psychological knowledge can be at least as great as where satisfaction and the mastery of inert ideas are viewed as the primary goals.

Sensitivity as an Educational Goal

A half century ago William James told college students: "The best claim that a college education can possibly make on your respect, the best thing it can aspire to accomplish for you, is this: that it should help you to know a good man when you see him." Members of every discipline have aspirations to contribute to this end: the anthropologist, to teach the differences between men of different cultures; the sociologist, the differences between men from different social backgrounds; the economist, the differences between men playing varying roles in the economy; and the political scientist, the differences between men identified with varying political institutions. The historian uses men of the past to describe the nature of man, and the English instructor uses the insights of the Shakespeares to explain it. The natural scientists, by their teaching and their model, demonstrate the differences between poor and good physicists, chemists, mathematicians, and scientists in general. Culture is a great storehouse filled with knowledge about men available for use in building an understanding of men.

How can these possibilities for improving sensitivity be realized? Whether a man comes from modern slums or Shakespeare's England, the errors we may make in judging him are the same. We may err because of too low or too high a level; because of too narrow or too wide a spread; because of too little or too much empathy; because of poor observation; because of ignorance of the similarities and differences between the group we are judging and the group to which we belong; and because of our inability to differentiate between individuals in the same group. The goals, therefore, are the same: to develop level and spread accuracy, empathic and observational accuracy, stereotype and individual accuracy. How, for example, do Nigerians see themselves? In what ways are they similar and in what ways are they different from us? How do they differ among themselves? Again: How do poets rate themselves? In what ways are they similar or different from us? How do they differ among themselves? These are the kinds of questions that students may learn to answer better as a result of education in anthropology or poetry.

All instructors might agree that the development of sensitivity is a worthy goal; none but the most optimistic feel that we are making much progress in achieving it. Teaching is content-centered rather than process-centered—instructors are much concerned with how the content is to be divided and presented; little concerned with the process by which students master and use it. Teaching is teacher-centered rather than student-centered—instructors are much concerned with what they say and do, little concerned with what students think and do about what is said and done.

The acceptance of sensitivity as a goal would not imply the elimination of traditional content; it would imply viewing the content in relation to its contribution to sensitivity. The mastery of content would be a means toward the development of sensitivity. In a similar way, the development of critical thinking as a goal could be attacked not in the abstract but in relation to thinking about people. The development of tolerance as a goal is also intimately related to increasing sensitivity.

The acceptance of sensitivity would not imply the elimination of any usual methods of instruction: lectures, small group discussions, independent study, films, programmed learning, etc. It would mean selecting the methods best suited to enhance the achievement of sensitivity. In fact, acceptance of sensitivity as a goal would not imply *any* drastic change, for real progress can only come by the slow molding of content to fit the goal. It requires assembling, and in some cases finding, knowledge about a group and the individuals in it. It requires translating this knowledge into forms suitable for effective presentation to students. Above all, it requires testing the effectiveness of these varying methods. The small unit of instruction, not the general course of instruction, is the most natural focus for these ends. The development of sensitivity requires not the solution of one big problem but the solution of many interrelated small ones.

BIBLIOGRAPHY

Abeles, N. The meaning and development of sensitivity in the training of therapists. Paper read at the International Congress of Psychology, Washington, D.C., 1963.

Albrecht, P. A., Glasser, E. M., and Marks, J. Validation of a multiple-assessment procedure for managerial personnel. *J. appl. Psychol.*, 1964, **48**, 351–360.

Allport, G. W. *Personality.* Boston: Houghton Mifflin, 1937.

Allport, G. W. Catharsis and the reduction of prejudice. *J. soc. Issues*, 1945, **1**, 3–10.

Allport, G. W. The general and the unique in psychological science. *J. Pers.*, 1962, **30**, 405–422.

Allport, G. W., and Kramer, B. M. Some roots of prejudice. *J. Psychiat.*, 1946, **22**, 9–39.

Armour, J. B. Student attitudes in relation to classroom achievement. Unpublished master's thesis, Michigan State Univer., 1954.

Asch, S. E. Forming impressions of personality. *J. abnorm. soc. Psychol.*, 1946, **41**, 258–290.

Bakan, D. Clinical psychology and logic. *Amer. Psychologist*, 1956, **11**, 655–662.

Bakke, E. W. Labor and management look ahead. American Management Association, Personnel Series, 1946, No. 98, 9–25.

Beier, E. G., and Stumpf, J. Cues influencing judgment of personality characteristics. *J. consult. Psychol.*, 1959, **23**, 218–225.

Bieri, J. Changes in interpersonal perceptions following social interactions. *J. abnorm. soc. Psychol.*, 1953, **48**, 61–66.

Bingham, W. V. Psychology as a science, as a technology, and as a profession. *Amer. Psychologist*, 1953, **8**, 115–118.

Blackman, N., Smith, K., Brokman, R., and Stern, J. The development of empathy in male schizophrenics. *Psychiat. Quart.*, 1958, **32**, 546–553.

Bloom, B. S. Thought processes in lectures and discussions. *J. gen. Educ.*, 1953, **7**, 160–169.

Boice, R. A programmed learning approach to training in group sensitivity. Unpublished article, 1965.

Bronfenbrenner, U., Harding, J., and Gallwey, Mary. The measurement of skill in social perception. In D. C. McClelland (Ed.), *Talent and society.* New York: Van Nostrand, 1958. Pp. 29–108.

Bronfenbrenner, U., and Newcomb, T. M. Improvisations: An application of psychodrama in personality diagnosis. *Sociatry,* 1948, **1,** 367–382.

Brown, C. T. Introductory study of breathing as index of listening. *Speech Monogr.,* 1962, **29,** 79–83.

Bruner, J. S., and Postman, L. J. On the perception of incongruity: A paradigm. *J. Pers.,* 1949, **18,** 206–223.

Bruner, J. S., Postmann, L. J., and Rodrigues, J. Expectations and the perception of color. *Amer. J. Psychol.,* 1951, **64,** 216–227.

Bruni, E. A film test of accuracy in observing people and its correlates. Unpublished master's thesis, Michigan State Univer., 1963.

Burks, Barbara S., and Roe, A. Studies of identical twins reared apart. *Psychol. Monogr.,* 1949, **63,** No. 5 (Whole No. 300).

Burnstein, E., Stotland, E., and Zander, A. Similarity to a model and self-evaluation. *J. abnorm. soc. Psychol.,* 1962, **62,** 257–264.

Burrow, T. *The social basis of consciousness.* New York: Harcourt, Brace, 1927.

Campbell, D. T. An error in some demonstrations of the superior social perceptiveness of leaders. *J. abnorm. soc. Psychol.,* 1955, **51,** 694–695.

Carson, R. C., and Heine, R. W. Similarity and success in therapeutic dyads. *J. consult. Psychol.,* 1962, **26,** 38–43.

Cattell, R. B. Validation and intensification of the 16 personality factor questionnaire, *J. clin. Psychol.,* 1956, **12,** 205–214.

Chance, June E., and Meaders, W. Needs and interpersonal perception. *J. Pers.,* 1960, **28,** 200–210.

Chelsea, Linda. A study of implicit personality theories. Unpublished manuscripts, 1965.

Chodorkoff, B. Self-perception, perceptual defense, and adjustment. *J. abnorm. soc. Psychol.,* 1954, **49,** 508–512.

Cline, V. B. Ability to judge personality assessed with a stress interview and sound film technique. *J. abnorm. soc. Psychol.,* 1955, **50,** 183–187.

Cline, V. B., and Richards, J. M. Variables related to accuracy in interpersonal perception. Second Annual Report, Office of Naval Research, Contract NE 171–146, Univer. of Utah, 1959.

Cline, V. B., and Richards, J. M. Accuracy of interpersonal perception: A general trait? *J. abnorm. soc. Psychol.,* 1960, **60,** 1–7.

Cline, V. B., and Richards, J. M. Components of accuracy of interpersonal perception scores and the clinical and statistical prediction controversy. *Psychol. Rec.,* 1962, **12,** (4), 373–379.

Close, Mary. A test of stereotype accuracy in judging differences in marital couples. Unpublished manuscript, 1963.

Cobb, S. Personality as affected by lesions of the brain. In J. McV. Hunt (Ed.), *Personality and the behavior disorders.* New York: Ronald, 1944. Pp. 550–581.

Cofer, C. N, and Dunn, J. T. Personality ratings as influenced by verbal stimuli. *J. Pers.,* 1952, **21,** 223–227.

Cole, Luella. *The background of college teaching.* New York: Farrar and Rinehart, 1940.

Covner, B. Studies in phonographic recording of verbal material. *J. consult. Psychol.,* 1942, **6,** 105–113.

Coyle, E. Psychology and slycology. *Amer. Psychologist,* 1955, **10**, 87.

Cronbach, L. J. Processes affecting scores on "understanding of others" and "assumed similarity." *Psychol. Bull.,* 1955, **52**, 177–193.

Crow, W. J. The effect of training upon accuracy and variability in interpersonal perception. *J. abnorm. soc. Psychol.,* 1957, **55**, 355–359.

Crow, W. J., and Farson, R. E. The effect of training upon accuracy and variability in judging others, California: Western Behavioral Sciences Institute, Report No. 9, 1961.

Crow, W. J., and Hammond, K. R. The generality of accuracy and response sets in interpersonal perception. *J. abnorm. soc. Psychol.,* 1957, **54**, 384–390.

Dailey, C. A. The effects of premature conclusions upon the acquisition of understanding a person. *J. Psychol.,* 1952, **33**, 133–152.

Daniels, H., and Otis, J. A method of analyzing employment interviews. *Personnel Psychol.,* 1950, **3**, 425–444.

Dore, R. The development and validation of forced-choice scales measuring attitudes toward leadership methods. Unpublished master's thesis, Michigan State Univer., 1960.

Dymond, Rosalind F. A scale for measurement of emphatic ability. *J. consult. Psychol.,* 1949, **13**, 127–133.

Dymond, Rosalind F. Interpersonal perception and marital happiness. *Canad. J. Psychol.,* 1954, **8**, 164–171.

Engel, E. Binocular methods in psychological research. In F. P. Kilpatrick (Ed.), *Explorations in transactional psychology.* New York: New York University Press, 1961. Pp. 290–305.

Estes, S. G. Judging personality from expressive behavior. *J. abnorm. soc. Psychol.,* 1938, **33**, 217–236.

Fenichel, O. *The psychoanalytic theory of neurosis.* New York: Norton, 1945.

Fey, W. F. Acceptance by others and its relation to acceptance of self and others: A reevaluation. *J. abnorm. soc. Psychol.,* 1955, **50**, 274–276.

Fiedler, F. E. *Leader attitudes and group effectiveness.* Urbana: Univer. of Illinois Press, 1958.

Fiedler, F. E. Leadership and leadership effectiveness traits: a reconceptualization of the leadership trait problem. In L. Petrullo and B. M. Bass (Eds.), *Leadership and interpersonal behavior.* New York: Holt, 1961.

Flanagan, J. C., and Burns, R. K. The employee performance record. In T. L. Whisler and Shirley F. Harper (Eds.), *Performance Appraisal.* New York: Holt, 1962. Pp. 262–271.

Fleishman, E. A., Harris, E. E., and Burtt, H. E. Leadership and supervision in industry; an evaluation of a supervisory training program. *Bur, Educ. Res. Monogr.,* 1955, No. 33. Columbus, Ohio: Ohio State University Press.

Fox, R. E., and Goldin, P. C. The empathic process in psychotherapy: a survey of theory and research. *J. nerv. & ment. Dis.,* 1964, **138**, 323–331.

Frenkel-Brunswik, Else. Intolerance of ambiguity as an emotional and perceptual-personality variable. *J. Pers.,* 1949, **18**, 108–143.

Fromm, E. Man is not a thing. *Saturday Review,* March 16, 1957. Pp. 9–11.

Gage, N. L. Explorations in teachers' perceptions of pupils. *J. Teacher Educ.,* 1958, **9**, 97–101.

Gage, N. L., Leavitt, G. S., and Stone, G. C. The intermediary key in the analysis of interpersonal perception. *Psychol. Bull.,* 1956, **53,** 258–266.

Gibb, J. R. Effects of role playing upon (a) role flexibility and upon (b) ability to conceptualize a new role. *Amer. Psychologist,* 1952, **7,** 310.

Giedt, F. H. Comparison of visual content and auditory cues in interviewing. *J. consult. Psychol.,* 1955, **19,** 407–416.

Giedt, F. H. Cues associated with accurate and inaccurate interview impressions. *Psychiatry,* 1958, **21,** 405–409.

Goldberg, L. R. Grades as motivants. *Psychol. in Sch.,* 1965, **2,** 17–24

Golden, M. Some effects of combining psychological tests on clinical inferences. *J. consult. Psychol.,* 1964, **28,** 440–446.

Gollin, E. Forming impressions of personality. *J. Pers.,* 1954, **23,** 65–76.

Gollin, E. S. Organizational characteristics of social judgment: A developmental investigation. *J. Pers.,* 1958, **26,** 139–154.

Gollin, E. S. Cognitive dispositions and the formation of impressions of personality. In J. B. Peatman and E. L. Hartman (Eds.), *Festschrift for Gardner Murphy.* New York: Harper, 1960, 157–170.

Gollin, E. S., and Rosenberg, C. Concept formation and impressions of personality. *J. abnorm. soc. Psychol.,* 1956, **52,** 39–42.

Gottlieb, B., and Kerr, W. A. An experiment in industrial harmony. *Personnel Psychol.,* 1950, **3,** 445–453.

Gough, H. G. *A preliminary guide for the use and interpretation of the California psychological inventory.* Berkeley: Univer. of California Institute for Personality Assessment Research (manual), 1954.

Gross, Cecily. Intrajudge consistency in ratings of heterogeneous persons. *J. abnorm. soc. Psychol.,* 1961, **62,** 606–610.

Grossman, B. A. The measurement and determinants of interpersonal sensitivity. Unpublished master's thesis, Michigan State Univer., 1963.

Guilford, J. P. An experiment in learning to read facial expression. *J. abnorm. soc. Psychol.,* 1929, **24,** 191–202.

Haire, M. Role-perceptions in labor-management relations: An experimental approach. *Industr. Labor Relat. Rev.,* 1955, **8,** 204–216.

Hariton, T. Conditions in influencing the effects of training. Unpublished doctoral dissertation, Univer. of Michigan, 1951.

Harris, W. The relation of observational to inferential accuracy in judging people. Unpublished master's thesis, Michigan State Univer., 1962.

Hartlage, L. C. Differences in the listening comprehension of the blind and sighted. *Int. J. for the Educ. of the Blind,* 1963, **13,** 1–6.

Hershey, G. L. College grades in relation to inventory measures of personality. Unpublished master's thesis, Michigan State Univer., 1958.

Hershey, G. L. The relative effectiveness of discussion groups with dominant and submissive members. Unpublished research report, 1960.

Hughes, J. L., and McNamara, W. J. A comparative study of programmed and conventional instruction in industry. *J. appl. Psychol.,* 1961, **45,** 225–231.

Hunt, W. A., Schwartz, M. L., and Walker, R. E. The correctness of diagnostic judgment as a function of diagnostic bias and population base rate. *J. clin. Psychol.,* 1964, **20,** 143–146.

Hyink, P. The adverse effects of repeated evaluations upon subsequent understanding. Unpublished master's thesis, Michigan State Univer., 1965.

Ittelson, W. H., and Cantril, H. *Perception: A transactional approach.* New York: Doubleday, 1954.

Johnson, D. M., and Smith, H. C. Democratic leadership in the college classroom. *Psychol. Monogr.* 1953, **67**, No. 11 (Whole No. 361).

Johnson, R. L. Correlates of a test of group sensitivity. Unpublished master's thesis, Michigan State Univer., 1963.

Johnson, W. B., and Terman, L. M. Personality characteristics of happily married, unhappily married and divorced persons. *Charact. & Pers.* 1935, **3**, 290–311.

Jones, E. E. Authoritarianism as a determinant of first impression formation. *J. Pers.*, 1954, **23**, 107–127.

Jones, E. E., and deCharms, R. Changes in social perception as a function of the personal relevence of behavior. *Sociometry*, 1957, **20**, 75–85.

Jones, E. E., and Thibaut, J. W. Interaction goals as bases of inference in interpersonal perception. In R. Tagiuri and L. Petrullo (Eds.), *Person perception and interpersonal behavior.* Stanford: Stanford Univer. Press, 1958. Pp. 151–178.

Kaess, W. A., and Witryol, S. L. Memory for names and faces: A characteristic of social intelligence? *J. appl. Psychol.*, 1955, **39**, 457–462.

Kahn, M. W., and Santostefano, S. The case of clinical psychology: a search for identity. *Amer. Psychologist*, 1962, **17**, 185–189.

Katz, R. L. *Empathy.* New York: Free Press of Glencoe, 1963.

Kelley, H. H. Warm-cold variable in first impressions. *J. Pers.*, 1950, **18**, 431–439.

Kellogg, M. S. New angles in appraisal. In T. L. Whisler and Shirley F. Harper (Eds.), *Performance Appraisal.* New York: Holt, 1962. Pp. 88–95.

Kelly, E. L. Consistency of the adult personality. *Amer. Psychologist*, 1955, **10**, 659–681.

Kelly, E. L., and Fiske, D. W. The prediction of performance in clinical psychology. Ann Arbor: Univer. of Michigan Press, 1951.

Kepes, S. Y. Experimental evaluations of sensitivity training. Unpublished doctoral dissertation, Michigan State Univer., 1965.

King, G. E., Ehrmann, J. C., and Johnson, D. M. Experimental analysis of the reliability of observations of social behavior, *J. soc. Psychol.*, 1952, **35**, 151–160.

Lamming, G. The pleasures of exile. *The Tamarack Review,* 1960, **14**, 32–56.

Lawson, C. *Brain mechanisms and human learning.* New York: Houghton Mifflin, 1966.

Leventhal, H. Cognitive processes and interpersonal predictions. *J. abnorm. soc. Psychol.*, 1957, **55**, 176–180.

Levinger, G. Social desirability in the ratings of involved and neutral judges. *J. consult Psychol.*, 1961, **25**, 554.

Levy, D. M. Anti-Nazis: Criteria of differentation. *Psychiatry*, 1948, **11**, 125–167.

Linden, J. The self-centered orientation in interpersonal relationships. Unpublished master's thesis, Michigan State Univer., 1965.

Lindgren, H. C., and Robinson, Jacqueline. An evaluation of Dymond's test of insight and empathy. *J. consult. Psychol.,* 1953, **17**, 172–176.

Lindzey, G., and Rogolsky, S. J. Prejudice and identification of minority group membership. *J. abnorm. soc. Psychol.,* 1950, **45**, 37–53.

Livensparger, D. *Empathy inventory.* Unpublished manuscript, 1965.

Luft, J. Implicit hypotheses and clinical predictions. *J. abnorm. soc. Psychol.,* 1950, **45**, 756–759.

Lundy, R. M. Assimilative projection and accuracy of prediction in interpersonal perceptions. *J. abnorm. soc. Psychol.,* 1956, **52**, 33–38.

McClelland, D. C., and Atkinson, J. W. The projective expression of needs. *J. Psychol.,* 1948, **25**, 205–222.

McClelland, W. A preliminary test of role-playing ability. *J. consult. Psychol.,* 1951, **15**, 102–108.

McGregor, D. *The human side of enterprise.* New York: McGraw-Hill, 1960.

McKeachie, W. J. Lipstick as a determiner of first impressions of personality. *J. soc. Psychol.,* 1952, **36**, 241–244.

McKeachie, W. J. (1963). Research on teaching at the college and university level. In N. L. Gage (ed.), *Handbook of research on teaching.* Chicago: Rand McNally, 1963. Pp. 1118–1172.

MacLeod, R. B. The teaching of psychology and the psychology we teach. *Amer. Psychologist,* 1965, **20**, 344–352.

Mahoney, S. C. The literature empathy test: Development of a procedure for differentiating between "good empathizers" and "poor empathizers." *Dissert. Abstr.* 1960, **21**, 674.

Maier, N. R. F., Hoffman, L. R., and Lansky, L. Human relations training as manifested in an interview situation. *Personnel Psychol.,* 1960, **13**, 11–30.

Martin, H. W. Effects of practice on judging various traits of individuals. *Psychol. Bull.,* 1938, **35**, 690.

Masling, J. M. The effects of warm and cold interaction on the interpretation of a projective protocol. *J. proj. Tech.,* 1957, **21**, 377–383.

Maslow, A. H., and Mittelman, B. *Principles of abnormal psychology.* New York: Harper, 1951.

Maugham, W. S. *The summing up.* New York: Doubleday, 1938.

Mead, G. H. *Mind, self, and society.* Chicago: Univer. of Chicago Press, 1934.

Meehl, P. E. *Clinical versus statistical prediction.* Minneapolis: Univer. of Minnesota Press, 1954.

Meehl, P. E. When shall we use our heads instead of the formula? *J. consult. Psychol.,* 1957, **4**, 268–273.

Meehl, P. E. A comparison of clinicians with five statistical methods of identifying psychotic MMPI profiles. *J. counsel. Psychol.,* 1959, **6**, 102–109. (a)

Meehl, P. E. Some ruminations on the validation of clinical procedures. *Canad. J. Psychol.,* 1959, **13**, 102–108. (b)

Miles, M. B. Human relations training: Processes and outcomes, *J. counsel. Psychol.,* 1960, **7**, 301–306.

Miles, M. B. *Innovation in education.* New York: Bureau of Publishers, Teachers College, Columbia Univer., 1964.

Mullin, J. Reliability and validity of a projective film test of empathy. Unpublished master's thesis, Michigan State Univer., 1962.

Newbigging, P. L. The relationship between rate of reversal of figures of reversible perspective and empathy. *Canad. J. Psychol.*, 1953, 7, 172–176.

Newcomb, T. M. The prediction of interpersonal attraction. *Amer. Psychologist*, 1956, 11, 575–586.

Newcomb, T. M. Stabilities underlying changes in interpersonal attraction. *J. abnorm. soc. Psychol.*, 1963, 66, 376–386.

Nichols, R. G., and Stevens, L. A. *Are you listening?* New York: McGraw-Hill, 1957.

Oakes, R. H., and Corsini, R. J. Social perceptions of one other self. *J. soc. Psychol.*, 1961, 53, 235–242.

Olmsted, D. W. The accuracy of the impressions of survey interviewers. *Publ. Opin. Quart.*, 1962, 25, 635–647.

Oskamp, S. W. The relation of clinical experience and training methods to several criteria of clinical prediction. *Psychol. Monogr.*, 1962, 76, No. 28 (Whole No. 547).

Oskamp, S. W. Overconfidence in case-study judgments. *J. consult. Psychol.*, 1965, 29, 261–265.

Parker, J. W., Taylor, E. K., Barrett, R. S., and Martens, L. Rating scale content. *Personnel Psychol.*, 1960, 13, 11–30.

Pemberton, Carol L. The closure factors related to temperament. *J. Pers.*, 1952, 21, 159–175.

Perry, R. B. *The thought and character of William James.* Boston: Little, Brown, 1935.

Plath, D. W. Physique and personality differences between male college cigarette smokers and non-smokers. Unpublished maser's thesis, Michigan State Univer., 1959.

Porter, E. H. *An introduction to therapeutic counseling.* Boston: Houghton Mifflin, 1950.

Pressey, S. L. Teaching machines (and learning theory). *J. appl. Psychol.*, 1963, 47, 1–7.

Proust, M. *Swann's way.* London: Chatto and Windus, 1922.

Reade, W. H. V. *The problem of inference.* Oxford: Clarendon, 1938.

Rodgers, D. A. Relationship between real similarity and assumed similarity with favorability controlled. *J. abnorm. soc. Psychol.*, 1959, 59, 431–433.

Rogers, C. R. *Becoming a person.* Boston: Houghton Mifflin, 1961.

Rokeach, M. *The open and closed mind.* New York: Basic Books, 1960.

Sarbin, T. R., Taft, R., and Bailey, D. E. *Clinical inference and cognitive theory.* New York: Holt, 1960.

Scott, J. P. The place of observation in biological and psychological science. *Amer. Psychologist*, 1955, 10, 61–64.

Secord, P. F. Facial features and inference processes in interpersonal perception. In R. Tagiuri and L. Petrullo (Eds.), *Person perception and interpersonal behavior.* Stanford: Stanford Univer. Press, 1958.

Secord, P. F. Stereotyping and favorableness in the perception of Negro faces. *J. abnorm. soc. Psychol.*, 1959, 59, 309–314.

Secord, P. F., and Berscheid, Ellen. Stereotyping and the generality of implicit personality theory. *J. Pers.*, 1963, **31**, 65–78.

Shapiro, M. I. Teaching observational skills in child psychiatry to mental students. *Amer. J. Orthopsychiat.*, 1964, **34**, 563–568.

Showel, M. Interpersonal knowledge and rated leader potential. *J. abnorm. soc. Psychol.*, 1960, **61**, 87–92.

Siipola, E. M. A group study of some effects of preparatory set. *Psychol. Monogr.*, 1935, **46** (Whole No. 210).

Silkiner, D. S. A cross-cultural study of the measurement, determinants, and effects of stereotype accuracy. Unpublished master's thesis, Michigan State Univer., 1962.

Smith, H. C. Team work in the college class. *J. educ. Psychol.*, 1955, **46**, 274–286.

Smith, H. C. *Personality adjustment.* New York: McGraw-Hill, 1961.

Smith, H. C., and Dunbar, D. S. The personality and achievement of the classroom participant. *J. educ. Psychol.*, 1951, **42**, 65–84.

Soskin, W. F. Bias in postdiction and projective tests. *J. abnorm. soc. Psychol.*, 1954, **49**, 69–74.

Soskin, W. F. Influence of four types of data on diagnostic conceptualization in psychological testing. *J. abnorm. soc. Psychol.*, 1959, **58**, 69–78.

Stagner, R. Dual allegiance as a problem in modern society. *Personnel Psychol.*, 1954, **7**, 41–47.

Stelmachers, Z. T., and McHugh, R. B. Contribution of stereotyped and individualized information to predictive accuracy. *J. consult. Psychol.*, 1964, **28**, 234–242.

Stock, Dorothy. A survey of research on T groups. In L. P. Bradford, J. R. Gibb, and K. D. Benne (Eds.), *T-group theory and laboratory method.* New York: John Wiley, 1964, 395–411.

Stone, G. C., Leavitt, G. S., and Gage, N. L. Two kinds of accuracy in predicting another's responses. *J. soc. Psychol.*, 1957, **45**, 245–254.

Stotland, E., and Dunn, R. E. Empathy, self-esteem, and birth order. *J. abnorm. soc. Psychol.*, 1963, **66**, 532–540.

Stotland, E., Zander, A., and Natsoulas, T. Generalization of interpersonal similarity. *J. abnorm. soc. Psychol.*, 1961, **62**, 250–256.

Strayer, F. K. Empathy and social perception. *Dissert. Abstr.*, 1960, **21**, 244.

Sullivan, H. D. *Conceptions of modern psychiatry.* New York: Norton, 1956.

Symonds, P., and Dietrich, D. Effects of variations in the time interval between an interview and its recording. *J. abnorm. soc. Psychol.*, 1941, **36**, 593–598.

Taft, R. Some correlates of the ability to make accurate social judgments. Unpublished doctoral dissertation, Univer. of California, 1950.

Taft, R. The ability to judge people. *Psychol. Bull.*, 1955, **52**, 1–23.

Tagiuri, R., and Petrullo, L. *Person perception and interpersonal behavior.* Stanford: Stanford Univer. Press, 1958.

Tannenbaum, R., Weschler, I. R., and Massarik, F. *Leaderhip and organization: a behavioral science approach.* New York: McGraw-Hill, 1961.

Thornton, G. W. The effect upon judgments of personality traits of varying a single factor in a photograph. *J. soc. Psychol.*, 1943, **18**, 127–148.

Thurstone, L. L. Primary mental abilities. *Psychometr. Monogr.*, 1938, No. 1.

Thurstone, L. L. *A factorial study of perception.* Chicago: Univer. of Chicago Press, 1944.

Tobias, S., and Weiner, M. Effect of response made on immediate and delayed recall from programmed materials. *J. Programmed Instruction,* 1963, **2**, 9–13.

Toch, H. H., Rabin, A. I., and Wilkins, D. M. Factors entering into ethnic identifications: An experimental study. *Sociometry,* 1962, **25**, 297–312.

Toch, H. H., and Schulte, R. Readiness to perceive violence as a result of police training. *Brit. J. Psychol.,* 1961, **52**, 389–393.

Travers, R. M. E. A study of the ability to judge group-knowledge. *Amer. J. Psychol.,* 1943, **56**, 54–65.

Trier, H. E., Smith, H. C., and Shaffer, J. Differences in food buying attitudes of housewives. *J. Marketing,* 1960, **25**, 66–69.

Trumbo, D. A. The development and analysis of a test of the ability to predict behavior. Unpublished master's thesis, Michigan State Univ., 1955.

Viteles, M. S. "Human-relations" and "humanities" in the education of business leaders: Evaluation of a program of humanistic studies for executives. *Personnel Psychol.,* 1959, **12**, 1–28.

Wakeley, J. H. The effects of special training on accuracy in judging others. Unpublished doctoral dissertation, Michigan State Univer., 1961.

Wallen, R. Individual's estimates of group opinion. *J. soc. Psychol.,* 1943, **17**, 269–274.

Watson, D. L. On the role of insight in the study of mankind. *Psychoanalyt. Rev.,* 1938, **25**, 358–371.

Wedeck, J. The relationship between personality and "psychological ability." *Brit. J. Psychol.,* 1947, **37**, 133–151.

Wedell, C., and Smith, K. V. Consistency of interview methods in appraisal of attitudes. *J. appl. Psychol.,* 1951, **35**, 392–396.

Weingarten, Erica M. A study of selective perception in clinical judgment. *J. Pers.,* 1949, **17**, 396–406.

Weiss, J. H. Effect of professional training and amount and accuracy of information on behavioral predictions. *J. consult. Psychol.,* 1963 **27**, 257–262.

Whisler, T. L., and Harper, Shirley. (Eds.) *Performance appraisal.* New York: Holt, 1962.

Whitehead, A. N. *The aims of education.* New York: Macmillan, 1929.

Witryol, S. L., and Kaess, W. A. Sex differences in social memory tasks. *J. abnorm. soc. Psychol.,* 1957, **54**, 343–346.

Young, K. *Social Psychology.* New York: Appleton, 1944.

Zavala, A. A test of Stereotype accuracy. Unpublished master's thesis, Michigan State Univer., 1960.

Zax, M., Lowen, E. L., Budin, W., and Biggs, C. F. The social desirability of trait descriptive terms: Applications to an alcoholic sample. *J. soc. Psychiat.,* 1962 **56**, 21–27.

NAME INDEX

Abeles, N., 105, 205
Albrecht, P. A., 70, 205
Allport, G. W., 35, 36, 43, 118, 140, 153, 154, 188, 205
Armour, J. B., 201, 205
Asch, S. E., 34, 36, 38, 39, 205
Atkinson, J. W., 113, 210

Bailey, D. E., 154, 155, 164, 165, 211
Bakan, D., 101, 205
Bakke, E. W., 145, 205
Barrett, R. S., 71, 211
Beier, E. G., 99, 205
Berscheid, Ellen, 39, 40, 211
Bieri, J., 98, 205
Biggs, C. F., 18, 213
Bingham, W. V., 68, 205
Blackman, N., 4, 205
Bloom, B. S., 178, 205
Boice, R., 147, 205
Bradford, L. P., 212
Brokman, R., 4, 205
Bronfenbrenner, U., 26, 30, 103, 112, 205
Bruner, J. S., 114, 206
Budin, W., 18, 19, 113, 206, 213
Burns, R. K., 126, 207
Burnstein, E., 98, 206
Burrow, T., 122, 206
Burtt, H. E., 44, 207

Campbell, D. T., 65, 139, 206
Cantril, H., 114, 209
Carson, R. C., 102, 206
Cattell, R. B., 168, 206

Chance, June, 29, 96, 99, 100, 104, 105, 176, 178, 182, 206
Chelsea, Linda, 40, 41, 206
Chodorkoff, B., 46, 206
Cline, V. B., 11, 27, 30–32, 45, 84, 100, 162, 163, 176–179, 206
Close, Mary, 140, 206
Cobb, S., 5, 206
Cofer, C. N., 121, 206
Cole, Luella, 200, 201, 210
Corsini, R. J., 142, 211
Covner, B., 126, 206
Coyle, E., 193, 206
Cronbach, L. J., 12–15, 21, 81–83, 207
Crow, W. J., 8, 10, 11, 63, 77, 78, 85, 86, 207

Dailey, C. A., 72, 207
Daniels, H., 123, 207
DeCharms, R., 124, 209
Dietrich, D., 125, 212
Dore, R., 139, 207
Dunbar, D. S., 201, 212
Dunn, J. T., 121, 206
Dunn, R. E., 100, 212
Dymond, Rosalind, 30, 65, 66, 96, 194, 207

Ehrmann, J. C., 76, 115, 209
Engel, E., 114, 207
Estes, S. G., 7, 33, 44, 207

Farson, R. E., 85, 86, 207
Fenichel, O., 93, 207

Fey, W. F., 64, 207
Fiedler, F. E., 97, 100, 207
Fiske, D. W., 7, 165, 166, 176, 178, 180, 209
Flanagan, J. C., 126, 207
Fleishman, E. A., 44, 207
Fox, R. E., 4, 207
Frenkel-Brunswick, E., 81, 207
Freud, S., 167
Fromm, E., 6, 207

Gage, N. L., 62, 65, 134, 194, 195, 207, 208
Gallway, Mary, 26, 30, 103, 177, 205
Gibb, J. R., 198, 208
Giedt, F. H., 102, 128–130, 208
Glasser, E. M., 70, 205
Goldberg, L. R., 18, 208
Golden, M., 166, 208
Goldin, P. C., 4, 207
Gollin, E. S., 37, 78–81, 179, 181, 208
Gottlieb, B., 64, 208
Gough, H. G., 104, 208
Gross, Cecily, 62, 78, 208
Grossman, B. A., 8, 45, 46, 59, 67, 77, 81, 157–160, 162, 176, 208, 209, 212
Guilford, J. P., 76, 208

Haire, M., 145, 208
Hammond, K. R., 10, 11, 63, 77, 78, 207
Harding, J., 26, 30, 103, 177, 205
Hariton, T., 44, 208
Harper, Shirley, 181, 213
Harris, E. E., 44, 207
Harris, W., 113, 208
Hartlage, L. C., 116, 208
Heine, R. W., 102, 206
Hershey, G. L., 168, 179, 208
Hoffman, L. R., 47, 124, 125, 210
Hughes, J. L., 147, 208
Hunt, W. A., 164, 208
Hyink, P., 72, 185, 209

Ittelson, W. H., 114, 209

James, William, 178
Johnson, D. M., 76, 115, 201–203, 209
Johnson, R. L., 136, 139, 143, 160, 209
Johnson, W. B., 140, 209
Jones, E. E., 45, 121, 124, 209

Kaess, W. A., 46, 118, 209, 213
Kahn, M. W., 9, 209
Katz, R. L., 109, 209
Kellogg, M. S., 71, 72, 209
Kelley, H. H., 121, 209
Kelly, E. L., 7, 62, 165, 166, 176, 178, 180, 209
Kepes, S. Y., 123, 161, 162, 209
Kerr, W. A., 64, 208
King, G. E., 76, 115, 209
Kramer, B. M., 140, 205

Lamming, G., 143, 209
Lansky, L., 45, 47, 124, 210
Lawson, C., 35, 149, 209
Leavitt, G. S., 62, 134, 208, 212
Levinger, G., 70, 209
Levy, D. M., 81, 209
Linden, J., 41, 127, 168–170, 209
Lindgren, H. C., 66, 210
Lindzey, G., 116, 210
Livensparger, D., 93–97, 101, 210
Lowen, E. L., 18, 208
Luft, J., 7, 210
Lundy, R. M., 124, 210

McClelland, D., 113, 210
McGregor, D., 160, 161, 210
McHugh, R. B., 87, 88, 90, 134, 135, 212
McKeachie, W. J., 38, 184, 201, 210
MacLeod, R. B., 200, 210
McNamara, W. J., 147, 208
Mahoney, S. C., 49, 210
Maier, N. R. F., 47, 124, 125, 210
Marks, J., 70, 205
Martens, L., 71, 211
Martin, H. W., 76, 210
Masling, J. M., 120, 210
Maslow, A. H., 62, 210
Massarik, F., 23, 52, 53, 212

Maugham, S., 78, 79, 210
Mead, G. H., 93, 210
Meaders, W., 29, 96, 100, 104, 105, 176, 178, 182, 206
Meehl, P. E., 83, 84, 154, 164, 165, 185, 210
Miles, M. B., 108, 177, 190, 191, 210
Mittelman, B., 62, 210
Mullin, J., 106, 107, 211

Newbigging, P. L., 46, 211
Newcomb, T. M., 45, 97, 112, 165, 205
Nichols, R. G., 116, 211

Oakes, R. H., 142, 211
Olmsted, D. W., 143, 211
Oskamp, S. W., 73, 88, 89, 211
Otis, J., 123, 207

Parker, J. W., 71, 211
Pemberton, Carol, 81, 211
Perry, R. B., 178, 211
Plath, D. W., 167, 211
Porter, E. H., 110, 111, 211
Postman, L. J., 114, 206
Pressey, S. L., 148, 149, 211
Proust, M., 42, 211

Rabin, A. I., 140, 213
Reade, W. H., 154, 211
Richards, J. M., 11, 27, 31, 32, 84, 100, 162, 163, 178, 179, 206
Robinson, Jacqueline, 66, 210
Rodgers, D. A., 96, 211
Rodrigues, J., 114, 206
Rogers, C., 93, 195, 203, 211
Rogolsky, S. J., 116, 210
Rokeach, M., 183, 211
Rosenberg, C., 80, 208

Santostefano, S., 9, 209
Sarbin, R. R., 154, 155, 164, 165, 211

Schulte, R., 75, 213
Schwartz, M. L., 164, 184, 208
Scott, J. P., 19, 211
Secord, P. F., 38, 39, 211
Shaffer, J., 179, 213
Shapiro, M. I., 22, 212
Showel, M., 116, 139, 194, 212
Siipola, E. M., 113, 114, 212
Silkiner, D. S., 98, 102, 103, 138, 143, 212
Smith, H. C., 157, 168, 179, 201, 212
Smith, K. V., 4, 7, 205, 213
Soskin, W. F., 7, 23, 70, 74, 212
Stagner, R., 64, 212
Stelmachers, Z. T., 87, 88, 90, 134, 212
Stern, J., 4, 205
Stevens, L. A., 116, 211
Stock, Dorothy, 199, 212
Stone, G. C., 62, 134, 208, 212
Stotland, E., 98, 100, 206
Strayer, F. K., 96, 97, 212
Stumpf, J., 99, 205
Sullivan, H. S., 93, 212
Symonds, P., 125, 212

Taft, R., 8, 154, 155, 164, 165, 211, 212
Tannenbaum, R., 23, 52, 53, 212
Taylor, E. K., 71, 211
Terman, L. M., 140, 209
Thibaut, J. W., 121, 209
Thornton, G. W., 183, 184, 212
Thurstone, L. L., 12, 81, 212
Tobias, S., 46, 47, 213
Toch, H. H., 75, 140, 213
Travers, R. M., 137, 138, 213
Trier, H. E., 179, 213
Trumbo, D., 8, 27, 28, 118, 177, 213

Viteles, M. S., 55, 56, 213

Wakeley, J. H., 145, 149, 213
Walker, R. E., 164, 184, 208
Wallen, R., 137, 213

Watson, D. L., 6, 213
Wedeck, J., 28, 177, 213
Wedell, C., 7, 213
Weiner, M., 47, 213
Weingarten, Erica, 107, 213
Weiss, Janis, 8, 9, 14, 15, 32, 213
Weschler, I. R., 23, 52, 53, 212
Whisler, T. L., 181, 213
Whitehead, A. N., 197, 213

Wilkins, D. M., 140, 213
Witryol, S. L., 46, 118, 209, 213

Young, K., 23, 213

Zander, A., 98, 206
Zavala, A., 138, 213
Zax, M., 18, 213

SUBJECT INDEX

Accuracy, empathy, 100–104
  individual differentiation, 155–161
  level, 67–69
  observation, 123–130
  spread, 81–83
  stereotypes, 135–139
Affective complexity, 105, 106
Assumed similarity, 93–97
Authoritarianism, 45–46

Base rates, 88, 89
Behavioral flexibility, 5

Cancerous hypothesis, 183, 184
Case of Earl and Frank, 156
Case studies, typical, 149–151
Change, facilitation of, 44–46
Clinical training, sensitivity in, 195–197
Clinicians, maladjustment bias, 75, 76
Components of sensitivity, 12–15, 175
  (*See also* Empathy; Individual accuracy;
      Level; Observation; Spread; Stereo-
      types)
Control groups, uses of, 54–56
Criteria, of sensitivity, 48–50
  in teaching, 201, 202

Defensiveness, reduction of, 51, 52, 188,
    189
Differentiation, definition of, 20

Education, sensitivity as goal in, 203, 204
Empathic accuracy, 100–104

Empathic accuracy, improvement of, 22,
    104–112
  level of, 103
Empathic drive, 105–107
Empathy, definitions of, 19, 93
  level of, 22
  measurement of, 93–97
  traits related to, 99, 100
Empathy Inventory, 94, 95
Evaluation of training, 53–56, 108, 109,
    189, 190
Experimental designs, 53–56

Face-to-face interactions, 26, 27
Feedback, 46, 47
  in Sensitivity Training, 110
Filmed interviews, 26, 27
Formula for optimum spread, 82, 83

Generalization in empathy, 98
Goals of training, 47, 48
Grossman Test, 157–160

Human relations, teaching, 4
Hypothesis, the cancerous, 183, 184

Identification, 4
  in empathy, 97, 98
Implicit theories, 37–39, 129, 130
Impressions, formation of, 35–42, 72, 73

Individual accuracy, Grossman test of, 157–160
  improvement of, 24, 161–168
  measurement of, 155–160
Inferences about individuals, 154
Insensitivity, causes of, 180–184
  (*See also* Sensitivity)
Interviewers, sensitivity of, 12–14

Judgments, premature, 72, 73

Knowledge of results, 46–47, 179

Leadership, military, 116
  and stereotype accuracy, 139, 140
Leadership attitudes, measurement of, 139, 140
Learning, 177–180
  to observe, 114
  principles of, 35–42
  programmed, 146–149
  theory, 35
Level, definition, 17
  elimination of, 69, 70
  generality of, 61–65
  measurement of, 59–61
  rigidity of, 180, 181
  test of, 60
  traits related to, 65–67
Level accuracy, 67–69
  improvement of, 20, 21, 70–76
Listening (*see* Observation)

Marriage, sensitivity in, 194
  stereotypes in, 141
Measurement, of empathic accuracy, 100–104
  of individual accuracy, 155–159
  of level, 59–61
  of level accuracy, 67–69
  of observational accuracy, 115–118
  of spread, 77, 78

Measurement, of stereotype accuracy, 135–139
  values of, 48–50
Method(s), of evaluating training, 53–56
  forced-distribution, 69, 70
  paired-comparison, 69
  of presenting person, 26–30
  of recording predictions, 32–34
Motivation, 177

National Training Laboratory, 5, 197–200
Norm flexibility test, 89
Norms, development of internal, 87–89

Observation, definition, 19
  of inconsistent facts, 89, 90
  interactional approach to, 114, 115
  nature of, 113–115
  by psychologists, 182
  relation to role, 122, 123
  sex differences in, 118, 119
Observational accuracy, improvement of, 22, 23, 123–130
  measurement of, 115–118
Observations, recording of, 125–126
Orientations to people, 61–65, 127, 128

Perception of people, 35–42
Perceptional accuracy (*see* Observation)
Perceptual defenses, 46
Personality, in empathy, 99, 100
  in individual accuracy, 159, 160
  in level, 65–67
  in observation, 118, 119
  in sensitivity, 176–180
  in spread, 78–81
  in stereotype accuracy, 139, 140
  traits of, 168–170
Photographs, 26, 28, 29
Prediction, clinical versus actuarial, 83–85
  stereotypes in, 163
  theory as determiner of, 41–42
  types of, 30–32
Predictive accuracy (*see* Accuracy; Sensitivity)

Programmed learning, 146–149
Projection, 4
Propinquity, Law of, 99
Psychiatry, training in, 22, 23
Psychoanalysis, 6
Psychological-mindedness, 104, 105
  dangers of, 181, 182
Psychologists, prediction of success as, 165, 166
  stereotype test of, 144
Psychology, enrollments in, 6
  teaching of, 4, 200–203
Psychotherapists, aim of, 167
  role of, 122
  sensitivity of, 195–197
Psychotherapy as process, 4

Ranking method, 34
  within individuals, 73
  value of, 184, 185
Rating method, weaknesses of, 32–34
Reinforcement, 46–47
Relational thinking, 78–81
Reliability, 48, 49
Reward, 46–47
Rigidity of levels, 180, 181
Role playing, 111, 112, 123–125
Roles versus traits, 160, 161

Scientist, values of, 155
Selection of sensitive people, 184–186
Self-orientation, 61, 62
Sensitive people, selection of, 184–186
  traits of, 176–180
Sensitivity, antecedents and consequences, 5
  components of, 12–15
  definition, 3
  generality of, 10, 11
  as goal, of teaching, 200–204
    of therapy, 196, 197
  influence of training on, 7–10
  in marriage, 194
  nature of, 175
  as process and outcome, 4

Sensitivity, in teaching, 194, 195
  theory of, 17–20
  value of, 193–195
Sensitivity training, 107–109, 197–200
  defensiveness in, 188, 189
  definition, 5
  evaluation of, 190, 191
  goals of, 20–24, 188–190
  improvement of, 186–191
  measurement in, 187
  sequencing in, 187, 188
Sequencing of goals, 50, 51
Sex differences in observation, 118, 119
Simple thinking, prevalence of, 181
Social sciences, source of stereotypes, 140–142
  teaching, 4
Spread, definition of, 18, 19
  measurement of, 77, 78
Spread accuracy, 81–83
  improvement of, 21–24, 86, 87, 142–144
Stereotype accuracy, and leadership, 139, 140
  measurement of, 135–139
Stereotypes, definition, 19
  faulty, 183
  nature of, 133–135
  programmed learning of, 146–149
  social sciences as source, 140–142
  training in use of, 145, 146
Stress, variation with training method, 51, 52
Sympathy, 4

Taped interviews, 26, 29
Teaching, sensitivity in, 194, 195
T-group, 197–200
  definition, 5
Theories, as determiners of predictions, 39–41
  empirical versus nonempirical, 166–168
  explicit versus implicit, 129, 130, 164–166
  implicit, 37–39, 160
  psychoanalytic, 167
Theory, of impression formation, 35–42
  of sensitivity, 17–20

Therapy, sensitivity as goal of, 196, 197
Thinking, relational, 78–81
Training, of Air Force officers, 85, 86
    evaluation of, 7–10, 53–56, 85, 86, 189, 190
    guides to better, 47–56
    of medical students, 86
    methods of, 35–56
    principles of, 42–47
Training method, fitting to goal, 52, 53
Traits, personality, 40–41, 168–170

Traits, versus roles, 160, 161
    of sensitive people, 176–180

Uniqueness, battle of, 153–155
Unity, seeing a person as, 35–37

Validity, 48–50

Written records, 26, 27